A Clear and Present Danger

NARCISSISM IN THE ERA OF DONALD TRUMP

Edited by
Leonard Cruz and Steven Buser

With Articles by

Jean Shinoda Bolen ~ Steven Buser ~ Leonard Cruz
Clarissa Pinkola Estés ~ Nancy Swift Furlotti
James Hollis ~ Alden Josey ~ Thomas Patrick Lavin
Kathryn Madden ~ Eve Maram ~ John McClain
Robert Moore ~ Laurence de Rosen ~ Susan Rowland
Nathan Schwartz-Salant ~ Thomas Singer
Jacqueline West ~ James Wyly

CHIRON PUBLICATIONS • ASHEVILLE, NORTH CAROLINA

www.ChironPublicatons.com

www.TrumpNarcissism.com

Cover design by Predrag Markovic.

Interior design by Cornelia G. Murariu

Printed primarily in the United States of America.

Waking Up! Malignant Narcissism: How Bluebeard and Hitler Came To Power by Dr. Clarissa Pinkola Estés, ©2016, and *Letter To A Young Activist During Troubled Times [Do Not Lose Heart, We Were Made for These Times.* ©2001, 2016, All Rights reserved. Permissions: ngandelman@gmail.com

ISBN 978-1-63051-395-5 paperback

ISBN 978-1-63051-396-2 hardcover

ISBN 978-1-63051-397-9 electronic

Library of Congress Cataloging-in-Publication Data Pending

Table of Contents

Dedication

"Friends, comrades and fellow South Africans, I greet you all in the name of peace, democracy and freedom for all. I stand here before you not as a prophet but as a humble servant of you, the people. Your tireless and heroic sacrifices have made it possible for me to be here today. I therefore place the remaining years of my life in your hands."

~ Nelson Mandela, February 11, 1990. Speaking on his release from Robben Island from the balcony of Cape Town city hall.

This book is dedicated to the memory of two great first presidents. President George Washington of the United States of America declined to serve more than the two terms and risk establishing a new monarchy. President Nelson Mandela of post-Apartheid South Africa served only one term before departing to private life. Their selfless examples continue to shine like a beacon for all who consider aspiring to high office.

Acknowledgments

As volume editors, we must first thank the authors who contributed to this book. Their timely response to our call for submissions was humbling and appreciated.

Our title, *A Clear and Present Danger: Narcissism in the Era of Donald Trump*, is borrowed from the 1919 Supreme Court case of Schenck v United States. The unanimous opinion was written by Justice Oliver Wendell Holmes:

> "The most stringent protection of free speech would not protect a man in falsely shouting fire in a theatre and causing a panic. [...] The question in every case is whether the words used are used in such circumstances and are of such a nature as to create a clear and present danger that they will bring about the substantive evils that Congress has a right to prevent."

The phrase, "clear and present danger" was once again heard in 2016 from Ariana Huffington in a CNN interview as she spoke about Donald Trump.

> "We think that he's a little bit like Kim Jong-un," Huffington said. "You know, he's both a buffoon, and he's dangerous. So, we started covering him as a buffoon, until the day when he proposed that we ban 1.6 billion Muslims from entering the United States. From that point on, we started covering him as a clear and present danger, with an editor's note at the end of each story." (http://mediamatters.org/video/2016/04/03/on-cnns-reliable-sources-arianna-huffington-exp/209709)

As we go to press on this book, our country finds itself at a critical crossroad. Our hope is that the chapters that follow will give cause for reflection in America in the upcoming months. Regardless of the outcome of the 2016 presidential election, this exploration of narcissism will prove to be a timely and timeless study.

Dr. Leonard Cruz
Dr. Steven Buser

Disclaimer from the Publisher

Let us be clear: The contributors, editors, and publisher have not engaged in diagnosis of any public figures mentioned in the pages that follow. Specifically, we are not claiming that any public figures or leaders mentioned have been diagnosed with Narcissistic Personality Disorder (NPD). To establish a diagnosis of any psychological disorder requires individual assessment by a qualified mental health professional. Proper diagnosis is reached only after thorough, individual diagnostic evaluation. The results of such an assessment are strictly confidential and would only be released with the examinee's consent. This book examines narcissism and its impact on others, on communities, and on society-at-large.

Many people can be seen to occasionally display characteristic traits of NPD. Qualities like arrogance, a sense of entitlement, a tendency to exploit others, an inflated sense of oneself, and other defining features of NPD sometimes arise in every one of us. NPD is a condition in which these and other defining traits remain persistent over time. That is what is meant by character or personality.

The 2016 United States presidential election process was without precedent. To many people this was a season where arrogance, entitlement, and narcissism were on full display. Thomas Jefferson said, "The government you elect is the government you deserve." Time will tell what the American electorate deserved. In the meantime, the events of the 2016 election cycle inspired the contributors to answer an invitation to write on narcissism. The timing of this book was inspired by the 2016 presidential election; however, it reaches beyond and beneath the surface of a particular moment in history to explore narcissism in a broader context. We hope it will also catalyze a confrontation of the narcissism we each carry within.

Introduction to *Narcissistic Personality Disorder*

BY LEONARD CRUZ, MD, AND STEVEN BUSER, MD

When one aspect of our psychic life manifests in extreme fashion, an opportunity arises to integrate that into consciousness. The extreme utterances and behaviors displayed by candidates like Mr. Trump may have shined a light on narcissism and perhaps given society a chance to confront this phenomenon head-on. We wish to reiterate that we are not proposing that Donald Trump suffers from Narcissistic Personality Disorder, nor are we proposing he does not. Yet we wish to thank him and other candidates in the 2016 presidential election for the opportunity to take an honest look in the mirror and confront our individual and collective narcissism.

Concern about the perils of narcissism on the national or global level has been expressed in newspapers, blogs, magazine articles, and a spate of recently released books. Political analysts have invoked the word narcissism. Therapists have begun to use contemporary public figures to illustrate narcissistic features. Narcissism is in the spotlight. Most, but not all of the contributors to this book, are rooted in the traditions of Analytical Psychology, the school founded by Dr. Carl Gustav Jung. Jung was a gifted psychiatrist whose vast learning and scholarship revealed that the unconscious is composed of a personal domain as well as a collective domain. The collective realm is the source of fairy tales, myths, recurring symbols, and perhaps recurring motifs in history. Leaders are uniquely susceptible to intoxicating and inflating forces that are projected onto them. When these forces remain unconscious, there is more danger of leaders succumbing to unhealthy narcissism and for those they lead to be led astray. We are sincerely grateful to the 2016 United States political process and the controversies it has stirred.

This book examines the many facets of narcissism. What are its psychological origins? What mythological roots can be discerned? Does literature have anything to say on the subject? How does healthy narcissism differ from malignant narcissism? How does narcissism affect our relationships? How does narcissism engage the masculine or feminine? How has narcissism shaped the course of world history, and what role does it play in the rise of fascism? What effect is narcissism exerting on contemporary politics and society? Above all, this book asks the question, how can narcissism be recognized and transformed?

An invitation went out to leading psychologists, psychiatrists, and academics to write chapters on these and other questions. Each contributor provided a unique perspective. It is left to the reader to uncover the threads that weave these varied essays together. Taken together, these chapters give us a rich and textured overview of narcissism as well as penetrating insights about contemporary culture. But first we offer a concise description of narcissism from a clinician's perspective.

Narcissism and the DSM-5

The *Diagnostic and Statistical Manual of Mental Disorders*, 5th Edition (DSM-5) describes the diagnostic criteria for various disorders including Narcissistic Personality Disorder.

Individuals diagnosed with a "personality disorder" have chronic, maladaptive ways of engaging with others. They tend to react to their environment in rigid and unchanging patterns that lead to negative consequences. Those suffering from personality disorders often have substantial difficulty in maintaining jobs and relationships. Individuals with Narcissistic Personality Disorder can achieve considerable career success. Dr. Michael Macoby, author of *The Productive Narcissist: The Promise and Peril of Visionary Leadership* points out, "When narcissists win, they win big. Narcissists create a vision to change the world: they are bold risk takers who think and act independently, pursuing their vision with great passion and perseverance." He goes on to ask what sort of person believes he or she can change things through his or her ideas and the force of his or her personality. In the final chapter of his book, he issues the following caution, "The narcissistic leaders who have fared the worst throughout history, from Napoleon to Messier, fell prey to unbridled greed and grandiosity, were puffed up by their own vision and initial success, and isolated themselves from advisers who could help them from self-destructing."

The DSM–5 defines people with *Narcissistic Personality Disorder* as having very specific attributes. They show enduring patterns of grandiosity, an absence of empathy, and a need for being admired by others throughout adulthood. People with grandiosity have a sense of superiority, viewing themselves as better than others. They often look at others with a sense of disdain and perceive others as inferior themselves. They see themselves as unique and overly important and often exaggerate their achievements. Lacking empathy, they are unmoved by others' suffering. They have difficulty seeing how their actions can harm others or how someone might feel in a particular situation.

To meet the criteria for *NPD*, the DSM – 5 requires at least 5 out of the following 9 characteristics to be met: grandiosity; fantasies of unlimited power and success; sees self as "special" and only associates with others of high status; needs admiration; has a sense of entitlement; is interpersonally exploitative; lacks empathy; is envious of others; or appears arrogant.

Even people who fail to meet 5 of the 9 the diagnostic criteria for *Narcissistic Personality Disorder*, those said to have *narcissistic traits*, may experience difficulties in the way they relate to the world. The distinction between narcissistic traits and narcissistic personality disorder is sometimes subtle and difficult to make.

The *Goldwater Rule*

Crossing the Border of Assessing Public Figures

BY LEONARD CRUZ, MD, AND STEVEN BUSER, MD

Barry Goldwater and the American Psychiatric Association

In 1964, a publication known as *Fact* magazine sent questionnaires to 12,356 U.S. psychiatrists asking their opinion on whether presidential candidate Senator Barry Goldwater was psychologically fit to be President. Exactly 2,417 psychiatrists responded (19.6%). The results were broken down as follows:

571 (23.6%) respondents	Did not know enough about Goldwater to make a conclusion.
657 (27.2%) respondents	Deemed Goldwater to be psychologically fit to be President.
1,189 (49.2%) respondents	Deemed Goldwater to not be psychologically fit to be President.

Space was provided for respondents to make comments, and some of the psychiatrists labeled Senator Goldwater as *impulsive, unstable, paranoid, dangerous lunatic, neurotic,* and even *psychotic.* Following the publication of the September-October 1964 [*The unconscious of a conservative: a special issue on the mind of Barry Goldwater. Fact 1:3–64,* 1964], Senator Goldwater filed suit against Ralph Ginzburg and eventually won a judgment of $1 of compensatory damages and $75,000 in punitive damages. The Supreme Court refused Ginzburg's appeal, but Justice Hugo Black recorded a dissenting opinion (joined by Justice William O. Douglas in which he stated, "The public has an unqualified right to have the character and fitness of anyone who aspires to the Presidency held up for the closest scrutiny."

In 1973, the American Psychiatric Association created what is now known as the *Goldwater Rule*, declaring it unethical to diagnose or comment on the mental state of a public official who has not been personally examined by the clinician. Section 7.3 of the *Principles of Medical Ethics* states:

> On occasion psychiatrists are asked for an opinion about an individual who is in the light of public attention or who has disclosed information about himself/herself through public media. In such circumstances, a psychiatrist may share with the public his or her expertise about psychiatric issues in general. However, it is unethical for a psychiatrist to offer a professional opinion unless he or she has conducted an examination and has been granted proper authorization for such a statement.

The 2015 version of this rule states:

> For some in our profession, psychiatry can extend beyond the physician-patient relationship into the broader domain of public attention: in administration, politics, the courtroom, the media, and the internet. Psychiatrists need to sustain and nurture the ethical integrity of the profession when in the public eye. A psychiatrist may render a professional opinion about an individual after an appropriate clinical examination and accompanying waiver of confidentiality and should not do so unless the examination and waiver have occurred. **When a personal examination has not been performed and when a psychiatrist is asked for a professional opinion about a person in light of public attention, a general discussion of relevant psychiatric topics—rather than offering opinions about that specific person—is the best means of facilitating public education.** In some circumstances, such as academic scholarship about figures of historical importance, exploration of psychiatric issues (e.g. diagnostic conclusions) may be reasonable provided that it has a sufficient evidence base and is subject to peer review and academic scrutiny based on relevant standards of scholarship. When, without any personal examination, the psychiatrist renders a clinical opinion about a historical figure, these limitations must be clearly acknowledged. Moreover, labeling public figures cavalierly with psychiatric conditions, based on limited or indirect clinical knowledge, is not consistent with this approach and undermines public trust in the profession of psychiatry. [APA *Commentary on Ethics in Practice;* December 2015; Topic 3.4.7 Public Statements]

In a 2016 article in the *Journal of Psychiatry and the Law*, Drs. J. Kroll and C. Pouncy "conclude that the Goldwater Rule was an excessive organizational response to what was clearly an inflammatory and embarrassing moment for American psychiatry." Though the Goldwater Rule cast a long shadow upon public psychological commentary by professionals, the guidelines seem to be changing.

Today, telepsychiatry permits diagnosis and treatment without a face-to-face contact between the clinician and patient. We pay particular attention to Justice Black's dissent when the the U.S. Supreme Court denied Ginzburg's *writ certiorari* (declined to hear the case). Moreover, it seems ill-conceived that laypersons with no formal training or experience should be free to opine on the psychology of public figures aspiring to high office, while trained, experienced professionals are gagged. Donald Trump has become a lightning rod of controversy. In the public's search for explanations about his unexpected trajectory to the Republican nomination for the Presidency of the United States of America, a growing number of professionals have offered opinions about Mr. Trump. Dr. Jerrold M. Post, a founding director of the Center for the Analysis of Personality and Political Behavior at the Central Intelligence Agency (CIA) wrote in *Washington Psychiatrist* (Summer 2015) that the APA guideline is a "masterpiece of internal contradiction."

In a landmark decision, *Tarasoff v. Regents of the University of California*, the California Supreme Court held that mental health professionals have a "duty to warn" that was later modified to a "duty to protect" an individual who is being threatened with bodily harm by a patient. Dr. Post suggests that when he furnished a political personality profile of Saddam Hussein, a profile that was scrutinized by the APA, he was discharging a duty to warn similar to the Tarasoff principle.

Statements from Donald Trump

Donald Trump's own words are often used to fashion impressions about his "political psychological profile." As an example of some of these statements from Mr. Trump, the following 10 assertions have been well-documented.

☛ *"I get along with everybody. People love me, and you know what? I've been very successful; everybody loves me."*

> ~ Donald Trump - in a July 2016 interview with Anderson Cooperon
> http://edition.cnn.com/videos/us/2015/07/08/trump-everyone-loves-me-intvw.cnn

☛ *"All of the women on 'The Apprentice' flirted with me—consciously or unconsciously. That's to be expected."*

> ~ Donald Trump - How To Get Rich, 2004

☛ *"The greatest builder is me, and I would build the greatest wall you have ever seen."*

> ~ Donald Trump - May 2015 at a speech in South Carolina found at http://www.bloomberg.com/politics/graphics/2015-how-trump-invented-trump/

☛ *"I've always been there. In school, I was always successful. In life, I was always successful. My father was a successful real estate developer and he was a very tough man but a good man. My father would always praise me. He always thought I was the smartest person. He said to one of the big magazines that everything he touches turns to gold. At a very young age. So I don't know."*

> ~ Donald Trump - in a December 2015 interview with The Washington Post on https://www.washingtonpost.com/politics/i-will-never-leave-this-race/2015/12/08/af1b1d46-9ad2-11e5-8917-653b65c809eb_story.html

☛ In response to Spy magazine's go-to qualifier of Trump as a "short-fingered vulgarian," Trump told Page Six, "My fingers are long and beautiful, as, it has been well-documented, are various other parts of my body."

> ~ http://nypost.com/2011/04/03/trump-card/

☛ *"If I were a liberal Democrat, people would say I'm the super genius of all time. The super genius of all time. If you're a conservative Republican, you've got to fight for your life. It's really an amazing thing."*

> ~ Donald Trump - in an August 2015 interview with "Meet the Press" host Chuck Todd https://www.washingtonpost.com/news/the-fix/wp/2015/08/17/donald-trump-on-meet-the-press-annotated/

☛ About the State Department: *"I used to use the word incompetent, now I just call them stupid. I went to an Ivy League school. I'm very highly educated. I know words — I have the best words — but there's no better word than stupid."*

> ~ Donald Trump - Campaign Rally in Hilton Head Island, SC, December 2015 on https://www.youtube.com/watch?v=7UIE_MRAhEA

☛ *"I would build a great wall, and nobody builds walls better than me, believe me, and I'll build them very inexpensively, I will build a great, great wall on our southern border. And I will have Mexico pay for that wall."*

> ~ Donald Trump - from June 2015 Trump's announcement that he was running for President on http://time.com/3923128/donald-trump-announcement-speech/

☛ *"I think apologizing's a great thing, but you have to be wrong. I will absolutely apologize, sometime in the hopefully distant future, if I'm ever wrong."*

> ~ Donald Trump - In September 2015 on The Tonight Show, found on http://www.usmagazine.com/celebrity-news/news/donald-trumps-craziest-quotes-the-2016-presidential-hopeful-speaks-201568

☛ *"I could stand in the middle of Fifth Avenue and shoot somebody and I wouldn't lose voters,"*

> ~ Donald Trump - at a rally in January 2016; found at http://edition.cnn.com/2016/01/23/politics/donald-trump-shoot-somebody-support/

How then should mental health professionals respond to such statements by a candidate vying for the Presidency of the United States of America? Is there a role for experienced professionals to educate others when they see strong, suggestive evidence of personality traits or behaviors that may bear upon a candidate's fitness for elected office? When Toronto Mayor Rob Ford's public descent into severe substance abuse became a nightly spectacle, was silence about how his vehement denials were part of his condition the ethical response? Quite a few clinicians have chosen to make public comments about some of Mr. Trump's statements and his conduct.

Clinical psychologist Dr. Joseph Burgo, author of *The Narcissist You Know* and instructor with an affiliate of the International Psychoanalytic Association is quoted in the *Huffington Post*, saying:

> "Narcissists like Donald Trump ... are constantly driven to prove themselves among the 'winners' of the world, often by triumphing over or denigrating other people as comparative 'losers.' ... If you examine Trump's language in his public statements as well as in the debates, you will hear him proclaim his winner status again and again while sneering at his detractors as losers."
>
> http://www.huffingtonpost.com/entry/donald-trump-psychologists_us_55f8e00be4b08820d9173a56

Vanity Fair's November 11, 2015, article by Henry Alford quotes multiple clinicians seeming to diagnose Mr. Trump as well. The first paragraph of his article quotes three different clinicians' views:

> For mental-health professionals, Donald Trump is at once easily diagnosed but slightly confounding. "Remarkably narcissistic," said developmental psychologist Howard Gardner, a professor at Harvard Graduate School of Education. "Textbook narcissistic personality disorder," echoed

clinical psychologist Ben Michaelis. "He's so classic that I'm archiving video clips of him to use in workshops because there's no better example of his characteristics," said clinical psychologist George Simon, who conducts lectures and seminars on manipulative behavior. "Otherwise, I would have had to hire actors and write vignettes. He's like a dream come true."

http://www.vanityfair.com/news/2015/11/
donald-trump-narcissism-therapists

Furthermore, a guest commentary in *Forbes* on March 30, 2016, written by psychiatrist Glenn Swogger, Jr., M.D., and Stanford University Fellow Henry Miller, M.D., pulls no punches in writing of their concerns:

> Like Trump, charismatic leaders often manifest signs and symptoms of Narcissistic Personality Disorder. ... We fear that Trump's egocentricity would be an insuperable obstacle to his effort to organize and lead a well-functioning, transparent government. As the Narcissist-in-Chief, it is far more likely that he would govern capriciously and "make the country more greatly divided," to coin a phrase.

http://www.forbes.com/sites/realspin/2016/03/30/
donald-trump-narcissist-in-chief-not-commander-in-
chief/#68e9b1f45595

One subject that continued to haunt Donald Trump's presidential bid concerns narcissism. In the introduction to Trump's own book, *Think Like a Billionaire*, Mr. Trump implies that he fits the description of a productive narcissist.

> Macoby's book *The Productive Narcissist* makes convincing argument that narcissism can be a useful quality if you are trying to start a business. A narcissist does not hear the naysayers. At the Trump Organization, I listen to people, but my vision is my vision.

A Clear and Present Danger: Narcissism in the Era of Donald Trump does not purport to diagnose a public figure. Instead, this book is composed of thoughtful essays on topics related to narcissism, including some chapters that speak more directly to the figure of Donald Trump who has galvanized conversation on this topic. To many observers this primary election has polarized the nation and provoked intense passion among voters. The psychology of C.G. Jung, Analytical Psychology, is uniquely poised to offer insights into the subject of narcissism and the phenomenon that unfolded during the run-up to the 2016 presidential election.

The reader should keep two principles of Analytical Psychology in mind, the *collective unconscious* and *transcendent function*. The *collective unconscious is* an archaic, unconscious realm that is not personal and present in all human beings across all cultures. It forms the deepest basis for what becomes our unconscious life and accounts for the recurring images, myths, and motifs found across different cultures and in different epochs.

The other principle that deserves a brief introduction is the *transcendent function*. This is the psychological function that allows a person to unify opposites. According to Dr. Craig Calquist, "Unless the energy of the collective unconscious is used consciously via the *transcendent function* (communing with the gods), it swamps the *ego* and causes collective psychic infections." This collection of essays is an invitation to explore narcissism in its many forms and venues.

Section 1
Opening Thoughts

Narcissus's Forlorn Hope
The Fading Image in a Pool too Deep

BY JAMES HOLLIS, PHD

This essay examines the conventional myth of Narcissus, surveys its usual forms in daily life, its amplification in Dostoyevsky's *Notes from Underground*, and moves toward an examination of the need for, the resistance to, and the ineluctable human desire to be seen, and concludes with the acknowledgement of the impossibility of any fixed self-imago.

> "What seest thou else
> In the dark backward and abysm of time?"
>> Shakespeare, *The Tempest*

> "The deep is the unsayable."
>> Ludwig Wittgenstein, *Philosophical Investigations*

We all know the outlines of the ancient story, and from afar have judged the self-absorption of the youth transfixed by his own image in the pool. We who might pause a moment in the restaurant's mirror, straightening the tie, fluffing the hair, freshening the makeup, can afford such largess for are we not all above such self-absorption as sank this ancient soul?

Narcissus was cursed to have been *seen in his flaw*, as we, perhaps, are not, and *Nemesis* chose to catch him up on his one-sidedness. Jung's simplest definition of neurosis was the one-sidedness of the personality, a trait for which we are well rewarded today, and often handsomely paid. Catching his image in the pond, he was captivated, possessed. Again, Jung's term for the experience of a complex was *Ergriffenheit*: seizure, or possession. So captivated by his own beauty Narcissus's libido turned inward, fed on itself, and he lost the vital erotic vector of life. Life is served by the desire for, the encounter with, the dialogue with the other. This self-absorption is a form of Hell. As poet Gerard Manley Hopkins put it, to be one's own sweating self is to be irredeemably mired in stasis without possibility of movement, dynamism, growth through the other.

Nemesis is not a god, but one of those impersonal forces—like *Dike*, and *Sophrosyne*—which course through the cosmos to which even the gods seem to bend. To the degree that any of us feels insecure, that insecurity will show up over and over and over in venue after venue. Nemesis is a harvest of consequences, consequences that flow from our numerous gaps in consciousness. And wherever we are unconscious, the play of possibility is immense. All cultures, for example, amid their carnival of possibilities, have an archetypal presence called "the trickster." The trickster is that figure, god, or animal, or humanoid *jongleur* whose purpose seems to be to upset our apple carts, to remind us that we are not gods, that we are not as knowing, not as much in charge, not as omnipotent as we might think we are. So, Nemesis enchants Narcissus, and he falls into the sickness unto death, the *mortificatio*, the stultification of libido that occurs whenever the dialectic is replaced by one-sidedness, ambiguity by certainty, probing enquiry by fundamentalism, democracy by fascism, and so on.

The first "modern" to really explore narcissism was Fyodor Dostoyevsky in his 1863 *Notes from Underground*. This perverse, countercultural analysis explored both the collective phantasy of meliorism, the doctrine of "progress," and the phantasy of moral improvement toward which the 19th century believed it moved so confidently. On the collective level, the underground man mocks the narcissistic self-congratulation of the first world's exhibition, the Crystal Palace outside of London, a hall of glass in which could be seen not only the tools of the new, progressive epoch, but the self-congratulatory genius that procured them. But the underground man imagines that same technology will be used in the century to follow to more efficiently kill more people than ever before. Little could he envision that the ruins of the Crystal Palace were later used as a navigational point by the Luftwaffe in its bombing runs over London, nor that that morally untethered technology would build concentration camps and nuclear weapons less than eight decades later.

But even more telling, the underground man turns his lens upon himself and describes his own naked emotions and uncensored agendas. "Now then, what does a decent man like to talk about most? Himself, of course. So, I'll talk about myself."[1] His honesty is to this day still astounding and justifies the appellation he grants himself: "the antihero."

He celebrates his capacity to make others miserable when he moans loudly from a toothache. He acknowledges that he has no self-worth because, of course, he is a man of superior intellect, and anyone of superior intellect will, of course, know how worthless he really is. He describes his vanities, his petty jealousies, his elaborate plots to exact revenge for presumptive insults, and considers torpor superior to the stupidities of those who are activists primarily because they are stupid. The underground

---

1   Fyodor Dostoyevsky, *Notes from Underground*, p. 93.

man's cumulative catalogue of contumely is overwhelming, but in the end, he turns it around by confronting the superior, judgmental reader by noting that he alone has the honesty to look at himself in the mirror and bear what looks back while the reader cannot bear to look in the mirror very long at all. Amid his catalogue of shame, the cauterizing virtue of honesty shines with stunning, compelling, and intimidating power on the reader.

In Dostoyevsky's trope of *the underground man*, we begin to approach the perspective of depth psychology at last. Perhaps having survived the hell of a Siberian gulag, Dostoyevsky could survive the hell of self-knowledge. To what degree can any of us bear to see ourselves through the glass darkly, to use the metaphor of Paul's *Letter to the Corinthians?* The pitiful truth of narcissism is that *the narcissist stares in the mirror and no one stares back.* This is why he or she must use others for reflecting surfaces. If that person is the parent, the child is used to bring positive regard to the parent. One has to think only of the stage-door mother, or the Little League father for cultural stereotypes of this pattern. If the narcissist is the employer, the employees do the hard work, and the boss takes the credit. If the partner is insecure, he or she depends on the other to make one feel good about oneself. In each of these relational deficits the heroic task is fled, the task that asks: "What am I asking of that other that I need to address for myself?"

I know a socialite who hired a publicist to be seen in the right places, with the right people until she became a *celebrity,* that is, somebody "known for being known." Now, propped up with surgeries and pancake makeup, she totters to the same old functions to hold court. How sad, how empty, how alone the child within must feel, even in that big house filled with servants and sycophants. When I once drove a member of a religious order through a particularly affluent neighborhood, my guest, who had devoted her life to the poor, noted with pity the terrible psychospiritual burden that dollar-driven ghetto placed on subsequent generations to produce and sustain such splendiferous facades. And always, she noted, the daily fear of the inhabitants that people like us might not drive through their "hood to see them and envy them."

Shakespeare noted how so many seek *the bubble reputation.* The frangible nature of fame as bubble is not lost on any of us these centuries later in this era of 15 minutes of fame, of selfies, of vulgarity paraded as the divertissement of the hour. Beneath all this is our universal desire to be seen, and every child's desperate plea to be valued. If we wish to judge the other, we must first recognize that need persists in ourselves. In earlier eras of Western civilization, and in many other parts of the world today, the grinding necessities of survival require a focus on the outer world in service to daily survival. Throughout most of history, one's place in the larger scheme of things is demonstrably tiny, insignificant. If there is a meaning to one's brief transit through this vale of tears, it is found in an afterlife, a place for a possible transformation through embrace by that transcendent Other. Practically speaking, the linkage to that transcendent Other is so attenuated today that most people have felt the ground shift beneath their feet, the stirrings of existential angst, and have inflated this moment, this hour, with an urgency far exceeding the *carpe diem* thread of classical Greece and Rome. If, as more and more suspect, the Other is not there, or looking elsewhere for a century or two, one must scour one's own image through some transient graffito in the shifting sands of the hourglass.[2]

How often we have heard people say, "I want to know myself," or even we have said it ourselves. But do we, really? Could we bear that? Could we bear the possible revelations that we are *human, menschliche, alle zu menschliche* after all, with all its anfractuosities, its capacities for brutality and compassion, for selfishness and generosity, for aggression and caregiving? Since most of us would like to think of ourselves as improvements on humanity's developmental history, could we bear to be simply the most recent iteration of the whole human project, as Vergil suggested: "*Nihil a me humanun alienum puto.*"

The ancients recognized our ambivalence before the vision in the pond. Could we afford to stare at our own darkness directly, or that of another, or that of divinity? We know what happened to those who looked at Medusa directly, and so Athena's bright shield provided a reflective surface, a distancing *metaphora* perhaps, through which to refract that primal power. As T.S. Eliot put it, "Humankind cannot bear too much reality." Jung recognized the role of resistance, the creation of those

> taboo regions which psychology must not touch. But since
> no war was ever won on the defensive, one must, in order
> to terminate hostilities, open negotiations with the enemy
> and see what his terms really are.[3]

For over two centuries now, philosophers, psychologists, phenomenologists, physicists, and others have been telling us that we cannot know things in themselves: Hume, Kant, Heisenberg, Husserl, and so on. All we can *know* is that we do not know; but we do experience, and we experience through various modalities, categories, and mediatorial vehicles. Poets and prophets have always known this. The poet knows he or she cannot speak of love or grief or anything worth it directly, so he or she will find a tangible object, which, because more nearly available to the corporeal senses, lends itself to the task of bridging to the essential but illusive other. Thus *the beloved other* is wholly *other* to Robert Burns, but he says his love is like a red, red rose, and we immediately get his angle

---

2   American soldiers left the phrase "Kilroy was here" everywhere in the world during World War II. "Kilroy" got around.
3   Jung, *The Practice of Psychotherapy*, CW 16., para. 374.

on her. Thomas Nashe, describing the terror of the approaching Black Death, writes: "Brightness falls from the air; / Queens have died, young and fair; / Dust hath closed Helen's eye."[4] We get the point. If you think you are exempt from the roving eye of Lord Death, think again. If we miss that point, he repeats the refrain, "timor mortis conturbat me."[5] So, even if we do not dimly see ourselves in that dark glass, we are, apparently, seen by an eye from which we cannot hide.

Remember when you, the reader, first stared into a mirror, perhaps as a toddler, amused to see another, a simulacrum, a funny other who moved limbs like you, yet not you, for they moved differently. How to explain that? Was it that an alternative world lay within, on the other side of that silvered surface? Could one step through into another world, just like this, but not, as through a black hole into an alternative universe? And if so, what did it say about the provisonality of this world, this universe, this I?

Narcissus is judged in our emotionally distanced place because he is captured by, possessed by his self-image, but are we not all captives to some extent? Is that not the problem for all of us? Is not the central task of psychotherapy to examine, identify, what stories, what concepts, what self-images have captivated us, led us to our current impasse, our suffering, and to bring them to the surface, challenge them, and perhaps replace them with something larger, more capacious? Freud called the process *Nacherziehung*, or re-education, given the need to repair, or redeem the original *paideia*, or *education*, which instructed us as to who we were and what we were to do with our lives.

When we are young, vulnerable, and utterly at the mercy of the world around us, we desperately "read" the world for clues as to who we are, who the other is, what the world is about, how we are to comport ourselves, and so on. The core perceptions assemble over time into a reticulated, anxiety-driven set of autonomous responses to life's challenges. Were there no psychopathology, namely, the revolt of the *Self* (Jung's metaphor for the deep natural wisdom of the whole organism) we would be nothing but a series of reticulated and adaptive mechanisms. The revolt of the Self tells us that there is an Other within, a transcendent Other. As it is transcendent to the ego consciousness, nothing particularly useful or informative can be said about it; thus, a respectful silence is best. As Wittgenstein put it, "*Wovon man nicht sprechen kann, darueber muss man schweigen.*"[6]

So, when we look in the mirror of the world, do we see ourselves, or do we not see through the distorting lenses of our complexes, those charged clusters of history, those fractal narratives that we assemble,

---

4 Thomas Nashe, *A Litany in Time of the Plague.*
5 *The fear of death troubles me.*
6 "Whereof one cannot speak, thereof one should remain silent." *Tractatus Logicus Philosophicus.*

some conscious, some not? Is not most of our life seeing what our history tells us, what our world told us, or we thought told us a long time ago? Is not much of our history a replication of the self-image we have thought reflected to us? I have a client currently whose mother repeatedly told him that he was the cause for her unhappy life. What was he to do with that? As a child, was he to take his own life, get out of the way? He thought of that, but then he thought of his younger brothers and knew he couldn't leave them unprotected. So, he labored on through the darkness—drove himself through a life of work, overcompensation, and caretaking of others, and only now, in the sixth decade, is beginning to think of his life reflected in a different pool. As he sends his child off to college, he knows he has made her feel welcome, safe, valued, and empowered to live her own journey. The person she sees in the mirror is quite different from the one her father sees every day. And she had no idea that her father sees himself, or has seen himself as the unworthy, unwanted impediment in his mother's life all these years. As she heads off to a different journey, I have suggested to him that he share with her something of what her father's life has been so that she can begin to see him as he is, not as the perhaps overcompensated great guy he has been, but as a person who is even more worthy of respect and cherishing than she imagines.

Just as the *Self* is a transcendent Other, so the encounter with the *Other* as God is unknowable. This makes *theology*, if one thinks it through carefully, untenable. The transcendent Other is that about which one cannot speak for only silence is respectful of the transcendence of the mystery; anything short of that is a construing by ego-consciousness and a distortion by complexes. As one wit put it, one may be pretty sure we have made the gods in our own image when they seem to hate the same people we hate. (And how much history and contemporary politics does that help explain)? Or, as the ancient Xenophanes observed, if horses could draw, the gods they would draw would look like horses. So, respecting the Self as transcendent Other means the best we ever get at it is a *sense of self*.

In the so-called narcissistic personality disorder, which is discussed elsewhere in this volume, the narcissist has essentially lost connection with the corrective ministries of the Self. Thus, he or she is consumed by a default program: namely, *self-inflation as compensation for the disconnect from the Self.* (This program for living was memorably critiqued by Pearl Bailey who noted, "Them what's thinks they is, ain't.") Most of us are simply garden-variety neurotics, which means we know we have erred, we suffer our disconnections, know we are at fault, and know we have to get back in line with some deeper principle within. This *knowing* represents our attenuated but still living thread to the Self.

Today, though we have forgotten much wisdom possessed by those who went before us, we also know too much to reconnect. Blake worried about this over two centuries ago and proposed *reorganized innocence*, an oxymoron if there ever was one. Wordsworth and Rilke grasped the sad solitude of certainties lost forever, of moments of *wholeness* never to be regained. (Perhaps fortunately, most of country music thrives on this dialectic of yearning, loss, and more yearning). And what is it we really long for? Robert Frost, in a poem titled "For Once, Then, Something," reports a moment in his reflection on the matter.

> Once, when trying with chin against a well-curb,
> I discerned, as I thought, beyond the picture,
> Through the picture, a something white, uncertain,
> Something more of the depths—and then I lost it.
> Water came to rebuke the too clear water.
> One drop fell from a fern, and lo, a ripple
> Shook whatever it was lay there at bottom,
> Blurred it, blotted it out. What was that whiteness?
> Truth? A pebble of quartz? For once, then, something.

That canny old Vermonter. He is not writing about a well, and we all know it. He is probing in his usual way what there is to probe, "beyond the picture, through the picture," the received story, the conventional ego frame, *something white*, momentarily visible. Something-there. *Da-Sein?* Something from the depths. Visible at last? But no, a drop of water from a branch effaces the surface, and the image crazes in fractured shards. "What was that whiteness? Truth?" Was it that? Was it the promised truth? The Promised One? Or merely a stone shard, another hoax, another distortion through the glass darkly? Frost's perplexity is ours as well.

I imagine that when we stare into the pool, we experience what, ultimately, Narcissus experienced to his dismay. He wasn't just entranced by his beauty; he was stunned by his complexity, his infinite number of selves, his compelling regression into the black hole of the timeless *Unus Mundi*. Like the Quaker on the box of Quaker Puffed Wheat holding a box of Quaker Puffed Wheat holding a box of Quaker Puffed Wheat that so amused, perplexed, and captivated me as a child at the breakfast table, our image in the pool fades in infinite replication, infinite regression, into a carnival House of Mirrors, a receding puzzle box, a *Matryoshka* doll within a doll within a doll, and so on. Narcissus wishes to be seen, and to be seen, wholly. And so do we. The religious affirm that only God has that power, that capacity, and perhaps they are right. Perhaps the Self is that capacious power within each of us that sees and holds us with care as we tumble though an infinite space into the depths of our own fathomless mysteries. It is a pool of great depth, a pool too deep for human sight to penetrate, but we urgently look, and never stop looking.

James Hollis, PhD, is a Jungian analyst in private practice in Washington, D.C., where he is Executive Director of the Jung Society of Washington, and author of 14 books.

Bibliography

Dostoevsky, Fyodor. *Notes from Underground*. New York: New American Library, 1961.

Frost, Robert. *For Once, Then, Something*, http://www.poetryfoundation.org/poem/173528

Jung, Carl. *The Collected Works of Carl Jung*. Princeton: Princeton University Press, 1953-1979.

Section 2
Narcissism in the Era of Donald Trump

The Trump Complex, the John Wayne Archetype and States of National Possession

BY STEVEN BUSER, MD

A central theme of this book is the idea that emotional *complexes* develop not only within an individual but within a nation as well. A complex in an individual can be defined as a cluster of charged ideas, feelings, and images that can trigger unconscious and problematic behavior. Complexes arise from the collision of a person's need to adapt with his or her inability to make suitable adaptations. In Jungian psychology, a complex is thought to be a component of the personal unconscious, which groups around an *archetype* that is a part of the collective unconscious. The collective unconscious is that domain of the unconscious that possesses qualities of universality, often evident in world mythology, symbols, and recurring motifs like the Trinity or death and resurrection.

Many complexes are familiar enough to have found their way into common usage. For example, phrases like *inferiority complex, martyr complex, hero complex, mother complex, Peter Pan complex*, and many others will sound familiar to the reader. It is commonly understood that someone with an *inferiority complex* is likely to struggle with low self-esteem and may display exaggerated reactions should anyone call attention to any perceived shortcomings.

A person struggling with a *hero complex* may go to great lengths to secure a spot as the hero who is always victorious. In the course of their unrelenting need to be the winner or to be perceived as a hero, such individuals may become vicious and even cutthroat.

The force and power exerted by a complex is often determined by the severity of difficult life experiences that created the complex. The wounds we sustain in life predispose us to developing complexes that can overtake us later in life. People can become so identified with a particular complex that it is as if they are possessed by it. Once a person is possessed by a complex, there is virtually no room for any other emotions or behaviors to be expressed. C.G. Jung wrote, "Everyone knows nowadays that people *have complexes.* What is not so well known, though far more important theoretically, is that complexes can *have us."* (CW 8, par. 200)

Suppose, instead of a complex affecting a single individual, we consider what happens if a complex affects an entire nation. Nations certainly suffer wounds. A nation may be called upon to adapt to these wounds yet be unable to meet the challenge adequately, thus leading to the formation of a national complex. There is evidence that a nation, or a group within a nation, can be overtaken by complexes that provoke unusual mass behavior. For example, the Rwandan Civil War witnessed an outbreak of genocidal behavior on the part of Hutu, who set about slaughtering Tutsis, who had been their friends and neighbors prior to the outbreak of war.

The last 15 years visited enormous psychological trauma on the United States of America. On September 11, 2001, the nation watched as a terrorist attack caused the collapse of the Twin Towers in New York City and the fiery crash on a portion of the Pentagon, a national symbol of the country's military might. In addition to the ceaseless obsession with terrorism, the nation plunged into two protracted wars. By 2008, the economy had lost its momentum, and a financial crisis that might have rivaled the Great Depression was narrowly averted. For nearly a decade, the Legislative and Executive branches of government in the U.S. have been deadlocked. During this same period, the world confronted Ebola, threats of climate change and global warming, deforestation, rising oceans, rampant pollution, and environmental degradation. What have these deep, unhealed wounds of the nation constellated in the psyche of the United States?

> If, for a moment, we look at mankind as one individual, we see that it is like a man carried away by unconscious powers. (CW 18, para 531)

Just as wounds create unconscious complexes within an individual, collective wounds sustained by a nation may cause cultural complexes within the nation's unconscious. The cumulative wounds suffered by the U.S. and other Western nations that once enjoyed a sort of world dominance have now led to a sense of powerlessness. Incessant wars, financial strains, and a frustrating inability to remove the terrorist threat has left nations feeling isolated and helpless. We are left to wonder if the soil has been tilled for a charismatic, self-promoting leader to tap into the deep complexes that formed around this sense of powerlessness experienced by a nation. Perhaps the United States is under the influence of a powerful complex. If so, we might call this the *Trump Complex.*

The *Trump Complex* arises from our nation's repeated injuries tracing back to 9/11, two languishing wars, the exportation of jobs, the influx of immigrants, and economic stagnation. This *Trump Complex* unleashes anger in the growing crowds while powerfully yet unconsciously compelling them toward a perceived solution of strength and nostalgia. The solution claims the need for a *strongman*, someone who will stand up to terrorists, immigrants, and *corrupt* politicians, while also returning us to the nostalgia of the *good old days*, when America viewed itself as strong and dominant on the world stage. The phenomenon nostalgically pulls people back to a time when notions of inclusion, diversity, and political correctness had not even entered the national consciousness. The *Trump Complex* compels many Americans to align with a leader embodying this image of strength and nostalgia.

Remembering that at the core of a complex is an archetype, I propose that the *Trump Complex* is rooted in the *John Wayne Archetype*. John Wayne was a famous screen actor who starred in countless Westerns in which he was depicted as the strong, rugged figure who never backed down from a fight, said exactly what he thought, and always knew who the bad guy was. He was a man who aimed straight and didn't hesitate to pull the trigger. This *John Wayne Archetype* animates the powerful emotions within the *Trump Complex*. Thus, at the core of the *Trump Complex* lies what I call a *John Wayne Archetype* that has gripped a nation so forcefully that an unlikely candidate who displays some of the features of the archetype stood poised to make a bid for the Presidency of the United States of America.

Steven Buser, MD, trained in medicine at Duke University and served 12 years as a physician in the US Air Force. He is a graduate of a two-year Clinical Training Program at the CG Jung Institute of Chicago and is the co-founder of the Asheville Jung Center. In addition to a busy psychiatric private practice, he serves as Publisher of Chiron Publications.

Healthy Presidential Narcissism Is that Possible?

BY NATHAN SCHWARTZ-SALANT, PhD

The 2016 presidential election is strikingly different from past campaigns. The facts—the candidates' histories and policy positions—seem insufficient to explain why people are so fervent in supporting Donald Trump, or Ted Cruz, or Bernie Sanders. What has been missing in the critique of all the experts who believed Trump's campaign had to collapse? Why did they think someone as widely disliked as Ted Cruz would command a serious position in the race? Or how could an old-time lefty like Bernie Sanders galvanize millions of voters and threaten the supremacy of Hillary Clinton, who from the start was the choice of pundits to easily win the Democratic Party's mantle?

Many answers have been given, notably that Donald Trump channels the extreme anger of the disenfranchised middle class; Bernie Sanders stands for radical change from a failed and corrupt political system, a change that especially resonates with younger voters; while Ted Cruz exemplified rock-solid conservative values and the religious fervor of evangelicals. All this is true enough but hardly defines the unusual nature of the campaign, for previous elections have also featured such elements.

Indeed, there is another influencing factor largely independent of real present-day and historical issues. It is the issue of *identity*, a sense of I Am. In a quest for understanding the forces driving this election, the slogan, "It's the economy, stupid," should be replaced by "It's identity, stupid."

When a person's job and capacity to put food on the table for their family is lost, or when people live in fear of that happening, or of losing their home as well, they suffer a severe narcissistic injury. Self-esteem and sense of purpose plummet, identity fragments, and the void is filled by despair, rage, and often by a very defensive grandiosity. How candidates respond to this injury to identity in the electorate is key to understanding why some have done so much better than expected and others have lagged behind.

The term *narcissism* has entered the campaign, but generally as a pejorative way of describing a candidate. However, the concept is far more subtle and important than name-calling. For narcissism is a term and body of thought that concerns the mystery of identity—Who am I?

Why am I here? Where am I going?—and addresses how its fallen sense can be restored.

Understanding narcissism further clarifies why, in this election, a candidate can propose what others see as *unrealistic*—great border walls being built; devastating, even nuclear, wars initiated if called for; financial institutions torn down; millions of residents deported; single-payer medical plans established; and so on. The question *"How will you do this?"* usually comes out with a tone of superiority that implies it's all pie in the sky, and destructive at that. Then there is bewilderment when, for the most part, the only ones nodding in agreement are those who approve the status quo and are a part of it.

Identity and the Self

In everyday life we tend to take our sense of identity for granted, as though it isn't a problem to care and wonder about. If asked, "Who are you?" people will likely answer by describing what they do: I am a teacher, a mother, an engineer, a physicist, a psychoanalyst, an athlete, a writer, a policeman. This adaptation, innocent about the depths and mystery of identity, works well enough, but if it fails, in its absence symptoms like depression and anger appear. *"What"* one did has been lost, and nothing has filled its place.

That leads us to the profound basis of identity, as when Moses asks the Old Testament God his name and is told: "I Am That I Am," or when the Hindu guru Maharaj answers the question, "Who are you?" with "I Am That," or when the Sufi master shows *divine pride* and celebrates his or her qualities and their origin. All these revolve around knowing and showing the ineffable center of our being, the *self*, for that is the source of identity.

The self is a subtle, inner presence, a guide that can be consulted when a person makes serious choices. The hero in a fairy tale comes to a crossroad and throws a feather in the air to determine which direction to take. The self provides such a spiritual attitude and guide within.

Through experiencing the self, a person meets what Socrates called his *Daemon*, Nietzsche his *Superman*, Emerson his *Genius*, Jung his *Philemon*, or the alchemist's *Stone of the Wise*, or Luke Skywalker's *The Force* in *Star Wars*. A long list could be drawn from history and literature of lives, young and old, that were inwardly informed, as if the power of a god spoke through the person. Furthermore, the relationship to this power could be nurtured and its presence counted on, even under highly stressful conditions.

But the aliveness, form, and presence of this mysterious orienting center of being can be greatly impeded. Abandonment or betrayal by a person, or institution, can cause the self to fragment and lose vitality, its positive features gone from awareness.

Without a connection to the self—at most a living, felt experience, or at least something we may intuit within that *backs us up* and infuses us with a sense of knowing ourselves, a sense we might call "instinctual"—we have no individual compass and little hold on identity. One is drawn to be part of a collective mind, uncritically attaching to collective values of power, fame, and money, those seductive and false indicators of self-esteem. A bloated ego then takes the place of the self.

Thus presidential candidates, especially in this election, must somehow represent and channel the energies of a deeper center. In mythical cultures a king or queen had this function. The health of the entire community depended on it. And while today's secular views dismiss such ideas, this is, nevertheless, the essential function of any world leader.

Their primary role is not offering realistic programs and laws, but being capable of animating the sacred center of the people, so that the *ordinary man or woman* feels uplifted, and rays of hope for the present and future emerge.

Certain candidates, notably Trump, Sanders, and to some extent Cruz, have been capable of representing the self to a crowd in dire need of restoring, if not discovering, a sense of identity. In the language of psychoanalysis, these candidates are not *real objects*, with positive and negative traits. They have a different status: They are *self-objects*.

The term jars sensibilities because its abstraction so diverges from the actual beauty and vastness of the self. But it is a useful term. It helps one focus on how a person who carries the projection of the self is different from a normal, real person. The latter has pros and cons, what is good and not so good. But interacting with the former, a self-object, is like looking into a mirror and seeing an image that can reflect aspects of who we really are.

Many religious and cultural institutions have been self-objects. Whether through revered figures in the world's great religions, or through modern-day programs such as Alcoholics Anonymous with its motto—"I can't, God can, I will trust God"—that mysterious sense of a self can be reached, even if largely on an unconscious level.

People may actually dream of a leader who represents the mystery of the self within. Even in a dream state that barely emerges into consciousness, the self can be enlivened. And from such depths lives can change. Most significantly, a person begins to feel a sense of identity, a unique "*I Am*" with an individual purpose, no longer just a cog in a collective wheel.

The subject of narcissism involves the nature of a person's inner link to the self. Is he or she identified with it? Or is the self an orienting factor that the conscious person relates to? And how does a self-object restore this related condition? Finally, how is a candidate, Donald Trump in particular, able to gain self-object status?

Narcissism—Healthy and Pathological

Everyone has narcissistic traits. It usually takes another person to point them out, which is always unpleasant and somewhat wounding. But if we are capable of seeing ourselves in a critical light, we have to recognize any number of these disagreeable characteristics. For example, we may have to acknowledge that at times we demand being admired and understood by another person to the exclusion of any concern for that person's feelings and thoughts. And we may also recognize that we are capable of feeling, if not exhibiting, a ruthless rage when such demands are not met. Or we may come to know that we tend, out of fear, to squelch this anger and then feel dejected, anxious, mildly depressed, and even for a day or two without the energy for goal-oriented tasks.

Such demands can render us grandiose and arrogant know-it-alls. This can take many forms, from trivial to weighty. Who among us has not lied about having read a book, when we only intended to read it? And do we not at times fail at empathy—that act of "feeling into" a person, or "getting into another person's shoes"—which is a crucial, defining trait of narcissism. If we are really honest, we may confess that we withhold empathy as part of a desire to retaliate for "not being seen," a phrase common to the jargon that attends the idea of narcissism.

To perceive someone as a narcissistic personality means that such traits define the person to a high degree. But the concept of narcissism is extremely complex, and diagnosing someone as narcissistic is not only a cheap shot, but explains nothing, even though the person in question may display glaring, negative-narcissistic qualities. For instance, that same person as a politician may innately, and to some degree consciously, relate to the terrible wounded narcissism of many in the electorate.

However, becoming identified with the self does lead to pathological negative narcissism, and with it all the well-known characteristics like grandiosity; controlling demands to be listened to while showing no genuine interest in, let alone empathy for, another person; and the inability to take criticism without growing angry and sadistic, or else withdrawn. This identification with the self leads to ego inflation, the outrageous arrogance of one who fails to recognize that they are being graced by energies of the self, taking this power to be their own.

It is only when a person lives the internal energy and wisdom of the self, while also feeling separate from it, that they exhibit healthy narcissism. They show the wonder of the self and its creative process, that is, not of the ego but of the mysterious other within. A state of healthy narcissism stands out in the story of Paul on the road to Damascus: "It is not I that do this but He that does this through me." That is the essence of healthy narcissism; one feels the self moving through one's being, informing one of a way to go or not go, of what to say or not say.

Healthy narcissism may not necessarily stem from a living awareness of the self, as in Paul's awareness of Christ working through him. It can appear more mundanely, and too easily be reduced by others to pathological narcissism.

For example, a man who occasionally works for me will tell me stories about his personal encounters, or how he solved a complicated mechanical problem, going on and on in seemingly endless detail. I like him and usually find the time to listen, although this is often difficult to manage. But I notice that I never feel controlled by him. At any moment I can say, "I'm sorry, but I have to leave now." I feel no pull from him to go on listening. He respects my need to leave. He will not be hurt. He will not withdraw and sulk. He will not be *narcissistically injured*.

In fact, he is not narcissistic in any negative sense. He is showing me the beauty and wonder of the creative process flowing within him and takes pride in this. Though he can stray into endless storytelling, even then his tone and feeling about a person he describes is not critical and filled with hate and envy but with intense interest. His narcissism is like the Sufi's divine pride; it is healthy narcissism.

Such healthy narcissism, engendered by social institutions, formed the American Dream—that belief in a person's inalienable right to shape his or her own destiny—through which citizens were empowered. The spirit of the nation could be roused by the oratory genius of Obama with his rallying cry of hope, or by Kennedy's challenge: "Ask not what your country can do for you—ask what you can do for your country."

But when, especially in 2007, the healthy narcissism of millions was undermined by failures of government and by self-seeking Wall Street executives who had had self-object status, the Dream died. Now its promise would largely fall on deaf ears. Those days of seemingly limitless possibilities for Everyman were over.

As a consequence, it was natural for many in the electorate to regressively identify with the self as a power source, and a very unstable condition arose. For a sense of strength and agency would seem available. But it could only be a false, inflated state, and with it came the enfeeblement accompanying pathological narcissism.

This is a trap lurking in the negative narcissistic condition. It is not as though one can ease away from the perils of identification with the self, notably the isolation, hubris, and damage created, and still maintain some of the good energy in a realistic way. Rather, the pseudo-identity one assumed completely disappears, as does the empowerment.

Here is the internal dilemma of narcissism: One cannot stay identified with the energies of the self, nor can one separate from them. The only way to avoid this intense suffering seems to be to replace inflation with a *negative inflation*, in which one falls into enfeeblement rife with anxiety, low energy, and depression. The glow of the self disappears, identity plummets, and despair takes over.

Barring the redemptive state of a mystical experience, this narcissistic condition is only transformed into a healthy *relation* to the self by experiencing a self-object.

Enlivening Healthy Narcissism: Becoming a Self-Object

Back to our starting point: What is it that allows candidates to flourish in this election against all *realistic* expectations? The answer, I believe, is that they manage to project themselves as self-objects. This explains the phenomenon of Donald Trump, and to a significant but lesser extent, Bernie Sanders. Ted Cruz achieved this standing to a degree, by virtue of identifying with the self-object status of the Constitution and conservative values.

A candidate felt as a self-object can trigger the regeneration of healthy narcissism and, with it, a regained sense of identity. Through this force, many of those dispossessed since 2008 began to feel the emergence of hope and ambition. This is strong medicine. And no matter how much a candidate's *real qualities* seem to jar, the one seen as a self-object has that "Teflon coating" so mystifying to the experts.

For example, Donald Trump has been criticized for being just a showman. But that misses the point. For to constellate the self-image for people in the political arena, one must engage and partially identify with roles that have a numinous quality, much as a great actor can. Some criticized Ronald Reagan for *playing the president*. They were unaware of the compliment they gave him; he played the part well.

Leaders must project something of a numinous power, far beyond human scale. In Jung's terms, they have to reflect an archetypal image. If they become inwardly identified with such power, that would mean pathological narcissism. Instead, to some degree, they must feel and project the energy of the self flowing through them. That is, some degree of healthy narcissism must also be present.

Notice the archetypal roles Trump is playing. He is surely like the court Fool who criticizes the King. Trump acts the fool in numerous ways, and all are *politically incorrect*. Now one might argue that he doesn't intend this at all and that he is a narcissistic buffoon who can't help himself. I doubt it. He plays the role adroitly, and while I hardly find him a beacon of consciousness or individuation, there is more to him than pathological narcissism.

Trump also takes on the archetypal strength of the Wise Old Man. His business experience is touted as the elixir of change; he knows how to make a deal. He Knows.

Trump channels suprahuman forces, proposing more than any mortal president could accomplish. He purports to do what a rational person would see as impossible, but mythological figures perform remarkable feats. And that is the energy Trump uses, mixed with his personality, which seems to teem with narcissistic traits. Yet, in it all there are strands of healthy narcissism, and from this blend he has been able to become a mighty self-object.

In a much different mode, but like Trump, Bernie Sanders is a self-object more than a real object. He rails away as an Old Testament prophet or revolutionary hero would, unmasking the evils of society and promising the destruction of the root of the problem—the greed and avarice of the 1 percent and Wall Street. And he is seen as a prophet by millions, both younger voters and lifelong critics of the dark side of capitalism.

Sanders projects powers and stands for changes that are beyond the scope of *real* programs; but no matter how much his proposals are assailed by sober economists or other candidates, notably Hillary Clinton, his popularity persists. Why? Because he catches a self-object projection and, against its aura, realities, things as they are, being pragmatic, seem irrelevant for those caught up in his crusade. Again like Trump, Sanders shows positive narcissism, but he is probably far less identified with the archetypal.

Trump takes on that element of narcissism called showing the "grandiose-exhibitionistic self," but he does it in a crafted way that resonates with the idea of divine pride. He is often just plain grandiose, but often not. When he says, "I am Very rich," is that the speech of someone merely boasting about his own fortune? It doesn't come across that way; something more is involved, a kind of just-so story about great wealth, about what is. Sanders plays a different polarity of narcissism, that of idealization. He becomes the idealized self-object and, as such, lifts up the demoralized masses. He is the courageous radical with lofty ideals.

But like Trump, Sanders has a way of projecting ideas and plans that resonate with divine pride—a pride in the message and its truth—without being totally identified with it. Neither is a madman, but both stray recklessly close to the power of the archetype.

Cruz didn't seem to live in these waters. His narcissism was legendary in the ways it turned so many people off. But he aligned with the powerful self-object of conservatism and evangelicalism. In that regard, despite his failings, his message also afforded a source of identity.

Unfortunately, over time, few leaders handle a self-object projection in a good and consistent manner. It is no small thing to be revered and not inwardly identify with this projection. Leaders tend to become overbearing and eventually tyrannical, if not criminal, outside the law. Very few gurus have escaped this, and very few personalities, whose self-object status led nations, have avoided becoming inflated and mad. One can point to Mao and Stalin, and perhaps Nixon, and thousands of priests, for starters.

Will the strength of the self-object projection endure for a candidate throughout the present election? Or will attacks that muster *facts* about the person, or assaults on their *unrealistic programs*, take their toll? Will a candidate, notably Donald Trump, take on the politically dangerous maneuver of becoming more realistic, or more *presidential*, to the exclusion of his showmanship and archetypal identifications? That could quickly diminish his self-object status.

It is all part of the drama playing out in the election of 2016. Identity, and the role of the self-object in renewing healthy narcissism, is the central feature.

Nathan Schwartz-Salant, PhD, is a Jungian Analyst and co-founder of Chiron Publications. He has authored numerous books including *The Black Nightgown, The Borderline Personality, Narcissism and Character Formation.*

Trump and the American Selfie
Archetypal Defenses of the Group Spirit

BY TOM SINGER, MD

I: Trump's Selfie

Donald Trump is currently carrying around a selfie stick with the longest reach in the world. And, for a long time, America has also been carrying around a selfie stick with the longest reach in the world. In a recent trip to a town as remote as Alice Springs in the middle of Australia, I noted that the charge in the dinner conversation shot through the roof at the very mention of Trump's name. Everybody is watching him and wondering what he is about, and he seems happy to have his image become a global dark hole, sucking up planetary time and energy.

Mysterious Forces of the Universe, by Matt Davies • DAVIES © 2016 Newsday. Dist. By UNIVERSAL UCLICK. Reprinted with permission. All rights reserved.

For the media, having Donald Trump run for president is as compelling as a terrorist bomb bringing down an airplane every day—huge, dire excitement that incites obsessive attention. After dominating daily Google searches for all of 2016, Trump was finally out searched for a few days in late May when Americans frantically Googled *gorilla* because zookeepers at the Cincinnati Zoo shot Harambe, a 17-year-old lowland gorilla, after a 4-year-old boy fell into the primate's enclosure.

[Screen shot from *Google Trends*]

Compare

Gorilla   Donald Trump   + Add term

Interest over time

Searches for "Donald Trump"

Searches for the word "Gorilla"

Donald Trump v. Gorilla Screen Shot Provided by Chiron Publications

How absurdly synchronous that Donald Trump and a gorilla were fighting it out for the nation's attention. How hungry and needy we are for stimulation! At this point, so many words have been written and spoken about Donald Trump, so many theories put forth, that I feel as if I am contributing to the pollution of the environment by adding even one more word or one more theory to the stew. But here I go because I, too, am obsessed and can't help it. I am joining the not-so-cottage industry that is riding the Trump brand.

The fact is we are all trying to make sense out of the Donald Trump phenomenon and just about everybody has become a talking head, pasting together various theories about what Donald Trump's attraction as a presidential candidate really means. Stephen Hawking, a man who knows the universe and mathematics well, is perhaps the only wise man among us when he admits to being baffled when asked on ITV's *Good Morning Britain* to explain Donald Trump: "I can't," he said. Hawking went on to comment, "He is a demagogue who seems to appeal to the lowest common denominator."

Early in the Republican primaries, *The Huffington Post*'s theory was that Trump was a buffoon. The editors pontificated that he didn't deserve coverage on the front page of their website and dismissed his candidacy as a folly that would shortly collapse. They vowed to their readers that they would only report his electioneering in the entertainment section. But the day after announcing that Trump was "entertainment," *The Huffington Post* ran a front-page story on him and has done so almost every day since, making false to their readers the promise of not giving him any more headline attention. Trump rolled over their pledge in less than 24 hours in the same way that he has crushed all Republican opposition. There was simply too much free-floating anger and frustration in the national psyche about the current state of affairs in the United States to be activated and exploited by a figure like Trump who appears to have an uncanny knack for pricking sacred cows. His early attacks on *political correctness* scored a direct hit on a hugely vulnerable spot in the national psyche.

There is widespread fear in our country that things are falling apart, from our infrastructure (Flint, MI) to our economic position in the world economy, to our ability to maintain a high standard of living and care for all our citizens, to our vulnerability to terror attacks and other forms of socio-economic disruption from outside and within our country. Trump's unique ability to capitalize on these fears could not be ignored by *The Huffington Post* or any other newspaper, journal, television or radio show, or other form of social media. Trump has the special ability to turn his campaign and person into a marketing spectacle, an irresistible circus fueled by his inflammatory comments on everything from the Mexicans to Muslims, women, his opponents, judges, and any other ready target of his apparently endless source of deep anger, aggression, suspicions, fears, and his seemingly unparalleled gift for bullying.

Trump's foundational cries of "Get 'em outta here!!!" and "Make American Great again!" are perfectly attuned to the hatreds and longings at the group level of the psyche of many Americans. No one has been able to avert their gaze or turn their cash registers away from Trump. He has managed to capture and dominate our national discourse and imagination. He has been able to mesmerize or stun nearly everyone who crosses his path, including his fellow candidates running for the Republican nomination. Les Moonves, president of CBS, speaking at a Morgan Stanley Technology, Media & Telecom Conference in San Francisco, let the cat out of the bag:

> It may not be good for America, but it's damn good for CBS. ... Man, who would have expected the ride we're all having right now? ... The money's rolling in, and this is fun. I've never seen anything like this, and this going to be a very good year for us. Sorry. It's a terrible thing to say. But, bring it on, Donald. Keep going. (Collins, 2016)

The hard-to-believe fact is that there are now many people in America (not just white males who didn't graduate from high school or lost their jobs to overseas manufacturing or who are *authoritarian types*) who believe Trump is good for them and that he is uniquely qualified to lead the country in a new, positive direction. The focus of this chapter is less on the narcissism of Trump or other world leaders. Rather it is more on the question of why Trump's gaudy self-parade is appealing to so many people. Trump's appeal—his apparent money, power, and celebrity status, and his brash willingness to shoot from the hip—seems to resonate with the collective psyche of many Americans. The more vulgar his appearance and self-congratulatory his behavior and rhetoric, the more some people appear to be drawn to him. Trump's campaign has been a three-ring circus of peddling Trump steaks and other bombastic poses, a charade of a campaign that looks and sounds liked a staged wrestling match, and it is working. That it is working says something about the tastes, the intelligence, and the needs of many Americans. Of course, what I and others see as Trump's *narcissism* and his self-aggrandizing display of opulent wealth and brute power, others see as success and the ultimate achievement of the American dream.

Kevin KAL Kallaugher, Baltimore Sun, Kaltoon.com

The Trump/anti-Trump showdown has become a kind of cultural complex in which the major attraction is surprisingly not so much Trump himself as a person but the national psychodrama playing itself out in the collective psyches of various groups in the country and their differing projections onto Trump, for which he is a perfect hook

The Huffington Post was not able to honor its high-ground stance to its readers to keep Trump off the front page any more than Trump presumably would be able to honor his promise, if elected president, to build a wall on the border between the United States and Mexico and have Mexico pay for it. But Trump's presence in the political arena has been all-consuming and has drawn to himself a kind of possession of the national and international psyche that defies reason. His manna has been a powerful medicine if you are for him or a truly toxic poison if you are against him. It is almost impossible for me to imagine what it feels like from the inside to embrace Trump. But in a way that is the challenge of trying to understand this irrational possession, whatever we label it and whatever origins/causes we attribute to it. There have been as many theories about Donald Trump's magnetic appeal or revulsion as there are theories about the causes of schizophrenia. Schizophrenia is not a bad analogy because Trump's candidacy has further revealed and amplified deep splits in the psyche of the country (and many parts of the world). For those of us profoundly disgusted and frightened by Trump—from his physical appearance and mannerisms to his worldview to his apparent beliefs and policies—it takes a considerable effort to understand or find empathy for those who have joined his movement. What causes a significant portion of our population to see Trump as a hope for America's and the world's future? That is the challenge of this chapter, which, Dear Reader, you must consider as a work in progress, as the verbal equivalent of a collage. The events and themes of riding the Trump rollercoaster are unfolding on a daily basis, and, for the individual, it is like being carried away by a flood in which one is lucky to come up for air just long enough to get a breath before being pushed under again.

II: Blind Monks Describing an Elephant

Trying to understand Trump reminds me of the well-known story from the Indian subcontinent of several blind monks touching an elephant to learn what it is like. But each touches a different part of its huge body, and the monks are in complete disagreement about what the elephant is. Trump is our elephant, and even though he says he's a Republican, he hardly acts like one.

Before putting forth my own theory, I want to offer a brief survey of some of the more interesting commentaries that have surfaced, variations of which have appeared just about everywhere. Each day, it seems, there is some new *take* on what Trump is really all about—both as a person and as a cultural/political phenomenon. I have divided these theories into various categories that might be helpful in terms of how to approach this beast.

Blind Men Appraising an Elephant, by Ohara Donshu, Edo Period (early 19th century), Wikipedia Image

The Demographics of Early Trump Supporters

The most basic information about Trump's early appeal came from demographic studies that gave clear indicators about Trump's core constituency. One sure thing is that the early Trump supporters who created the emotional energy and momentum for his surprising emergence as the dominant Republican candidate will be diluted considerably as that core constituency will be joined by most traditional Republicans (and other Hillary Clinton haters) who will present a much broader and more varied demographic profile in terms of income, socioeconomic position, and so on. In other words, Trump is going to have far more support than one would have imagined at the outset. Initially, the typical Trump supporter was white, without a high school diploma, born in the United States, frequently living in a mobile home, with an *old economy job,* often with a segregationist voting record, and quite likely an Evangelical Christian. A chart of the profile of early Trump supporters can be found at http://www.nytimes.com/2016/03/13/upshot/the-geography-of-trumpism.html.

The Character Type of Trump Supporters

Various notions of what motivates a Trump supporter have been put forward. Matthew MacWilliams, writing in *Politico*, argues that gender, age, income, race, or religion are not reliable predictors of an individual being a Trump supporter:

> Only two of the variables I looked at were statistically significant: authoritarianism, followed by fear of terrorism, though the former was far more significant than the latter.

> Authoritarianism is not a new, untested concept in the American electorate. Since the rise of Nazi Germany, it has been one of the most widely studied ideas in social science. While its causes are still debated, the political behavior of authoritarians is not. Authoritarians obey. They rally to and follow strong leaders. And they respond aggressively to outsiders, especially when they feel threatened. From pledging to *"make America great again"* by building a wall on the border to promising to close mosques and ban Muslims from visiting the United States, Trump is playing directly to authoritarian inclinations. (MacWilliams, 2016, paras. 5, 6)

About authoritarian types, Dan B. McAdams writes in *The Atlantic*:

> During and after World War II, psychologists conceived of the authoritarian personality as a pattern of attitudes and values revolving around adherence to society's traditional norms, submission to authorities who personify or reinforce those norms, and antipathy—to the point of hatred and aggression—toward those who either challenge in-group norms or lie outside their orbit. Among white Americans, high scores on measures of authoritarianism today tend to be associated with prejudice against a wide range of *out-groups*, including homosexuals, African Americans, immigrants, and Muslims. Authoritarianism is also associated with suspiciousness of the humanities and the arts, and with cognitive rigidity, militaristic sentiments, and Christian fundamentalism. (McAdams, 2016, *I. His Disposition*)

Trump's Character

Obviously, Trump's character has also been the object of many articles. The most thorough and thoughtful that I have seen is the one by McAdams in *The Atlantic*. His conclusions include the observations that Trump is a *highly extroverted, remarkably disagreeable, socially ambitious, very aggressive, angry, vigilant, fierce, tough, disciplined, narcissistic warrior*, with a desire *to win at any cost*. McAdams also observes that Trump seems to lack or is not burdened by the capacity for self-reflection and is apparently without a meaningful vision for himself or the country beyond his winning the presidency. It is well worth reading McAdams' complete analysis of Trump, as he combines both a trained psychological and historical perspective. About a possible Trump Presidency, he writes the following:

> In sum, Donald Trump's basic personality traits suggest a presidency that could be highly combustible. One possible yield is an energetic, activist president who has a less than cordial relationship with the truth. He could be a daring and ruthlessly aggressive decision maker who desperately desires to create the strongest, tallest, shiniest, and most awesome result—and who never thinks twice about the collateral damage he will leave behind. Tough. Bellicose. Threatening. Explosive. (McAdams, 2016, *I. His Disposition*)

McAdams, as well as others, has the impression that Trump is always playing a role—*Trump playing Trump*—and that the *real* Donald Trump remains elusive, mysterious, and perhaps doesn't even exist. Maybe he is a new kind of 21st-century personality, a character given over entirely to brand, illusion, and hyperbole—a reality TV character.

> Who, really, is Donald Trump? What's behind the actor's mask? I can discern little more than narcissistic motivations and a complementary personal narrative about winning at any cost. It is as if Trump has invested so much of himself in developing and refining his socially dominant role that he has nothing left over to create a meaningful story for his life, or for the nation. *It is always Donald Trump playing Donald Trump*, fighting to win, but never knowing why. (McAdams, 2016, *IV. His Self-Conception*)

The State of Our Culture

Three commentators have caught my attention in terms of placing Trump's candidacy in a cultural context. Andrew Sullivan, writing in *New York* magazine, lays out a disturbingly insightful theory that Trump represents the kind of leadership that emerges in the end stages of democracy. In *Democracies*

End When They Are Too Democratic, Sullivan harkens back to his early read-
ings of Plato in which Socrates says:

> ....that "tyranny is probably established out of no other
> regime than democracy."

> What did Plato mean by that? Democracy, for him, I
> discovered, was a political system of maximal freedom
> and equality, where every lifestyle is allowed and public
> offices are filled by a lottery. And the longer a democ-
> racy lasted, Plato argued, the more democratic it would
> become. Its freedoms would multiply; its equality spread.
> Deference to any sort of authority would wither; toler-
> ance of any kind of inequality would come under intense
> threat; and multiculturalism and sexual freedom would
> create a city or a country like "a many-colored cloak
> decorated in all hues."

> This rainbow-flag polity, Plato argues, is, for many people,
> the fairest of regimes. The freedom in that democracy has
> to be experienced to be believed—with shame and priv-
> ilege in particular emerging over time as anathema. But
> it is inherently unstable. As the authority of elites fades,
> as Establishment values cede to popular ones, views and
> identities can become so magnificently diverse as to be
> mutually uncomprehending. And when all the barriers
> to equality, formal and informal, have been removed;
> when everyone is equal; when elites are despised and full
> license is established to do *whatever one wants,* you arrive
> at what might be called late-stage democracy. There is no
> kowtowing to authority here, let alone to political experi-
> ence or expertise...

> And it is when a democracy has ripened as fully as this,
> Plato argues, that a would-be tyrant will often seize his
> moment.

> He is usually of the elite but has a nature in tune with
> the time—given over to random pleasures and whims,
> feasting on plenty of food and sex, and reveling in the
> nonjudgment that is democracy's civil religion. He makes
> his move by *"taking over a particularly obedient mob"*
> and attacking his wealthy peers as corrupt. If not stopped
> quickly, his appetite for attacking the rich on behalf of
> the people swells further. He is a traitor to his class—and
> soon, his elite enemies, shorn of popular legitimacy, find

a way to appease him or are forced to flee. Eventually, he stands alone, promising to cut through the paralysis of democratic incoherence. It's as if he were offering the addled, distracted, and self-indulgent citizens a kind of relief from democracy's endless choices and insecurities. He rides a backlash to excess—*"too much freedom seems to change into nothing but too much slavery"*—and offers himself as the personified answer to the internal conflicts of the democratic mess. He pledges, above all, to take on the increasingly despised elites. And as the people thrill to him as a kind of solution, a democracy willingly, even impetuously, repeals itself. (Sullivan, 2016, paras. 1–2, 4–5)

The second author whose trenchant analysis of American culture has caught my interest is Christopher Hedges. I find myself in sad agreement with his observations about who we have become as a people and a nation. First, Hedges dissects how we have increasingly lost the capacity to distinguish illusion from reality in our private and public lives:

We are a culture that has been denied, or has passively given up, the linguistic and intellectual tools to cope with complexity, to separate illusion from reality. We have traded the printed word for the gleaming image. Public rhetoric is designed to be comprehensible to a ten-year-old child with a sixth grade reading level. Most of us speak at this level, are entertained and think at this level. We have transformed our culture into a vast replica of Pinocchio's Pleasure Island, where boys were lured with the promise of no school and endless fun. They were all however, turned into donkeys—a symbol, in Italian culture, of ignorance and stupidity....When a nation becomes unmoored from reality, it retreats into a world of magic. Facts are accepted or discarded according to the dictates of preordained cosmology. The search for truth becomes irrelevant. Our national discourse is dominated by manufactured events, from celebrity gossip to staged showcasing of politicians to elaborate entertainment and athletic spectacles. All are sold to us through the detailed personal narratives of those we watch.

Pseudoevents, dramatic productions orchestrated by publicists, political machines, television, Hollywood, or advertisers... have the capacity to appear real, even though we know they are staged. They are effective because they can evoke a powerful emotional response which overshadows reality

> and replaces it with a fictional narrative that often becomes
> accepted as truth. (Hedges, 2009, pp. 44, 50)

If our unwillingness and inability to sort our illusion from reality is not enough in itself, it gets further hopelessly entangled with our cult of celebrity. Hedges does not spare us the dire consequences of our intoxication and possession with celebrity:

> Celebrity culture plunges us into a moral void. No one has any worth beyond his or her appearance, usefulness, or ability to *succeed*. The highest achievements in a celebrity culture are wealth, sexual conquest, and fame. It does not matter how these are obtained. These values, as Sigmund Freud understood, are illusory. They are hollow. They leave us chasing vapors. They urge us toward a life of narcissistic self-absorption. They tell us that existence is to be centered on the practices and desires of the self rather than the common good. The ability to lie and manipulate others is held up as the highest good.

> The cult of self dominates our cultural landscape. This cult has within it the classic traits of the psychopaths: superficial charm, grandiosity, and self-importance; a need for constant stimulation, a penchant for lying, deception and manipulation, and the inability to feel remorse or guilt.

> It is the misguided belief that personal style and personal advancements, mistaken for individualism, are the same as democratic equality. We have a right, in the cult of the self, to get whatever we desire. We can do anything, even belittle and destroy those around us, including our friends, to make money, to be happy, and to become famous. Once fame and wealth are archived, they become their own justification, their own morality. How one gets there is irrelevant. Once you get there, those questions are no longer asked. (Hedges, 2009, pp. 32–33)

If you didn't know otherwise, you would assume that Hedges is sketching a portrait of Trump, the Republican candidate, in the preceding description. But the fact is that Hedges' analysis of our cult of celebrity was written well before Trump's full-blown emergence on the national scene as a presidential candidate. Rather, Hedges is describing a generic kind of celebrity—whether politician, businessman, actor, or athlete. And generic celebrity is at the heart of our social, political, and cultural life. He is describing all of us, who we are as a people, who many of us would like to be.

Finally, the third author, Robert Reynolds, a former congressional staff person, a former trustee of the Marin Community Foundation, and a former Republican, offers this cogent analysis:

> Trump has survived the rhetorical equivalent of spitting on the Constitution and the American flag and yet he marches on with thousands flocking to his events and turning out to vote for him?
>
> So who are these people who are so angry that they would seemingly be willing to tear down the foundations of our government and social order and elect a man so manifestly unqualified to be President?
>
> Here in California and the salons of Manhattan and Washington it is said dismissively that the Trump supporters live in the *fly over places*. They are out of work and angry. They just don't understand or care about the consequences if Trump is actually elected. And that is exactly the point. This was the case in the late sixties when angry, disenfranchised blacks burned down their own neighborhoods and major cities in a stampede of violence and rage. They believed that it did not matter; they had lost hope and so they chanted, *"Burn, Baby! Burn!"* This is the case with much of the Arab world that feels betrayed and threatened by modernity. These red-blooded American Jihadists are willing to blow the country up in a nihilistic rage because they feel out of place and betrayed by a 21st century that has only brought war and diminished expectations.
>
> We are seeing two sides of the same coin in Trump and Sanders. It is the yin and yang of disenchantment with the establishment and its inability to address the needs of the common man. People, especially whites from the 20th century, have come to recognize that they are underserved by the old order and they are being left with less materially than they had expected. The promises and policies of both the Democrats and Republicans have been unfulfilled. Nothing incurs wrath and hatred like the imposition of lowered expectations. The rich get richer and everyone else gets angry. The anger is particularly pronounced among Republicans who have been distracted for over a decade by the social issues of gay marriage and abortion while their economic well-being was eroding from the march of technology and global competition. Then with the Great Recession of 2008, fortunes were lost in the form

of collapsed housing values, vanished 401ks and a new President who ran on the platform of Hope and delivered a sclerotic recovery and a continuing decade of war. The social issues that held them in electoral bondage proved to be a chimera; their marriages did not collapse as a consequence of gay marriage. Their marriages are collapsing because both husband and wife have to work two jobs to help support their kids who are saddled with college debt and are still unemployed. The massive income disparity infecting the country is mirrored by a mounting disparity in expectations. This will not end well. Meanwhile, many of the dividend-receiving upper middle class are living in comfort but watching the rise of Trump with horror. Some, who begin to understand how they are complicit in creating this debacle, are beginning to engage in a full-fledged naked belly crawl stampede out of the dark fetid cave that became the Republican Party. (R. Reynolds, personal communication, June 2016)

III: A Psychological Theory about Trump's Appeal. A Marriage of Shadow, Archetypal Defenses, and Self at the Group Level of the Psyche to Form a Cultural Complex

I am now going to add my own theory to all the others, each of which, like the blind monks describing the elephant, have partial claim to some truth. And I hope that on November 9, 2016, the day after the United States presidential election, that all of these theories and words—including my own—will become an irrelevant footnote to an absurd chapter in American history. I hope that the illusion of Trump that is becoming all too real will vaporize back into insubstantiality. But, even if Trump vanishes from sight (an unlikely possibility), what his candidacy has revealed will not. Those who have hoped for some sort of redemption through him will still be disenfranchised and angry.

You don't need to be a psychologist or psychiatrist to see Donald Trump as a narcissist. Ted Cruz—apparently not the most psychologically minded politician—relieved any mental health professional wary of a lawsuit for character assassination of that burden by announcing on May 3, 2016, the day of the Indiana Republican Presidential primary, that Trump was *a pathological liar, utterly amoral, a narcissist at a level I don't think this country's ever seen and a serial philanderer.* (Wright, Kopan, & Winchester, 2016)

But it is not Trump's narcissism that captures my attention as much as the narcissistic injury at the level of the group Self that I hypothesize about those who are so captivated by him. My focus then is not so much on Trump himself, but on how his personality seems to strike such a resonant chord in many Americans and speaks to what we can think of as the group psyche. In a series of papers over the past decade, I have explored various aspects of the group psyche and have developed a working model that may be useful in understanding Trump's appeal at this time. Keep in mind that in the following remarks, I am talking about the psyche of the *group*—what lives inside each of us as individual carriers of the group psyche and what lives between us in our shared group psyche. This group psyche engages with themes and conflicts that are not the same as our more personal psychological struggles. For better or worse, we all swim in a shared bath of collective psyche.

I want to explore what I perceive as a direct link between Trump's personal narcissism, grandiosity, and his attacks on various minority groups and the frightening growth in the number of American citizens who embrace Trump's perception of America and who feel that he understands and speaks to them. The following discussion is not a political analysis. It is a psychological analysis of what we can think of as the *group psyche*, which, of course, contributes enormously to and fuels political processes. But it is fundamentally about psyche and is based on the notion that there are certain psychological energies, even structures, at the level of the cultural or group psyche that are partly conscious and partly unconscious which are activated at times of heightened threats or perceived threats to the core identity of the group—what we might think of as the group Self. Three of these most important energies/structures[1] are the shadow, archetypal defenses of the group Self, and the group Self itself. I do not see these energies/structures as fixed entities but more as potential, dynamically shifting channels in the collective psyche through which huge affects and energies may pour when aroused. These energies/structures take shape around social, political, economic, geographic, and religious themes that are alive in specific contexts and with particular contents. This same type of analysis may currently apply in the Brexit crisis in Great Britain, or in the Palestinian-Israeli conflict with very different contexts and contents in which various groups can be seen as protecting their imagined or real, threatened, or wounded Self from being further injured by pursuing a defensive, aggressive attack against the dangerous enemy, which might be the Palestinians or the European Union.

---

1   Jean Kirsch, in a personal conversation, pointed out to me that characterizing certain phenomenon in the group psyche as *energies/structures* is analogous to the development of the wave/particle duality in physics where every quantic entity may be partly described as a particle and partly described as a wave to fully explain the different types of behaviors they exhibit. It may be similar when discussing archetypes or culture complexes in the group psyche, which can sometimes manifest as energies and sometimes as structures.

What is it about Trump that acts as an irresistible magnet sucking up most of the air in our cultural psyche, both drawing people to him or repelling them from him with such ferocious attraction or repulsion? Is Trump the end product of our culture of narcissism? Is he what we get and perhaps even deserve because he epitomizes the god or gods that we currently worship in our mindless, materialistic, consumerist, hyper-indulged cult of around-the-clock stimulation and entertainment? Here is how Christopher Hedges states it in *Empire of Illusion: The End of Literacy and the Triumph of Spectacle:*

> An image-based culture communicates through narratives, pictures, and pseudo-drama. Scandalous affairs, hurricanes, untimely deaths, train wrecks—these events play well on computer screens and television. International diplomacy, labor union negotiations, and convoluted bailout packages do not yield exciting personal narratives or stimulating images. A governor who patronizes call girls becomes a huge news story. A politician who proposes serious regulatory reform advocating curbing wasteful spending is boring. Kings, queens, and emperors once used their court to divert their subjects. Today, cinematic, political, and journalistic celebrities distract us with their personal foibles and scandals. They create our public mythology. Acting, politics, and sports have become, as they were in Nero's reign, interchangeable. In an age of images and entertainment, in an age of instant emotional gratification, we neither seek nor want honesty or reality. Reality is complicated. Reality is boring.
>
> We are incapable or unwilling to handle its confusion. We ask to be indulged and comforted by clichés, stereotypes, and inspirational messages that tell us we can be whoever we seek to be, that we live in the greatest country on earth, that we are endowed with superior moral and physical qualities, and that our future will always be glorious and prosperous, either because of our own attributes or our national character or because we are blessed by God. In this world, all that matters is the consistency of our belief systems. The ability to amplify lies, to repeat them and have surrogates repeat them in endless loops of news cycles, gives lies and mythical narratives the aura of uncontested truth. We become trapped in the linguistic prison of incessant repetition. We are fed words and phrases like *war on terror* or *pro-life* or *change*, and within these narrow parameters, all complex thought, ambiguity, and self-criticism vanish. (Hedges, 2009, p. 49)

It seems clear that Trump's apparent narcissism and his attacks on political correctness dovetail with deep needs in a significant portion of the American population to enhance their own dwindling sense of their place in the world and of America's place in the world. Trump's peculiar brand of narcissism is a perfect compensatory mirror for the narcissistic needs and injuries of those who support him. Or, stated in another way, there is a good fit between Trump's personal narcissism and the narcissism of our culture and the wounded collective Self of many Americans.

With this general formulation in mind, I want to analyze how Trump's candidacy speaks to three highly intertwined parts of the American group psyche:

- » To a woundedness at the core of the American group Self.

- » To the defenses mobilized in the groups that feel wounded who wish to protect themselves and the country against further injury to the shared group Self.

- » To the promise or hope of a cure for the wound.

Wound to the American Group Self

I would first like to address what I perceive as a wound at the core of the American group Self/spirit that is deeply felt by many, especially by those who have neither benefited from nor participated in the relative well-being of our nation's prosperity and by others who are relatively well off but keenly aware that our system of government and our way of life are threatened at the core of our collective being. Here is a working definition of the group Self or spirit that I put forth in an earlier paper:

> .... the group spirit is akin to what we Jungians might call the Self of the group. The group spirit is the ineffable core beliefs or sense of identity that bind people together. Sports teams have a group spirit and their fans often magically participate in it. Nation states have a group spirit and their citizens often magically and unconsciously participate in it—particularly in times of crisis. Religious faiths have a group spirit, often symbolized by a part human/part divine being. Ethnic groups, gender groups, and racial groups all have a group spirit that is frequently felt and identified with in a myriad of ways.

> The group spirit can be symbolized by animals, humans, inanimate objects and, in its most ineffable form, the refusal to symbolize it in imagery at all. The group spirit has many different elements that have come together in

a seamless, often wordless and even imageless, non-material whole that is known to its members through a sense of belonging, shared essential beliefs, core historical experiences of loss and revelation, deepest yearnings, and ideals. One can begin to circle around the nature of a group's spirit by asking questions such as:

What is most sacred to the group?
What does the group treasure most?
What binds the group's members together?

(Singer, 2006b, pp. 9–10)

Trump Hat: Make America Great Again. Photo By Chiron Publications

The group *Self* is best expressed through a symbolic image, which, in today's United States, often looks more like a brand that its creators hope will become a symbol:

Because a group's Self has so many pieces, many of which are contradictory, only a authentic symbol has a numinous quality that can contain all the tensions and conflicts. An authentic symbolic image can make a whole of the disparate parts.

Many in our country—on the left, right, and in the center—feel the country is in danger and may be beyond hope of being repaired or getting back on *the right course*. Profoundly divided, our group spirit at this stage in our history is less secure than it has been for some time. This nervousness about our essential well-being is deeply felt both by the progressive left and by the conservative right—those who feel alienated and angered by the current governing leaders (congressional, executive, and judicial branches of government), whom they oppose and see as destroying the country, whether the archenemy be Mitch McConnell of the Republicans or Barack Obama of the Democrats. On the right, the threat of terrorism (Muslims), the threat of immigrants (Mexicans), the threat of the global economy (China and international trade agreements), or the threat of our existing governing bodies and leaders (Congress) are seen as leading us to the brink. On the left, the threats to a sense of well-being and security in our national group Self come as the result of the growing disparity in the distribution of wealth and income; the mistreatment of minorities whether those of different races, colors, ethnicities, sexual identities or genders; our power relationships to other countries around the world; and, of course the treatment of the environment itself.

I postulate that these threats are amplified on all sides by an even deeper, less conscious threat that I call *extinction anxiety*. Extinction anxiety exists both in the personal and group psyche and, at this time, is based on the fear of the loss of white America as we have idealized it, the loss of America's place in the world as we have known it, and ultimately the destruction of the environment and the world itself. One might think of extinction anxiety as the cultural psyche's equivalent of the anxiety about death in the individual. I believe that this extinction anxiety is like a psychic radioactive background in our global society and that it fuels many of our concerns—whether we favor Clinton or Trump or neither. For instance, climate change deniers on the right may be seen as denying the very real possibility of the planet's destruction as a way of defending themselves against the fear of extinction. Aligning himself with this attitude, Trump offers to dispel *extinction anxiety* by denying it is real and appointing a well-known climate change denier as his energy adviser. As we all know, denial—whether at the individual or group level—is the most primitive defense in the psyche's arsenal of defenses to protect itself. This is not just about death of the individual—Freud's death instinct—this is about death of all life as we know it. This extinction anxiety belongs to all of us—to the collective psyche.

Here is how Joseph Epstein described the injury to the group Self/spirit of those attracted to Trump:

> Something deeper, I believe, is rumbling behind the astounding support for Mr. Trump, a man who, apart from his large but less than pure business success, appears otherwise entirely without qualification for the presi-

dency. I had a hint of what might be behind the support for him a few weeks ago when, on one of the major network news shows, I watched a reporter ask a woman at a Trump rally why she was supporting him. A thoroughly respectable-seeming middle-class woman, she replied without hesitation: "*I want my country back.*"

This woman is easily imagined clicking through TV news channels or websites and encountering this montage: Black Lives Matters protesters bullying the latest object of their ire; a lesbian couple kissing at their wedding ceremony; a mother in Chicago weeping over the death of her young daughter, struck by an errant bullet from a gang shootout; a panel earnestly discussing the need for men who *identify* as women to have access to the public lavatories of their choosing; college students, showing the results of their enfeebling education, railing about imagined psychic injuries caused by their professors or fellow students.

I don't believe that this woman is a racist, or that she yearns for immigrants, gays and other minorities to be suppressed, or even that she truly expects to turn back the clock on social change in the U.S. What she wants is precisely what she says: her country back.

The political rise of Donald Trump owes less to the economy, to his status as a braggadocio billionaire, to his powers of insult, to the belief that he can Make America Great Again, than to the success of this progressive program. What the woman who said she wants her country back really meant was that she couldn't any longer bear to watch the United States on the descent, hostage to progressivist ideas that bring neither contentment nor satisfaction but instead foster a state of perpetual protest and agitation, anger and tumult.

So great is the frustration of Americans who do not believe in these progressivist ideas, who see them as ultimately tearing the country apart, that they are ready to turn, in their near hopelessness, to a man of Donald Trump's patently low quality. (Epstein, 2016)

The Self or group spirit of America is built on more than 300 years of progress, success, achievement, resourcefulness, and ingenuity, accompanied by almost endless opportunity and good fortune. We love and believe in our heroic potential, our freedom and independence, our worship of height and speed, youth, newness, technology, our optimism, and eternal innocence. We have enjoyed the profound resilience of the American spirit, which has shown itself repeatedly through very difficult historical trials, including our Civil War, World War I, the Great Depression, World War II, the Vietnam War, the 9/11 attacks, the Iraq War, the financial collapse in 2008, and other major crises. As a country, we have been blessed in our capacity to transcend loss, failure, and the threat of defeat in the face of crisis time and again, and this has contributed to a positive vision of ourselves that has been fundamentally solid at the core for a long time. Of course, that Self-image is subject to inflation, arrogance, and grandiosity in our belief in our own exceptionalism and our blindness to our causing grave injury to other peoples at home and abroad. Again, this Self-image exists at the level of the group psyche. It is quite possible that Trump's personal inflation, arrogance, and grandiosity represents a compensatory antidote in our group psyche to a Self-image beginning to suffer severe self-doubt about our ability to navigate a highly uncertain future successfully and the nostalgic longing perfectly articulated in the phrase: "*I want my country back.*"

Archetypal Defenses of the Group Self

Second are the defenses mobilized by those feeling this woundedness who wish to protect themselves and their country against further injury to the shared group spirit. A significant number of people in our society feel cut off from what they believe to be their inherited, natural birthright as American citizens. Those for whom our cherished American group spirit seems endangered are ready to defend themselves—whether the perceived attack is coming from within or outside the country. Although they would not use this language, they are suffering a wound at the level of the group spirit or Self, even as they are also suffering individually. We can think of this as a narcissistic injury at the level of our group Self. I suggest that Trump has somehow intuited that injury and is playing to it, both as a carrier of the renewal of the group spirit and as a defender against those who would do further harm to it—be it terrorists, immigrants, Washingtonian political insiders, the established Republican Party, Obama, and perhaps above all else right now, Hillary Clinton and the Democrats.

Trump's attack on political correctness

Trump's particular political genius in this election cycle has been to launch his campaign with an attack on *political correctness*. With incredible manipulative skill, Trump's full-throated yawp of a barbarian New Yorker, "*Get 'em outta here!*" made its first appearance at his rallies when he urged the faithful in his crowds to get rid of protesters (one can't help but wonder if these *protesters* weren't, in fact, paid actors planted in the crowd). "*Get 'em outta here!*" also seems to be his pledge to rid the country of Mexicans, Muslims, and other groups that were portrayed as dangerous threats to the American Way of Life. His sneering attacks on *political correctness* and his willingness time and again to be *politically incorrect* have tapped into the shadowy feelings that many have about all the things they are supposed to be compassionate about—ethnic differences, racial differences, color differences, gender differences, religious differences. Trump's strategy has been shrewd: He seems to have sensed that *political correctness* could be the trigger word and target for unleashing potent levels of shadow energies that have been accumulating in the cultural unconscious of the group psyche. He rode a huge wave of pent-up resentment, racism, and hatred unleashed by his attacks on *political correctness* long enough to crush his Republican opponents and become the Republican nominee for president of the United States. The notion of a trigger word activating a complex goes back to Jung's early word association tests in which certain words detonated powerful emotions contained within personal complexes—such as the mother or father complex. Cultural complexes are also frequently triggered by a collective word association process that takes on a life of its own in the psyche of the group and which can be manipulated by skillful politicians who use specific trigger words to activate the primitive emotions that fuel cultural complexes. Trump is at his best when he is awful.

Trump's willingness to be politically incorrect has become a sign of his "truth-telling" to many. Trump embodies the truth of the shadow side of political correctness and that seems to be the primary truth that his core followers care about. Once Trump spoke to their emotional truth, the Trump faithful no longer cared whether he told other truths. Cultural complexes don't need or rely on facts to validate their particular perspective on the world. If it feels right, it must be so. In fact, it is a characteristic of cultural complexes that facts are just about the first thing to go when an individual or group becomes possessed by a complex. A group caught up in a cultural complex has highly selective memory—if any historical memory at all—and only chooses those historical and contemporary *facts* that validate their pre-existing opinion. In a wild inversion from Trump's seemingly frequent misrepresentation of the truth, people have apparently come to believe that Trump is *"telling it like it is"* in his attacks on the inept Washington politicians who know nothing about conducting business. For instance, in full tricksterish play with the truth, Trump glibly dismissed taped recordings of his own voice prior to the 2008 housing market collapse, pronouncing that he looked forward to a fall in prices as it represented a great buying opportunity for him at low prices. He said any good businessman would have looked for such an opportunity, and the movie *The Big Short* (2015) gives ample evidence of those who profited from others' traumatic losses. As infuriating as it is that facts don't seem to make any difference in Trump's self-presentation, it would be a huge mistake to underestimate how successfully he has mobilized the crude underbelly of long-standing American suspicions of people who are different from themselves. What a relief for so many to hear a politician speak their unspoken resentments and express their rage, which they could only mutter privately. Trump apparently tapped into the dirty little (or not so little) secret of our loathing of various minorities (even though we may all be minorities now) and especially of recent immigrants.

This kind of shadow energy is much more likely to be close to the surface of consciousness and available for exploitation if a group of people who previously saw themselves as having a solid place in American society now find themselves marginalized and drifting downward—both socially and economically—or as never having had a chance of making progress toward the American dream. In fact, they see the recent immigrants to this country as stealing the American dream from them.

Unholy marriage of shadow, archetypal defenses of the group Self, and the group Self

What makes Trump's unleashing of the shadow in the American psyche around political correctness even more dangerous is that these energies become linked or even identical with what I call *archetypal defenses of the group spirit*. Here is how I have defined "archetypal defenses of the group spirit":

> This phrase is a mouthful, but its purpose is to offer a precise psychological description of a level of collective emotional life that is deeply responsive to threat—whether the threat is real or simply *perceived* as real. When this part of the collective psyche is activated, the most primitive psychological forces come alive for the purpose of defending the group and its collective spirit or Self. I capitalize *Self* because I want to make it clear that it is not just the persona or ego identity of the group that is under attack but something at an even deeper level of the collective psyche which one might think of as the spiritual home or *god* of the group. The tendency to fall into the grips of an identification with an archetypal defense of the group spirit is universal, and almost every one of us has experienced such a *possession* at some time in our lives— at least in one if not many of the primary groups to which we belong simultaneously.

> The tribal spirit of the clan or of the nation often lies dormant or in the background, but when it is threatened, the defenses mobilized to protect it are ferocious and impersonal. The mobilization of such potent, archaic defenses is fueled by raw collective emotion and rather simplistic, formulaic ideas and/or beliefs. One can think of the more

virulent cultural complexes as being fed by a vast under-ground pool of the collective emotional life. Archetypal defenses of the group spirit are animated by the release of these heightened emotions of groups in distress....

Once a certain level of emotional intensity is achieved in the psyche of the group, archetypal defenses of the group spirit come to the forefront and begin to determine and even dictate how the group will think, feel, react, and behave.

These activated archetypal defenses of the group spirit find concrete expression in forms as varied as the unrest of divided populations over the legal status of foreign immigrants in countries around the world, the threatened development of nuclear weapons by nation states such as Iran or [North] Korea, the deployment of suicide bombers by terrorist groups, or the launching of massive military expeditions by world powers. And, these same kinds of archetypal defenses come alive in all sorts of skirmishes between diverse groups of people, who are not necessarily armed with explosive devices but perceive themselves in a threatened or disadvantaged position in which their most sacred values are in jeopardy—Gays, Blacks, Women, the Christian Right in the United States, Jews around the world, the Muslim Brotherhood throughout the Middle East.

The list of groups threatened at the core of their being or at the level of the group Self seems endless.[2] (Singer, 2006b)

From the point of view of the group psyche, Trump has aligned his attack on political correctness with the archetypal defenses of the group spirit. That is why I stress his two foundational mantras: "Get 'em outta here!" and "Make America Great Again!"—in other words, "Rid the country of all elements that threaten our sense of Self, and "Make the country white and powerful and rich again." The first statement speaks for the shadow/archetypal defense of the group spirit, and the second statement speaks for the repair to group Self. This constellation of group energies/structure puts the shadow very close to the Self, very close to what the group values most about itself and how it protects itself. This gives further license in the unconscious of the group to ride and act out these aggressive, hateful, and violent forces in the collective psyche. What makes Trump's

---

2 I have patterned this model of group dynamics on Donald Kalsched's groundbreaking work on trauma and the injury to the Self in the individual, especially his *The Inner World of Trauma: Archetypal Defenses of the Personal Spirit*, but my work has focused on what we might call *The Inner World of Group Trauma: Archetypal Defenses of the Group Spirit*. I argue that this is a particular variety of what I call a cultural complex (Singer, 2006b).

narcissism so dangerous in its mix of shadow (his attacks on all sorts of groups of people) and Self elements (his self-aggrandizing, inflated sense of himself) is that it plays to the unholy marriage of Self and shadow elements in the collective psyche.

Trump's example gives permission for shadowy thoughts, feelings, and actions on behalf of the Self. I think this underlying group dynamic explains the comparison of Trump to Hitler. Evoking an archaic image of the German Self, Hitler mobilized the most shadowy forces in modern history in the so-called service of that Self-image, which centered on the supremacy of the Aryan race—first the Brownshirts, then the Gestapo, SS, and other forces of the Third Reich, including its highly efficient bureaucracy. Trump seems to be toying with the collective shadow, apparently encouraging its acting out in the name of the Self. It is hard to imagine Trump leading the United States in the same direction that Hitler led Germany (I certainly hope I don't live to regret writing these words), but the thought of an America under the leadership of a grandiose and puffed-up character such as Trump is terrifying. From the point of view of analytical psychology, when the shadow, the archetypal defenses of the group spirit, and the group Self in any group get so closely aligned, there is great danger of violence, tyranny, and absolutism.

Most of the anger we have witnessed has been coming from Trump's supporters who join in his attacks on political correctness and immigrants. Even more dangerous in Trump's apparent indiscriminate activation of shadowy attacks on political correctness is the possibility that he will unleash equally destructive counterattacks on the other side of the equation—in those people who feel Trump's assault on them endangers their core identity and being as individuals and as groups. As of this writing (early June 2016), I believe that we have seen just the very tip of the huge store of collective emotional counter-responses to Trump. During the next several months leading up to the presidential elections, we may well witness increasing anger and violence erupting on both sides, and I sense that the fear, resentment, and hostility building up *against* Trump in the United States will be even greater than what he has mobilized on his own behalf. From those who see themselves as defending the American Self or soul against Trump, I fear that there will be increasingly virulent displays of hostility toward Trump as a compensatory counter-reaction to Trump as a false Self, to Trump as a false god, to Trump as a demagogue.

Curing the Wounded Self of America: Trump's Selfie and America's Selfie

The third and final component of this intertwined triad of forces in the group psyche is Trump's implicit promise of providing a cure for the wound at the level of the group Self. This is where Trump's narcissism is most prominent and most dangerous. I believe there is an unconscious equation between Trump's inflated sense of himself and the cure for the American group Self that many believe he promises. This equation can be most simply stated as the following: "I am the Greatness to which America may once again aspire. By identifying with how great I am, you can rekindle your wounded American dream and make yourself and America great again." Or even more bluntly, "I have achieved the American dream; I am the American dream; I am the incarnation of the Self that the country aspires to." This, of course, is a massive inflation. Trump identifies his personal being with the Self of America, and it is his source of demagogic appeal to authoritarians and others. He is encouraging those Americans who have lost a foothold in the American dream to place their trust in him as a mirror of their own potential—a potential that he personally has already achieved. If one is able to place themselves in that mindset, one can get a glimpse of Trump's magnetic appeal.

Synchronistically, the day after I wrote the preceding words in an attempt to imaginatively enter into the psyche of someone drawn into Trump's orbit, I came across the following quote from Trump, a statement that he made many years ago but that applies even more today, when the stakes are much greater:

> I play to people's fantasies. People may not always think big themselves, but they can still get very excited by those who do. That's why a little hyperbole never hurts. People want to believe that something is the biggest and the greatest and the most spectacular. I call it truthful hyperbole. It's an innocent form of exaggeration—and a very effective form of promotion. (Fisher & Hobson, 2016)

Trump's apparent money, power, fame, and his willingness to shoot from the hip seems to fit with the frustrated yearnings of many Americans. He has managed to catch the projection of a powerful and successful person who, by virtue of his alleged business acumen and ability to negotiate, is able to make things happen for his own betterment—rarely for the betterment of others despite his claims of giving generously to charities and creating untold jobs. F. Scott Fitzgerald might roll over in his grave at this comparison, but Trump brings to mind a latter-day Jay Gatsby whose overweening ambitions for fame, fortune, and social status are unlimited. Trump manages to project an image that he is everything Willy Loman in Arthur Miller's *Death of a Salesman* was not able to achieve. Trump has accomplished—at least in the minds of many Americans—what Jay Gatsby and Willy Loman could only dream of. In this sense, Trump presents himself as the embodiment of a form of the American Dream that, in his singular greatness and achievement, he can personally restore to America's wounded Self-image and to those Americans who have failed to achieve their dreams of greatness. It is almost as if Trump is saying, "My grandiosity is the greatness of America.

We can make America great again by following me and then, you, too, can be like me: aggressive, successful, big, powerful." This has tremendous appeal for many. This is the narcissism of Trump joining with the injured narcissism of those Americans who have seen their chances for well-being and security rapidly slipping away. In that sense, Trump is not only speaking for the shadow; he is also speaking for the Self of America—or, at least his version of it. His version is the materialistic power version of the American dream—of the big man who has made himself rich and, through his wealth and strength of personality, powerful. He is free to speak his own mind and to pursue, without limits, his own self-aggrandizing goals.

The negative aspects of Trump's narcissism strike those who have been repelled rather than attracted by him as a symbolic mirror of everything negative about America's culture of narcissism. Just as some think that Trump is the embodiment of everything that has made America great in the past and will make us great again, some see Trump as the very embodiment of everything awful that we have become as a nation. Undoubtedly, this is also what many in the rest of the world see as the worst of who we have become. In this view, we can see the shadow of the American "selfie" as:

» A self-promoting brand
» Arrogant bullies in our conduct of business and other relations
» Very limited in our capacity for self-reflection
» Filled with hubris and a lack of humility
» Self-absorbed with little sensitivity for the needs of others
» Possessed by greed and consumerism
» So entitled in our good fortune that we have come to believe this is our natural due

These seven features are core characteristics of the American cultural complex in which the shadow, archetypal defenses of the American Spirit, and the American Self get all mixed up with each other in the most noxious stew and we find ourselves betraying that very Self or spirit on which the nation and its constitution were founded. And how dreadful to think that Trump's narcissism is a perfect mirror and archetypal embodiment of our national narcissism. And what if it is also a mirror of our own shadowy, personal narcissism to boot? Ultimately, I believe that the Trump phenomenon is less about Trump than it is about us—about who we are as a people. From this perspective, the elephant in the room turns out to be "We the People of the United States." How terrifying to think that our politics and our lives today have gotten horribly confused with reality TV, social media, computer and cellphone technology, and their infinite capacity to turn reality into illusion, Self into narcissism.

IV: A Perverted Echo of Walt Whitman

"Do I Contradict Myself?"

Just as F. Scott Fitzgerald and Arthur Miller have come to mind as I contemplate how Trump's narcissism plays to the injured narcissism of America's group Self, Walt Whitman, the ultimate bard of the American soul comes to mind, as some of Whitman's words have a strange, disorienting resonance with how Trump presents himself. Several pundits have played with the notion of Donald Trump being some sort of twisted mirror image of Walt Whitman. For instance, Zenpundit sardonically points to the similarity between how Trump behaves and what Whitman says about himself in the lines:

> Do I contradict myself?
> Very well then, I contradict myself.
> I am large, I contain multitudes.
> (Cameron, 2016)

Trump is so large and powerful that he doesn't have to be predictable. He can change his mind if he wants.

"Song of Myself"

In "Song of Myself," one of Whitman's most famous poems from *Leaves of Grass*, the poet gets as close to evoking the soul/Self of America as any American has in his visionary lines:

> I celebrate myself, and sing myself,
> And what I assume you shall assume,
> For every atom belonging to me as good belongs to you.
>
> I loafe and invite my soul,
> I lean and loafe at my ease observing a spear of summer grass.
> My tongue, every atom of my blood, form'd from this soil, this air,
> Born here of parents born here from parents the same, and their parents the same,
> I, now thirty-seven years old in perfect health begin,
> Hoping to cease not till death.[3]
> (Section 1)

---

3 "In the poem: Whitman emphasizes an all-powerful "I" which serves as narrator, who should not be limited to or confused with the person of the historical Walt Whitman. The persona described has transcended the conventional boundaries of self: 'I pass death with the dying, and birth with the new-washed babe ... and am not contained between my hat and boots' (section 7)." Wikipedia Contributors, 2016).

It is easy to imagine Trump also saying "I celebrate myself. I sing myself." Everything Trump says and does seems to be a celebration of himself. We know, intuitively, that Trump's "song of myself" is not the same one that Whitman sings. Trump sings a self-congratulatory song; Whitman sings a Self-affirming song. One song is of and for the whole nation; the other song centers on the triumph of Trump himself and for all those individuals who would appropriate his claim to superiority for themselves.

"I am the poet of the Body and I am the poet of Soul"

In *Leaves of Grass*, Whitman proclaims himself the bard of the American soul when he writes: "I am the poet of the Body and I am the poet of the Soul" (Section 21). Whitman likens the body and soul of America to a blade of grass whose very existence mirrors the "journey work of the stars" in its immortality. Trump claims himself to be the body and soul of America in the Trump Casinos, the Trump Towers, Trump University, and even Trump steaks—shoddy pretenders to what is best and most soulful in America.

"I Sound My Barbaric Yawp Over the Roofs of the World"

Whitman sings his mystical, transcendent vision of America as he compares himself to the spotted hawk who soars above the sacred land:

> The spotted hawk swoops by and accuses me, he complains
> of my gab and my loitering.
> I too am not a bit tamed, I too am untranslatable,
> I sound my barbaric yawp over the roofs of the world.
>
> (Section 52)

Trump echoes these sentiments as he proudly presents himself to the world as "untranslatable." He, too, shouts his own "barbaric yawp" over the roofs of the world[4]. In Whitman's imagination, the essence of the American soul is neither civilized nor verbal. The "barbaric yawp" is the fierce "voice" of a soul that is unrestrained and exulting in its self-expression. It gives expression to a primitive enthusiasm in the form of a non-verbal cry from the essential nature of a living being. Allen Ginsberg's *Howl* and Bob Dylan's voice, once described as "a coyote caught in barbed wire," can be considered grandchildren of Whitman's "barbaric yawp" of the American soul. So, too, is Jimi Hendrix's rendition of the "Star Spangled Banner."

---

4   *Barbaric* means "without civilizing influences, primitive" and a *yawp* is a "loud, harsh cry."

Steven Herrmann, a Jungian with a deep, scholarly interest in Whitman, wrote to me:

> Whitman's "yawp" is a *conscious* cry from the Soul of America to make the barbarian in American political democracy conscious! The "barbaric yawp" is Whitman's call from the depths of the American Soul to awaken the possibility of hope in a brighter future for American democracy....The aim of Whitman's "barbaric yawp" was to sound a new heroic message of "Happiness," Hope, and "Nativity" over the roofs of the world, to sound a primal cry which must remain essentially "unsaid" because it rests at the core of the American soul and cannot be found in "any dictionary, utterance, symbol" (*Leaves*, Section 50). The "barbaric yawp" is a metaphorical utterance for something "untranslatable" from the depths of the American Soul for the emergence of man as a spiritual human being in whom the aims of liberty and equality have been fully realized and in whom the opposites of love and violence, friendship and war, have been unified at a higher political field of order than anything we have formerly seen in America. His "yawp" is an affect state, a spiritual cry of "Joy" and "Happiness" prior to the emergence of language. (Steven Herrmann, personal communication, January, 2007)

Trump's "barbaric yawp" ("Get 'em outta here!") may sound tinny in comparison to those who came before him, such as Whitman, Ginsburg, Dylan, Hendrix, and many others who have tapped into a primal energy that is essentially American. At great risk, however, one could too quickly discount the fact that Trump also has his own instinct for a primal source of American "barbaric" enthusiasm.

I cannot help but wonder if Donald Trump and his inarticulate utterances, which make so many of us cringe, have not been heard by many in America as a modern version of Whitman's "barbaric yawp" from our country's "body and soul." However reluctantly, we have to accept the fact that Trump may speak directly to the American soul of many in our country, just as our more progressive sensibilities can link Barack Obama's measured oratory to the American soul. Who are we to suppose we know who speaks for the American soul? Who has a legitimate claim on the American soul anyway? Is it possible that Donald Trump has found in his crude utterances a resonance with the American soul that says more to many Americans' identities and yearnings than many of us can imagine?

Comparing Trump to Whitman may seem sacrilegious to the memory of the great American poet. But there is a logic to such a comparison as

Trump is the shadow or dark mirror to the best things in America, sung so eloquently by Whitman. Trump's "song of myself" is truly a "song of myself." Whitman sings of what is best in us and Trump's horrific bluster displays what is worst in us. What is sacred in Whitman's "barbaric yawp" becomes profane in Trump's perverted echo of that yawp.

I leave the reader with a question, given that I believe both Whitman and Trump identify themselves with the soul or Self of America. What is the difference between Whitman's "I celebrate myself, I sing myself" and Trump's version of that same song in "Make America Great Again"? It is worth grappling with this question as a way of differentiating that kind of narcissism in which the ego gets inflated and identifies with the Self and its archetypal defenses versus that kind of rare but blessed, over-flowing exuberance, integrity, and love in which the ego is connected to but not identified with the Self. What is real about Trump's selfie is the unexpurgated expression of both his own and America's grandiose, narcis-sistic, misogynistic, racist, materialistic, shadowy abuse of power. What is authentic about Whitman's barbaric yawp as a Self-portrait of America is its life affirming, primitive vitality, which is not to be confused with Trump's cheesy Bronx cheer as an American selfie.

Thomas Singer, MD, is psychiatrist and Jungian analyst who practices in the San Francisco Bay area. He has spent the last several years researching the cultural complex theory in different parts of the world, including Australia, North America, Latin America, Europe and a new project in Asia. He has co-edited the following books on the topic: *The Cultural Complex, Placing Psyche* (Australia), *Listening to Latin America,* and most recently, *Europe's Many Souls.* In addition, he has co-edited two books on Ancient Greece/ Modern Psyche based on conferences in Santorini, Greece. Beginning in 2000, he has organized five consecutive conferences at the San Francisco Jung Institute on politics, culture and psyche during presidential election years. Dr. Singer currently serves as President of ARAS (The Archives for Research in Archetypal Symbolism) which explores symbolic imagery from all cultures since the beginning of human history.

References

Cameron, C. (2016, May 5). *Trump as Walt Whitman.* Zenpundit.com. Retrieved from http://zenpundit.com/?p=50041

Collins, E. (2016, February 29). *Les Moonves: Trumps run is damn good for CBS.* Politico. Retrieved from http://www.politico.com/blogs/on-media/2016/02/les-moonves-trump-cbs-220001

Epstein, J. (2016, June 10). *Why Trumpkins want their country back.* Wall Street Journal. Retrieved from http://www.wsj.com/articles/why-trumpkins-want-their-country-back-1465596987

Fisher, M., & Hobson, W. (2016, May 13). *Trump masqueraded as publicist to brag about himself.* Washington Post. Retrieved from https://www.washingtonpost.com/politics/donald-trump-alter-ego-barron/2016/05/12/02ac99ec-16fe-11e6-aa55-670cabef46e0_story.html?hpid=hp_rhp-top-table-main_no-name%3Ahomepage%2Fstory

Hedges, C. (2009). *Empire of illusion: The end of literacy and the triumph of spectacle.* New York: Nation Books.

MacWilliams, M. (2016, January 17). *The one weird trait that predicts whether you're a Trump supporter.* Politico Magazine. Retrieved from http://www.politico.com/magazine/story/2016/01/donald-trump-2016-authoritarian-213533

McAdams, D. P. (2016, June). *The mind of Donald Trump.* The Atlantic. Retrieved from http://www.theatlantic.com/magazine/archive/2016/06/the-mind-of-donald-trump/480771/

Singer, T. 2006a. *The cultural complex: A statement of the theory and its application. Psychotherapy and Politics International,* 4(3), 197–212. DOI: 10.1002/ppi.110.

Singer, T. 2006b. Unconscious forces shaping international conflicts: Archetypal defenses of the group spirit from revolutionary America to confrontation in the Middle East. *The San Francisco Jung Institute Library Journal,* 25(4), 6–28.

Sullivan, A. (2016, May). Democracies end when they are too democratic. *New York.* Retrieved from http://nymag.com/daily/intelligencer/2016/04/america-tyranny-donald-trump.html

Whitman, W. (1973). Song of myself. *Leaves of grass.* New York: W. W. Norton & Co.

Wikipedia Contributors. 2016. Song of Myself. Wikipedia. Retrieved from https://en.wikipedia.org/wiki/Song_of_Myself

Wright, D., Kopan, T, & Winchester, J. (2016, May 3). Cruz unloads with epic takedown of "pathological liar," "narcissist" Donald Trump. CNN Politics. Retrieved from http://www.cnn.com/2016/05/03/politics/donald-trump-rafael-cruz-indiana/

Trumplestilskin
Narcissism and the Will to Power

BY LEONARD CRUZ, MD

Trumplestilskin: A Fairy Tale

Once there was a poor miller who had nothing to his name but one beautiful daughter. He went to speak with the king, and in an effort to seem more important than he felt himself to be, he told the king that he had a daughter who could spin gold out of straw. The king said, "If she really can do as you say, bring her to me tomorrow so that I can see for myself."

The next day, when she arrived, she was taken to a room that was full of straw and was seated in front of a spinning wheel and told by one of the king's men, "Get to work; If by morning you have failed to spin all this straw into gold, the king will put you to death." He led her into a room that was quite full of straw and gave her a wheel and spindle, and said: "Now set to work, and if by the early morning thou hast not spun this straw to gold, thou shalt die." The door was locked from the outside, and the poor miller's daughter was left alone without a clue as to what she should do. She began to cry and grew frightened.

All at once the door flew open, and in walked a little man with tiny hands who greeted her with the sort of smile a man displays when a juicy piece of mutton is placed before him. "Good evening, miller's daughter. Why are you crying?"

"Oh!" the miller's daughter said, "I must spin this straw into gold by morning, or I shall die. But, you see, I know nothing about how to spin and certainly not how to spin straw into gold," and she resumed her weeping. The little man said, "Suppose I spin it for you. What will you give me?"

"My necklace," she replied. The little man with his tiny hands snatched the necklace from her and promptly sat before the wheel and just before daybreak, the straw was gone. Stacked against the wall were bobbins full of gold thread.

The king was astonished and quite pleased; but being the sort whose appetites grew the more he acquired, he led the miller's daughter into another room that was much larger than the first and also full of straw.

She was placed before another wheel and told, "Spin all this straw into gold by morning, or you shall die." With that, he sealed her shut in the room. Once more the miller's daughter began to weep. Soon, the door flew open again, and there was the same little man. He seemed shrunken and somewhat deformed, as if someone had stomped him with their foot when he was still young, causing him to cease growing upward and upright. The little man with the tiny hands dispensed with pleasantries and asked straight away, "What will you give me if I spin this straw into gold before morning?"

"The ring from my finger," she replied. He took the ring and began to spin the wheel around, and by morning all the straw was spun into glistening gold.

The king was positively radiant at the sight, but as he could never have enough, he had the miller's daughter taken into a still larger room full of straw, and said: "If you are able to spin all this straw into gold in one night, then I shall make you my wife and queen." Although she certainly was not a royal, he considered that he might never find anyone richer in the whole world. As soon as the miller's daughter was alone in the room, the little man appeared for the third time and said: "What will you give me if I spin the straw for you this time?"

"I have nothing left to give," replied the miller's daughter. The little man looked right at her belly and said, "Then you must promise me the first child you have after you are queen." The poor miller's daughter thought, "I have nothing, and who knows if I will even bear a child." Not knowing what else to do, she agreed to give the man what he asked. Once more he set about spinning the straw, and by morning all the straw was gone, and in its place was gold. When the king found everything just as he had hoped, he arranged to wed the miller's daughter, who became his queen.

One year later, she gave birth to a child and had long ago forgotten the promise she made until one day her chamber door flew open, and there stood the little man saying, "I've come to collect what you promised me." The queen was horrified and tried to persuade him to accept untold riches instead.

"No, I would rather have something living, something of yours, than all the riches in the world." The queen sobbed and wailed so loudly that the little man took pity upon her and said, "I will give you 3 more days with the child, and if after 3 days you cannot call me by my name, then you must give the child to me."

That night the queen was unable to sleep. In the wee hours of morning, she left the castle and as if in a dream she found herself walking by a river. She heard the murmur of the water or perhaps the spirits that dwell beside a shushing stream. She returned to her bed and was awakened from her dreams when the door flew open, and there stood the little man.

The queen began reciting names—"Are you called Regis, Donald, Beezelbub," and more—but after she spoke each name, the little man said, "That is not my name."

The second day she asked her servants to question the villagers and neighbor and to make a list of the most unusual names they knew. In the evening she could not sleep and once more went for a walk by the river. This time she began to cross to the other side, but when she reached the other shore, she turned back and fell into a deep sleep with all the names she'd heard circling around in her head. When the little man arrived, she recited the names. "Perhaps you are called Bernard, or Boris, or Vladimir, or even Hillary?" Each time he simply said, "That is not my name."

On the third day one of her servants returned and said, "I have no new names for you, but last night while I was on the other side of the river, I came upon a little house on a hill, and outside stood a little, deformed, comical-looking creature, perhaps a man, who hopped on one leg and was chanting something." That evening, though the queen was exhausted, she went for a walk and this time crossed the river. Once on the other side, she climbed the bank, and there before her was the house, and the little man who was dancing gleefully around an open fire pit. As he hopped about, he cried out.

> "Today do I bake,
> tomorrow I brew,
> The day after that the queen's child comes in;
> And oh! I am glad that nobody knew
> That the name I am called is Trumpelstiltskin!"
> You cannot think how pleased the queen was to hear that name, and she quietly returned to her chambers and slept soundly that night.
> When the little man walked in, he said, " What's my name?"
> "Are you called Jack?" the queen asked.
> "No," answered he.
> "Are you called Harry?" she asked.
> "Oh no," he replied with a grin.
> And then she said: "Is your name, by any chance, Trumpel-stiltskin?"
> The little man flew into a rage. "The devil told you that, didn't he?" In his anger, he began to stomp his right foot so hard that it was driven into the ground all the way up to his knee. He could not free himself; somehow calling him by his proper name had unleashed a furious storm of anger. Stuck as he was, he reached down to grab the leg that was free and with both hands pulled so hard that he split in two, and that was the end of him.

~ ~ ~

I am a fan of the National Public Radio program *Car Talk*. The call-in radio show features two brothers who purport to run an automobile repair shop. Callers present a problem, and the two brothers proceed to diagnose the caller's problem with efficiency and humor. It is a mysterious thing for an untrained, uninformed listener. However, behind the mystery lies a fact that automobiles and their internal combustion engines typically break down in predictable ways. To the uninformed and untrained person, there appear to be an infinite number of possible causes for each vehicle. After all, there are countless models, tremendously varied driving conditions, different driving patterns, different histories for each vehicle, and some problems only arise after a certain amount of wear and tear on a vehicle. But the truth is there are a finite number of ways that automobiles run into problems and undoubtedly some are much more common than others. The same can be asserted about human beings and our psychology.

It is important to establish this principle at the outset before making certain propositions about public figures one has never met face-to-face. With a good knowledge and experience of human psychology, mental health professionals, or any layperson for that matter, can be equipped to formulate impressions and make inferences about another person's behavior, whether or not they had ever met the individual in person. It might be presumptuous to compare the diagnostic skills of any contributor to this book, myself included, to the highly refined diagnostic acumen displayed by the Magliozzi brother week after week. Nevertheless, here we go.

Two aspect of narcissism are the focus of this chapter: the unconscious sense of inadequacy that lies beneath the prideful, self-absorbed, self-aggrandizing veneer of a narcissist; and the way narcissists treat others like inanimate things. Additionally, this chapter proposes that certain reactions evoked in the individual who comes into contact with narcissists can be extrapolated to the wider domain of the collective. According to the Jungian analyst Daryl Sharp, the collective unconscious is "distinctive from the personal unconscious, [and] consists in archetypes or primordial images"; whereas, the personal unconscious is composed of the material that is personal to us and repressed into the unconscious.

Road Map of Narcissism

A brief road map of the developmental influences and roles played by narcissism is depicted below along with a synopsis of what may result when individuals sustain narcissistic wounds that lead to later displays of narcissistic distortion. This chapter will focus on second and third stages of this road map.

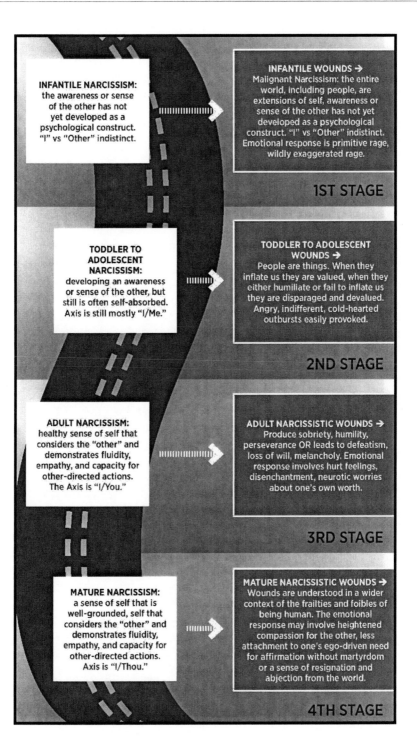

The road map highlights certain aspects of narcissism as it progresses along normal developmental lines. To the right of each synopsis of normal development in the roadway is a brief description of what occurs when an individual sustains narcissistic wounds. Just as a sapling whose trunk is marred early in life will forever show the evidence of that early wound, the developing human being who is injured in the early years of development may later display pronounced features in their personality deriving from those early wounds.

Sometimes life makes its demands upon you, and you find yourself struck by a deep uncertainty that you will have within you what you need to meet the challenge. In such moments, there are several possible trajectories you may follow. You may advance toward the challenge before you and do your best to take it on. If you succeed in meeting that challenge, you are likely to find that your self-esteem is enhanced. Such moments create a foundation or reservoir that can be relied upon in future encounters with life's demands.

Of course, things may not turn out so well for you. You may fail to master whatever demands life put before you. On those occasions, the interpretation you give to your failures to master life's challenge can exert profound and lasting impact on your personality development and your course in life.

Personal Vignette

In seventh grade as I was making a mad dash to exit the locker room for gym class so that I would not be the last one and receive the ritual paddling administered by the coach to the last one out, a classmate punched me in the gut right before I reached the doorway, and I doubled over in pain. He made a hasty exit. When I finally caught my breath, I stood up to find the coach ready to execute swift punishment. I walked out on the playground tearful and humiliated.

Years later when I was in the second two years of medical school and approaching my black belt test in karate, I entered a classroom where I was assigned the role of preceptor for first-year medical students learning physical exam skills for the first time. One of the freshmen students was my seventh-grade classmate.

I felt a sense of unadulterated power as I gave this young medical student a knowing look. It was clear he recognized me too, and I do not know if he made the same connection to that critical day in seventh grade. I prolonged my stern, fierce look designed to menace him. I allowed a few minutes of silence to punctuate the moment. When his frightened look confirmed to me that the tables had turned and now he was the vulnerable one whom I could bring to tears in front of his peers, I allowed my face to soften. I greeted him by name and mentioned to his classmates that we went to middle school together. I turned to him and made it clear that I had just been toying with him and all was well between us. His relief was almost palpable.

The lingering effects of narcissistic wounds manifest in patterned ways that depend upon the severity and timing of the wounds an individual receives. People, like automobiles, develop problems in predictable ways. On this basis, conjectures about public figures can be justified without making asserting any claims about a diagnosis.

Adler, Jung, and Inferiority

Nearly a century ago, the Viennese psychoanalyst Alfred Adler broke ranks with Freud and developed a different school of thought that came to be known as individual psychology. One of the underlying tenets of individual psychology is that each of us struggles with feelings of inferiority and our psychological development is shaped by the way we negotiate these struggles. Adler developed the idea of *social interest*, a feature that involves an individual's personal interest in furthering the welfare of others. Where Freud and many of Adler's contemporaries emphasized the personal, intrapsychic realm when formulating theories, Adler placed greater importance on the social dimension of personality development. C. G. Jung also broke ranks with Freud. One of the many ideas he introduced was the concept of a collective unconscious that undergirds everyone's psychology. He traced the origins of myths, fairy tales, and symbols within dreams to a deeply rooted domain of the collective unconscious. Jung erected a psychology of complexes that was expansive and encompassed not just psychopathology but took account of the farther reaches of human psychology. He was a pioneer of the transpersonal psychologies. However, Jung's psychology has remained primarily a psychology of the individual.

Despite the name *Individual Psychology*, Adler taught extensively about the social roots of individual psychological development. In fact, one of the characteristics of a well-adjusted individual, according to Adler, was the capacity to collaborate and cooperate with others. His approach recognized a sort of soft determinism whereby genetics and environment shaped, but did not absolutely determine, the choices and path an individual's life traversed.

Adler understood that feelings of inferiority are fundamental and part of normal development. They provide the impetus for a compensatory drive to improve oneself in order to avoid inferiority feelings in the future. When feelings of inferiority become fixed, maladaptive features of the personality, we can say that the person suffers from an *inferiority complex*. Such individuals seem convinced of their inherent worthlessness, and this is displayed in their speech, demeanor, body habitus, facial expression, and style of living. Certain that they will fail in whatever they attempt, people with *inferiority complexes* tend to retreat from the challenges presented by life.

Adler's and Jung's ideas about complexes have many things in common. They used the term to describe emotions, experiences, and styles of engaging the world that coalesce around central, organizing images, symbols, or ideas. Where Jung identified archetypes at the core of the complex, Adler's notion of a *superiority complex* was rooted in universal feelings of inferiority. This *superiority complex* reveals itself in an excessive, relentless degree of striving to overcome others, and this bears a striking similarity to narcissistic personality disorder.

Adler's notion of a *superiority complex* is a compensation for what might otherwise develop into an *inferiority complex*. The *inferiority complex* tends to paralyze an individual, mostly obstructing his or her effort toward self-improvement and superiority. By contrast, the *superiority complex* becomes a style of living that is insensitive to others, does not promote collaboration or cooperation, and is focused upon disproving and disavowing feelings of inferiority. The superiority complex, like narcissistic personality disorder, exists in opposition to community. Accomplishments in work, athletics, and relationships are driven by an incessant need for securing admiration from others. It is not sufficient for a person with NPD or a *superiority complex* to strive to perfect himself or herself; such people must exceed whatever they see others attaining. Other people function as reflections of the person with NPD or a *superiority complex*.

C. G. Jung's psychology can be understood as a psychology of narcissism, and in many ways Jung anticipated the later developments in psychoanalysis that are subsumed by the term self-psychology. Jung expanded Freud's concept of libido beyond the confines of sexual libido. Libido encompassed the life-affirming energy that fuels the process of becoming the person one is destined to be, individuation. This energy may be directed outward, and this is referred to as extraversion. It may also be directed inward as introversion. When libido is directed toward the Self in an excessive manner, it may lead to the narcissistic disorders. Jeffrey Satinover attempted to recover Jung's lost contributions pertaining to narcissism.

> 'In Jung's view the "narcissistic neuroses" consist of a withdrawal of energy from extraversion and a consequent "excess" of introversion. But it is an "excess" only in

the symptomatic, self-curative sense that, for instance, a reactive leukocytosis is an "excess" of white blood cells. In narcissistic (and psychotic) disturbances, the withdrawal of energy from the reality function is in response to the inadequacy of the "false self." The withdrawal constitutes a regression of ego energy. It leads to the relativization, or destruction, of that self (the mythic motif of the death of the god-hero in Jung's Jarbuch articles) in the face of reactivation of unintegrated, primordial archetypes, that is, of ego nuclei. Thus, the symptoms of these disturbances— the introversion of ego energy, the loss of reality function, archaic fantasy, and grandiose self-images—represent a homeostatic process by which a more comprehensively integrated self-representation is sought—"regression in service of the self," if you will.

In normal individuals, introversion is a background process by which a more or less stable self-representation is maintained' (Satinover, 1986)

In the narcissist, introversion is not only excessive, but it becomes identified with the Self. The Self is an organizing archetype in the collective unconscious that also serves as a template for the formation of the ego. When libido is withdrawn and becomes identified with the Self, a person experiences a sense of inflation, grandiosity, and he or she no longer feels the need to consider others. This is the foundation of the narcissist's dilemma. Such identification with the Self quickly becomes an identification with the lesser aspects of self. Here, the individual is not surrendering to the higher call of the Self, but is instead prone to believe that whatever arises in himself or herself deserves to be reflected in the outer world. The world becomes like an enormous mirror whose function is to constantly reflect the grandeur and impressiveness of the narcissist. Jung's perspective was teleological, that is, it assumed there exists a principle that directs the development of the individual. Adler also believed that there was a principle toward which the individual inclined.

Adler described a trajectory that moved toward greater degrees of collaboration and cooperation with others along with a movement toward equality and justice. Adler might have been expected to agree with Dr. Martin Luther King Jr. when he said, "The arc of the moral universe is long, but it bends towards justice." According to Adler, the well-adjusted human being is capable of living in harmony and cooperation with others and acts on behalf of the greater good of society. This is called *social interest* and consists of an individual's personal interest in furthering the welfare of others. When this quality is well-developed, it can progress to benefit society as a whole.

Narcissism, Mirroring, and the Narcissistic Wound

Narcissism as a process involves the psychological need to be mirrored by another human being. To a great extent, a healthy sense of self depends upon an individual receiving good enough mirroring. Mirroring consists of looking into the face of another person and having that person resonate accurately enough to be soothing and affirming. Good enough mirroring is preferred to perfect mirroring. In fact, the occasional failures of mirroring are thought to be critically important to process of healthy ego development. The quality of a parent's response to a child's needs and wants, whether it is a child's hunger, his or her need for touch/soothing, his or her need for correction, or many other parent-child interactions, become the building blocks of self-esteem—they determine the course of narcissism's development. When the child expresses a need or want, sometimes the parent is attuned and responds quickly and effectively. At other times, the parent misses the mark, and the child is left to experience a sense of his or her own inadequacy and helplessness. Parental failures may contribute to a child's developing narcissism. Modest parental failures are necessary for the individual to develop self-reliance and self-soothing abilities. Extreme parental failures, in which the parent's needs and wants supersede the child's, constitute narcissistic wounds. These can take the form of outright disregard for the child but may also occur when parents demand that a child mirror them, acclaim them, adore them. Parents given to gratifying their own narcissistic needs at the expense of their children tend to inflict on their children the similar wounds to those they sustained.

Hereafter, narcissistic wound will be used to signify those parental failures whereby a child or adolescent is treated like a thing, not a person. When a thing serves its purpose of mirroring and glorifying the parental figure, it is treated with regard; when the thing fails to fulfill its purpose, the thing is devalued. Too often, narcissism begets narcissism. A parent who suffered narcissistic wounds demands that his or her child mirror the parent's needs instead, rather than the other way around. The result is that the child is prevented from successfully negotiating his or her own inferiority. This child will be at enormous risk of being something of a bully and may become an overbearing, exaggeratedly competitive, often condescending adult.

The Narcissist

Viewed through an Adlerian lens, the narcissist has gone awry and cannot consider others, cooperate with others, or strive for the welfare of others. The veneer applied to the narcissist consists of superiority, avarice, and incessant need to prove himself or herself better than the rest. From a

Jungian perspective, the narcissist has become identified with the self. In this process, narcissists become inflated, grandiose, and tyrannical. This identification with the archetypal core, the self, fosters fantasies of power, glory, and celebrity. Whereas the self is ideally that organizing core of an individual that teleologically moves the individual's overall development, when a person becomes identified with this psychological element in the psyche, there is a tremendous risk of ego-inflation. This is the person who acts as if *My will be done.*

Narcissists often appear callous and insensitive. They demand that others affirm them, acclaim them, and treat them as if they are special. Those who dare to refuse the narcissist's demands will be dealt with harshly and with either indifference or overt rage. When narcissists are productive, they will often attain positions of power, they may in fact excel, and they may demonstrate superiority over others. Perhaps it is because the feelings of inferiority are ubiquitous that it is so easy for narcissists to demand that others conform to and obey their wishes. At the root of the narcissist's dilemma are inferiority and wounds that were rooted in the disavowal of the narcissist's personhood.

Remember that the narcissistic wound occurs when the individual's personhood is overwhelmed, pushed aside, ignored, and otherwise mistreated. The earlier an injury is sustained, the more pervasive and disruptive are the consequences.

The Narcissistic Dance

> *Sure he (Fred Astaire) was great, but don't forget Ginger Rogers did everything he did backwards...and in high heels!*
>
> ~ Bob Thaves

Something powerful and disturbing occurs in the encounter with the narcissist. It is not easy to flee from a narcissistic individual. Narcissists can prove to be very attuned to other people, not because they are moved by social interest, but because the other person has something they want. If the other person is someone of high standing, the narcissist will strive to associate himself or herself with that person. The person who is willing to affirm, aggrandize, and kowtow to the narcissist is a useful thing. However, if at any point the thing loses its value and function, the narcissist will cast the person aside the way one might discard a Kleenex tissue full of mucus. Once a person crosses the narcissist or once a person loses value for the narcissist, that person becomes like a thing that has no more usefulness.

Trumplestilksin Revisited

There are motifs in the Trumplestilksin fairy tale that resonate with the events of the 2015-16 campaign for the presidency of the United States of America. In Trumplestilksin, we encounter a figure who is small and almost comical. That he is a little man suggests the struggles with inferiority feelings. He is able to take straw and convert it into gold. It seems to me that there is an analogy here to Mr. Trump, who has seemingly endless gifts at making himself the centerpiece of the daily news cycle. What begins as straw, that is, the vacuous celebrity who reaches his or her zenith in reality television shows, has been spun into political gold. He may have started out a comical little man, but he has delivered on his promise of making gold despite having no sensible policies.

There are several elements to the Trumplestilskin story I wish to examine. Trumplestilksin is not satisfied with a necklace, nor a ring, nor even the untold riches the queen offers to bestow upon him—why should he be?—Trumplestilskin can spin straw into gold. Trumplestilskin is an exemplar of the "self-funded" one who strives. Ultimately, he seeks what is most precious to the queen, her child. This is the very soul of a woman, and that is what he wishes to possess. What is the soul of the United States of America? President Lincoln inscribed the words "a new birth of freedom" into the fabric of this nation after it had been torn apart by the Civil War. The freedom we enjoy, the inclusiveness that is established in the nation's motto *e pluribus unum* (out of many, one), and history of immigrants drawn by a beacon of hope, all this in the aggregate is the soul of the nation. It seems to me that this is what Donald Trump has been striving to possess.

Finally, Trumplestilskin cannot tolerate the moment when he is called by his real name, Is this not true of those who are bullies, that they will not tolerate being labeled what they are? Likewise, narcissists will not tolerate being identified as such. Any attempt to do so may provoke an angry backlash, a sort of counterpunch. Time and again, it has seemed that Donald Trump will raise his voice, interrupt, or simply disavow statements made by other people about his character and temperament.

In the end, the fairy tale Trumplestilskin character flies into such a rage that he ends up stomping his leg so hard that he becomes stuck. Unable to free himself, he begins to pull on his own limb and before long he tears himself in two. Trumplestilskin's fate may foretell how Mr. Trump will meet the demise of will to power. It seems that every time Donald Trump stomps his foot in an angry, indignant rant, he appears to become more stuck than before. In an effort to extricate himself from these moments, he has tended to become even more extreme in his posturing. Some pundits have foreseen Donald Trump's eventual self-destruction.

A Nation Showed Up to the Narcissism Dance with Donald Trump

An individual entering the gravitational field surrounding a narcissist, especially a seemingly successful narcissist, has trouble getting away. Perhaps the same is true for a nation ensnared in the gravitational field of a charismatic, narcissistic leader. History bears witness to the potential dangers when narcissistic leaders mobilize a large enough contingent of the population. How might this offer some explanations of the phenomenon that unfolded during the presidential election season of 2016? I speculate that the universal struggle with feelings of inferiority and an apparent deficiency of social interest on the part of Donald Trump resonated with a segment of the American public. The syndicated columnist Leonard Pitts Jr. wrote about the undercurrent Donald Trump tapped. (*Killing Donald Trump Won't Kill his Ideas*, June 21, 2016, Miami Herald, Op-Ed)

> America's problem has nothing to do with him [Trump], except to the degree he has made himself a focal point.
>
> No, America's problem is fear. Fear of economic stagnation, yes, and fear of terrorism. But those are proxies for the bigger and more fundamental fear: fear of demographic diminution, of losing the privileges and prerogatives that have always come with being straight, white, male and/or Christian in America. It was the holy quadfecta of entitlement, but that entitlement is under siege in a nation that grows more sexually, racially and religiously diverse with every sunrise.

During the primary season, it appeared that Donald Trump pounced on different candidates with a style worthy of a schoolyard bully. He dubbed Governor Bush "low energy," labeled Senator Rubio "little Marco," Senator Cruz became "Lyin' Ted," and Senator Graham was branded "an idiot." Once Donald Trump became the presumptive nominee, he set about using this same strategy to take on the Democratic leaders with names that included "Crazy" for Senator Sanders, "Goofy" for Senator Warren, and "Crooked Hillary" for Secretary Clinton. Senator Warren earned a second insulting nickname, "Pocahontas." This strategy allowed Mr. Trump to advance toward the nomination like Richard Hatch, the first winner of the reality television show, *Survivor*, who became the most hated character on the show for his unabashed ruthlessness that was likened to a snake. Because everyone wrestles with feelings of inferiority, such bullying behavior can be successful. Those viewing this conduct may identify with the aggressor. Neuroscientists have shown that we have a class of cells known as mirror neurons that experience something witnessed as if it is something we have actively carried out the action observed. This may be how we learn behaviors. In medicine, there is an adage about how trainees learn procedures: "See one, do one, teach one."

Possibly, Donald Trump's tactics allowed viewers who have been bullied and struggled with their own feelings of inferiority to relate to being the bully. Donald Trump has not seemed to be hindered by social interest. He has repeatedly espoused ideas like "The wall just got 10 feet taller" that are deeply flawed but kindle a deeply satisfying emotional response in his supporters.

Donald Trump seems to have shrewdly singled out one group after another—undocumented Mexicans, people with disabilities, Native Americans, and of course Muslims—and made them targets. In a sense, he seems to be an equal opportunity hater. This strategy may have allowed him to ignite the anger and resentment of a wide swath of voters. This strange interplay between charismatic leader who displays narcissistic traits and the public may be understood as a drama of first engaging the public's inferiority complex, then offering a promise of being able to remedy such feelings. One problem with this dynamic is that the compensation for an inferiority complex is too often a superiority complex. "Make America great again" hints at a promise of superiority that is premised on power and international standing is a zero sum game. Adler's notion of social interest seems to be absent from Donald Trump's worldview. America, like Donald Trump, should expect to overcome all its competitors, to be crowned the survivor. This is particularly dangerous in our profoundly interconnected world.

Many complex systems like politics, economics, and the environment are best understood by the science of Chaos and Complexity Theory. This field of study involves how small changes in initial conditions can produce extraordinary, powerful effects. It is symbolized by the idea that theoretically a hurricane could result from the initial cause of a butterfly flapping its wings at a distance. In light of this emerging field, Donald Trump's assertions that he can "make America great again" at the expense of others on the planet not only appears shortsighted, it may establish initial conditions that will not easily be managed.

Jungians recognize that large groups of people can be overtaken by archetypal energies. Possession by an archetype is capable of unleashing tremendous collective force. According to Jung, possession is a state of mind in which "complexes take over the control of the total personality in place of the ego, at least temporarily, to such a degree that the free will of the ego is suspended." This can be a centerpiece of sacred rituals whereby the individual is elevated into a larger drama. The sacrament of communion provides a familiar example. In the Gospel account of the Last Supper and later in 1 Corinthians, the ritual is described: "This cup is the new covenant in my blood; do this, whenever you drink it, in remembrance of me." Through this act of remembrance, an individual may enter the mystery of the death and resurrection of the Christ.

Culturally, strong, charismatic leaders can engage archetypal energies, and people can become possessed by such energies. Deeply embedded in the American psyche, the collective unconscious repository of the American experience, dwell ideas about triumphing against great odds and taming hostile forces. From the nation's birth secured by small numbers of rebels triumphing over a much stronger British military, to the Manifest Destiny that undergirded the conquest of the Western regions and the inhabitants, to the victory in World War II, something brash and unyielding is part of the fabric of the nation. Sadly, America has also demonstrated a pattern of brutal, discriminatory conduct and rhetoric directed against Native Americans, Africans forcibly enslaved in the Americas, and repeated waves of immigrants. A leader who is able to wed the vicious, brutal collective unconscious elements of the American psyche to the noble, hopeful, triumphant elements will be able to unleash powerful forces. The question that people within a nation stuck in the throes of such a drama should ask is: "To what end are these forces being unleashed?"

When Dr. Martin Luther King Jr. gave his "I Have a Dream" speech before an assembled crowd on the National Mall, he unleashed deep, collective forces. His words were crafted to inspire, to uplift, and to arouse what President Lincoln called "the better angels of our nature." Dr. King embeds his dream in the context of the American Dream: "I still have a dream. It is a dream deeply rooted in the American Dream. I have a dream that one day this nation will rise up, live out the true meaning of its creed: We hold these truths to be self-evident, that all men are created equal." Dr. King sought to connect with archetypal forces in order to bend that arc of the moral universe toward justice.

Contrast this with Donald Trump's apparent goals. Like Dr. King, the Donald makes known that he has a dream of triumph over 17 competitors and then Secretary Clinton that he has portrayed as part of the powerful elite that rigs the system. The irony of a man who boasts of being very rich and having attended the best schools leveling accusations of elitism against Secretary Clinton is striking. Mr. Trump seems to display considerable skill in conflating American's deeply rooted resentment toward King George III (or any modern facsimile) with his promise of restoring America to a triumphant state. He appears to have a singular purpose in tapping into collective, archetypal energies to win. In a speech delivered in April

2016 Trump informed his audience that "You'll say, 'Please, please, it's too much winning. We can't take it anymore. Mr. President, it's too much' And I'll say, 'No, it isn't.'" Take a careful look at that remark and notice that the focus is still on the person of Donald Trump. Adler's notion of social interest is conspicuously absent from Mr. Trump's rhetoric and actions. Instead, it seems that his goal in tapping into the archetypal realms is to promote Donald Trump. In this regard, he has demonstrated consistency, he has appeared to be a relentless promoter of the Trump brand and persona. The impetus for connecting with archetypal forces seems to be about self-inflation. Donald Trump's promise goes something like this:

Donald Trump's promise goes something like this.

If Donald Trump were simply a compelling figure whose apparent narcissistic traits drew incessant attention to himself, there might be no cause for concern. In my opinion, what makes Donald Trump a clear and present danger is his ability to inflame deep, archetypal energies for ignoble purposes. He does not appear to be driven by the pursuit of social interest. He has spent years building his brand and mystery and power of his brand in his name. There are certain elements in my retelling of the classic tale of Rumplestilksin that may shed light on the figure of Donald Trump. Trumplestilskin is smallish because beneath the larger-than-life appearance of a figure like Trump may dwell a person whose superiority complex is best understood as a compensation. In addition,

Trumplestilskin turns away from more riches, and he is seeking to capture the very soul of the miller's daughter. It appears to me that Donald Trump will not stop until he takes possession of the soul of America, and despite polls claiming that he is deeply disliked, he maintains that various groups who have been the target of his disparaging remarks "love" him. The danger Trump presents is properly located in the reaction people have to him. While narcissistic leaders do what all narcissistic individuals do, they differ in that the responses they evoke occur at very large scales. Whether viewed through an Adlerian lens as an attempt to overcome inferiority feelings or viewed through a Jungian lens as possession by archetypal forces, many of Donald Trump's supporters may be caught in the clutches of dancing with narcissism.

According to Jung, "The cooperation of conscious reasoning with the data of the unconscious is called the 'transcendent function.'.... This function progressively unites the opposites." My sincere hope is that as a result of the 2016 presidential election season and how it revealed America's potential to turn toward a figure like Donald Trump, the people of the United States of America may be poised to unify opposites, to enlist the transcendent function, and to engage in a mature fashion our own struggle with inferiority and the compensatory urge to superiority. If individuals and the nation itself pursue such lofty ambitions, that is, if we individuate as a nation, we will reduce our collective vulnerability to being led to questionable wars, to racist or misogynist rants, and we will be better equipped to contend with a complex, nuanced world. Then we may look back at this era of Trump as one of the best things that ever happened to the United States of America. For this to happen, we may need to call Donald Trump and the phenomenon he has loosed by name. Calling this entire phenomenon by name has been the primary intent of this chapter and this book.

Leonard Cruz, MD, in addition to maintaining a busy practice of psychiatry, he is the Editor-in-Chief of Chiron Publications, co-founder of the Asheville Jung Center, Chairman of the Mission Institutional Review Board. He co-authored *DSM-5 Insanely Simplified* and is a contributor to an upcoming Chiron book, *The Unconscious Roots of Creativity*. He is currently at work on a short story collection and a nonfiction work on globalization, sustainability and human rights.

Fascist Style in Narcissistic Fashion

BY JOHN McCLAIN, PhD

Make Italy Great Again! ~ Anonymous

This chapter will discuss the political theory and practice of Fascism in its original incarnation, Benito Mussolini's Fascist Italy. The chapter proposes that Italian Fascism has become a basic and influential component in the spectrum of political modernity. Specifically, the chapter emphasizes Fascism's "aesthetic." Fascism became fashionable in Italy by fixating on the images and actions of a single, idealized ruler, Il Duce. The chapter's main goal is to interpret Mussolini's appeal. It suggests that his appeal can be tied to a particular kind of audience, one with perhaps narcissistic traits; hence the title: "Fascist Style in Narcissistic Fashion." But *suggests* is the operative word here, for the chapter's conclusion is open-ended, one for the reader to decide. If the evidence provided here makes sense, and if the circumstances of Italians' receptivity to Fascism are repeatable elsewhere, then a Mussolini-like solution might be found elsewhere, too.

A quote from Giovanni Gentile is pivotal for this discussion of Fascism's possible recurrence. Gentile is not as well-known as Mussolini but is as important for how Italian Fascism achieved the influence this chapter claims for it. He was at various times under Mussolini the Minister of Education, the President of the Supreme Council of Public Education, a professor of philosophy at the University of Rome, and the main editor for the *Enciclopedia Italiana*. He was the philosopher of Italian Fascism and remained loyal to Mussolini even after the, ironically, Fascist coup that removed Mussolini from power. Gentile was assassinated by anti-Fascist partisans in 1944, as Mussolini himself would be in 1945.

Gentile begins to answer the question for how Mussolini succeeded, and for as long as he did. Gentile wrote, "Fascist philosophy is not a philosophy that is thought, it is rather one that is done. ...From this fundamental character of Fascist philosophy derives those qualities that are spoken of as Fascist *style* – a style of literary expression and a style of practical conduct..." (2002, p. 34). This chapter is about the story of Italian Fascism's rise and development as an official political movement, a political party that ruled Italy for just over 20 years under the leadership of Mussolini.

But it also wants to discuss what it labels "f"ascism—a technique, a method, a style, of political leadership, in large part created in Italy. The chapter suggests that this style has become a method that contemporary politicians, all over the world, frequently use to govern and to get elected to office. Most of this chapter will be about Fascism in Italy, but it proposes, too, the reality of this more implicit form of fascism, fascism with a small "f" that has become a part of everyday political life, thus its relevance for today.

Italy has often been interpreted as the weak partner in the Axis, the alliance with Germany and Japan that fought against the Allies in World War II. This view is correct. Italy was in fact the weak link in that alliance, militarily and economically. However, one can argue, and this chapter wants to, that Italian Fascism as a style of political leadership has in the long run had more influence than Nazism, e.g., in terms of its influence in the vocabulary of modern political discourse. For example, one should remember that Italian Fascists coined the term "totalitarian." As Mussolini wrote, "Besides the single political party there must be a totalitarian State ..." (1975, p. 25). Of course, there is the word "fascism" itself, now a common word in political conversation.

There is also the language of advertising and governing, as in the powerful role of "image" in politics today. Italian Fascism can be seen and used as a prophetic framework for understanding contemporary fascist-looking movements. The chapter claims, in sum, that Italian Fascism created and mastered a vocabulary of symbols, a political language of images, and image control that are now accepted as routine. What was an Italian form of discourse is now a model for the way political ideas, and the politicians articulating them, communicate with the public generally. Italian Fascism and its children are an indisputable part of political modernity and of the contemporary political experience.

The chapter follows a three-part structure. First, as Italian Fascism self-consciously saw itself within history, so its own history should be discussed. The second part presents Fascism's adoption of historical symbols from which they hoped to attain political and moral legitimacy. Part three analyzes Fascist doctrine, the cult of Mussolini that centers it, and suggests Fascism's mobile utility beyond Italy and World War II.

I: Some Fascist History - from Luck to Myth

It should be appreciated from the start that Italian Fascism developed out of political anxiety across most of the social boundaries in Italy. Fascism was a reaction, the impetus for its existence a negative one, born of disappointment in the present, fear and uncertainty about the future, and resentful anger toward the immediate past. Thus, to state it most simply, Fascism was better understood for what it opposed than for what it supported. Italian

Fascist actions, and then Fascist identity itself, operated on expediency, opportunism, an exploitation of a general "sense" that there was an emergency in the making, along with doubts that Italy's governing status quo was capable of thwarting it, or even seeing it.

Before World War I, the Kingdom of Italy was, at its best, a barely second-rate European power, economically and politically. World War I exasperated this condition. In World War I, Italy was on the winning Allied side with the British Commonwealth, France, and the USA, against the major Central Powers, the German, Austro-Hungarian, and Ottoman Empires. Italy, in an effort to increase its prestige on the continent, had switched its allegiance from the Central to the Allied powers. But *Italians* did not feel like winners in the aftermath of World War I. The war was tremendously costly for Italy, in casualties and financially, but Italy felt ill-compensated regarding reparations and territorial benefits.

Many Italians perceived a lack of respect for what had been immense risk-taking in the war, in particular against Austria-Hungary. Italy's efforts seemed underappreciated, especially when compared to the spoils of war given to France, for example. Italy's history, too, as the depository of Western Civilization—ancient Rome, the Roman Catholic Church, the Renaissance—seemed no more than a record of achievement noted by scholars and tourists, Italy's present political status an inferior asterisk in its own history, as well as in comparison to the high-stakes modern political players to their north and across the Atlantic.

It is indisputable that Italy was in disarray economically post-World War I. The central government seemed out of touch and inept at fixing financial problems (this is before the Great Depression). Communism was gaining more adherents. These factors led to alliances between three groups: a Vatican terrified and horrified by atheistic communism, industrialist capitalists terrified and financially threated by labor unions (communist-inspired and not), and Fascists. Fascists were an assortment of alienated individuals of many stripes, especially disenfranchised (and unemployed) World War I veterans, a group exasperated by the perception of Italy as weak, and of themselves as weak, their heroism in war heretofore unrewarded in peace. All three groups had firm constituencies but were not singularly powerful enough to dominate the central government.

One also needs to appreciate that in 1922 Italy as a modern nation-state was still a new, unfamiliar, not always popular experiment in the views of many Italian and Italian institutions. Italy was not completed as a modern nation-state until 1871, with a constitutional monarchy and parliament, and constitution rooted in many principles of classical liberalism, rights, and equality. This was the first time since the ancient Roman Empire that a majority of "Italians" were united under a central authority. King Victor Emmanuel III was titular leader in 1922 and remained so officially throughout the *de facto* Fascist dictatorship of Mussolini. But many Italians remained committed regionalists, their political identities, narrowly defined (as party voters), remaining rooted in local traditions and deep cultural identifications. This context provided for an uncanny, perfectly stormy atmosphere for which Fascists might seem a calming and concrete solution.

In 1922, the paramilitary wing of Mussolini's Fascist party, the flashy "Black Shirts," accomplished their infamous and audacious March on Rome. This was a publicity stunt. It was not an attempted military coup to take over Rome and overthrow the official monarchy. It was not clear what these Fascists were marching for, exactly. But it was clear what they were marching against: malaise, a moribund Italian spirit, governmental stagnation. At least, so it seemed to many Italians, Fascists were doing *something*; they showed verve, decisiveness, manliness. All of this functioned as a kind of evidence in itself for something potentially different and positive. If Fascists were bullies, and they were, that aggressiveness could be seen as a form of self-defense against chaos. Also, they put on a grand show; Fascism was entertaining and dramatic. The March on Rome in 1922, with its posturing and swaggering arrogance, showed a theatrical and intimidating contempt for the political class, the ruling political elites. Fascists threw down the gauntlet at BOREDOM with the political status quo. They offered a diverting "spectacle."

It was not clear if Fascism was the politically appropriate solution for Italy's ills, or if it even had a clear content that any opposition to it could find to debate. Fascism seemed beyond and above rational discussion. One needs to appreciate Fascism's psychological resonance. It was *affectively* correct given the Italian mood of political disquiet. Words from Carl Jung, though in a different context, make this point. "Logical arguments simply bounce off the facts felt and experienced. ... [there are] "emotional facts" (1989, p. 48).

This bluff, one of the most breathtaking political ones in the 20th century, froze the reigning political establishment. The unpopular and fragile central government, with its ineffectual bureaucracy, had no clear direction, no quick reaction. Not because of actual civil strife (or perhaps civil war), but because of the fear of it, King Victor Emmanuel III invited Mussolini to lead "his" government. In 1922, Mussolini, at the age of 39, became the youngest Prime Minister of Italy in history. He remained so until 1943.

II: Fascist Aesthetics

Fascists, along with their "triumphant" attitudes and actions, found symbols for them that, again affectively, and *viscerally*, resonated with a majority of Italians. They created a Fascist aesthetic. It is essential to appreciate that this aesthetic was not a rejection of modernity. Certainly, Fascists venerated and mythologized parts of Italian history. But Fascists loved modern technology and modern materials, too.

The place to begin understanding Fascist aesthetics is with the word "fascism." From the ancient Latin, fasces were a tied roped bundle of pruned branches that contained an ax. It was a symbol for ancient Romans of unity and authority. Mussolini appropriated it as the symbol for his modern political party, the Fascist, but then remade it, literally, with modernist style and materials for his contemporary audience. One sees this adaptation, for example, in the Exhibition of the Fascist Revolution in Rome, which ran from 1932-34.

The exhibition was created to celebrate the 10th anniversary of Mussolini's rise to power. At the front of the building housing the exhibit were four 75-foot-tall "fasces," but as no ancient Roman had seen them: They were tin-plated, shiny, streamlined, almost abstract renderings of the traditional symbol, sleek like submarine periscopes, but with the sharp edges of an ax blade at their tops. Framing them were colossal, 18-foot-diameter "X's," Roman numerals in the symbol for 10.

This exhibition contained a maze of rooms and passages that led its visitors eventually to its inner sanctum: The Chapel of the Martyrs. Here, Fascist designers appropriated the Christian symbol, the cross (not a crucifix), one made of metal standing on a blood-red pedestal. Engraved on it were the words "for the immortal fatherland." In the background, soft Fascist folk anthems played continuously.

The exhibition was a huge, almost delirium-inducing success. It was supposed to run for six months; it ran for two years. Nearly four million Italians came from all over Italy to see and enjoy this Fascist fair: a Fascist victory of *style*: ancient Roman symbols, an ancient Christian symbol, abstractly rendered, constructed of modern industrial materials for a modern political purpose.

Another example of this politically correct political aesthetic is the Palace of Justice, built in Milan between 1932 and 1940. It remains standing and functions as a Hall of Justice; it houses the offices of Milan's district attorney. The exterior is neo-classical and of monumental size. In fact, it is a monument of Fascist aesthetic expression, with clean and pure lines, the neoclassical style stripped down to its barest essentials, an unadorned and uniform geometry.

This modernized neoclassical structure contains a modernist interior. It is in the art deco style, the decorative, international "power" style of interior decoration in the 1920s and 1930s. One can find it all over Europe and North America—and occasionally in European colonies such as Italy's in Africa. Fascist architects and politicians found art deco to be a useful style because it was so adaptable for their own "power" style of political coding, as witnessed in their ancient Roman referencing.

Art deco made use of expensive materials, some traditional, e.g., wood and marble and bronze. Fascist designers added modernist touches, especially the incorporation of glass, an omnipresence of glass in vivid colors. The interior is all very up-to-date: glass, wood, marble, and bronze, joined symmetrically in contemporary lines of taste and elegance, integrated with ancient-style reliefs (paintings which are fresco-like), sculptures and carvings of fasces, eagles and so on. Fascist designers blended such ancient Roman motifs within an overall art deco aesthetic.

The message: Power is glamorous. Italian Fascists connected icons from the past to the needs of the present, all of this as an imagining of the future with style. This style is not the surface of things, but a self-conscious arrangement of images with an agenda: authority, hierarchy, and power, rendered architecturally. This building is beautiful and shiny and intimidating. It has a reflecting sheen of power about it, the sheen of conspicuous and shiny success.

One should note two more Fascist constructions, and like the Palace of Justice, ones still standing: the "cubed colosseum" and the *Foro Italico*. The *Palazzo della Civilta Italiana*—the "cubed colosseum"—is perhaps the quintessential example of the Fascist aesthetic. Mussolini thought of his Rome, Fascist Rome, as the third Rome. First came the Caesars of the ancient world; second came the Popes of the Roman Catholic Church in the Middle Ages and Renaissance; and third came Mussolini's Fascist and *modern* Rome. With this narrative in mind, Mussolini had constructed the EUR, the *Esposizione Universale Romana*, a site and suburb to the south of Rome proper. It was to be the location of the 1942 World's Fair, but World War II intervened. The site's "temple" is a modernist rendering of the ancient Roman colosseum's circularity, squared offed, cubed. It is a cubist work of art, literally a cubed building on a pedestal of steps surrounded by blunt Fascist copies of seminude ancient Roman athletes.

This Fascist obsession with athleticism, especially muscular masculinity, was no more aptly used than at an actual athletic facility, the enormous *Foro Italico*, originally built under Mussolini's auspices and named, unsurprisingly, the *Foro Mussolini*. A variety of sporting events can be held there today: track, swimming, tennis (it is the long-term home of the Italian Tennis Open.). Like the Fascist colosseum, it is decorated with many brutish male nudes and seminudes, the prowess and physicality of Fascism's many strengths (moral and political) displayed "classically." The Fascist designers of the *Foro Mussolini* went even further past Rome to Egypt. At the entrance to the site, to this day, is an Egyptian-style stone obelisk with "MUSSOLINI DUX" carved into its surface. Under Fascists, their "present" acquired the architectural language and legitimacy of the *past*, synthesizing time into "now." All of these sites were evidence of a renewed self-confidence, but also a kind of hysterical optimism that dared to be "now and then" simultaneously, creating a hope that targeted the future.

III: The Mussolini Cult and its Faithful

Fascists formulated their doctrines by looking back, first to their own recent past of success, a past already being described by them as the deeds and courage of living legend; and second, by framing the personal stories of their achievement, especially Mussolini's, within the scope of Italian history. The cult of Mussolini, and the images of his self-mastery that "document" his strengths, transformed him into a model that all Italians should emulate. The images of his biography became a kind of scripture.

Fascism's success must have had an inexplicable, magical quality even to Fascists—perhaps especially so! How then to formally codify an account of what had happened? How were they to offer an intellectual explanation, a reasonable account for success when *intellect*, especially in any sort of philosophical (or rational) garb, was excused? "One might consider Fascism a method, more than a philosophical system, because in ordinary language the term system is understood to mean a developed doctrine containing theories fixed in propositions or theorems ..." (2002, p. 24). Mussolini, in less clinical terms, but crisper and more dramatic ones—such as a former journalist like him might write—stated, "The years preceding the March on Rome cover a period during which the need for action forbade delay and careful doctrinal elaborations. ... A doctrine—fully elaborated ... may have been lacking, but it was replaced by something far more decisive—by a faith" (1936, p. 17).

To turn faith into clear doctrine was a puzzle and a danger for Mussolini and Fascists generally. Grammatical and clear statements are necessary for governing—whatever the emotional brouhaha of their tone. To articulate the principles that supposedly back specific policy decisions is governance. But Fascists must be careful; language and doctrine must be flexible enough so as not to suppress the spontaneity, the creative, courageous, and virile risk-taking of a Mussolini, traits that got him and them into the position of political supremacy in the first place. Referring to Mussolini's flexible use of the truth, Carl Jung writes, "Quite often *the great plan* plays the leading role [make Italy great again!], and it is only when it comes to the ticklish question of bringing this plan into reality that every opportunity is exploited. ..." (1979, pp. 61-62). To most Italians, Fascists had proved their mettle. Had Mussolini only made it up as they went along?

Following Gentile's characterization of Fascism, "a style of practical content," Fascists had to find the core tenets that, practically speaking, would fit their communicator, ones he could perform (believe?) convincingly. This chapter's working definition of Fascism is somewhat fractured, admittedly, but it seeks to show how, in the end, its tenets are held together by its *true* core, Mussolini himself.

Fascism is:

1. a faith-based political ideology;

2. an ideology that understands humans as unequal;

3. a totalitarian ideology; society and culture are its jurisdiction, in addition to politics;

4. a state-centered ideology, run by a single political party and its elite; (a multiparty system would "structure" disunity);

5. "patriotism" understood as nationalism defined by an elite;

6. an elite that are "charismatic" due to the spectacle contrived to surround the "leader" with images that merge a mythic past with a vivid and exciting present, all aimed at the future;

7. militarism;

8. militarism that leads to a nationalism-based foreign policy along modern lines of imperialism: extraction of resources from abroad and colonization to "convert" indigenous peoples to the Fascist cause;

These "articles" can have different priorities at different times, allowing the elite to behave in a catch-as-catch-can manner as determined by contingency. This ability also satisfies the Fascist ethos: its mood and appetite for spectacle.

It should be noted that these "articles" are in reaction to the then two dominant paradigms of political thought in the West: socialism or Soviet-style communism, and classical liberalism. Gentile stated, "The Fascist State may be defined in negative terms affirming what it is not rather what it is. That is because the Fascist State has arisen as antithetical to the socialist and liberal conception" (2002, p. 34). Many of Mussolini's initial supporters—literally, investors—were industrialists petrified by socialist unions. And to Mussolini, the human, inalienable equal rights of classical liberalism ("We hold these truths to be self-evident...") were not "self-evident" at all; they were only assumptions, and ones that in fact had failed their Italian test, for example with the parliamentary, constitutional monarchy in place since 1871.

Mussolini became a kind of oracle for an alternative: Fascism. He was the high priest of Italian Fascism. Fascism depended on control of the image of that spiritual, cultural, as well as political, leader. How did Mussolini project himself? One can find images of him in all of the following roles, all of which he is shown to "master":

» He was a family man often photographed with his wife and children.

» He was an athlete—a swimmer, a fencer, a horseman.

» He was an advocate of modern technology: he was a motorcyclist, a pilot, a master of the modern tractor (by Fiat).

» He was a supporter of the arts, attending the opera; a musician (he played the violin); and an art collector and patron in his own right. From his personal collection: a new sculpture in the style of an ancient Roman relief: title, "It is the plow that draws the sickle but it is the sword which defends it."

» Mussolini was a supporter of religion. In 1929 in the Lateran Accords, Mussolini signed a concordant with the Vatican in which Roman Catholicism was named the official religion of Italy in exchange for the recognition of the Holy See's independent sovereignty, (and thus de facto acceptance of the unification of Italy as a modern nation-state).

What was Mussolini? He was the modern Renaissance Man: the force for social evolutionary progress; the icon of political faith; a giant who could leap continents in a single bound. Finally and in sum: He was modernity, masculinity, machinery, and technology: he was sauce Bolognese; he was tiramisu.

Consequences and Conclusions

Although Mussolini reigned as long as he did in Italy—over 20 years—his rule might have lasted much longer had it not been for, in retrospect, *the* mistake: his allying Italy with Hitler's Nazi Germany. At first Mussolini and Hitler did not get along. There were long-term geo-political animosities, rivalries between Italy and Germany over the newly created territory post-World War I for Austria (in the Tyrol region), Italy having acquired German-language majorities in the region. When Hitler became chancellor over the winter of 1932-33, Mussolini had already been in power for a decade. Hitler was seen by Mussolini as a quite meagre crude Germanic copy. Following Mussolini's successful March on Rome in 1922, Hitler attempted a similar ploy, on a smaller scale, with the Beer Hall Putsch in Munich in 1923, an attempted coup against Bavarian government offices that failed, ending with Hitler's arrest, trial, conviction, and imprisonment.

Mussolini did not respect Hitler personally. He was as an ill-educated ruffian. Mussolini saw himself as an intellectual and "sophisticate."

Also, Hitler was an anti-Semite. This difference between them is crucial to understand. One example of this difference: Guido Jung, a Jew, was named the Minister of Finance under Mussolini in 1932. Traditionally,

Italian society had far less of an issue with Italians of Jewish origin than did Germany. Again, in 1932, after a full decade of ruling Italy, Mussolini would state: "We too have our Jews. There are many in the Fascist Party, and they are good Fascists and good Italians. ... A country with a sound system of government has no Jewish problem." (Michaelis, 1978, p.56). In fact, two Jews had been Prime Minster of the Kingdom of Italy: Alessandro Fortis (1905-06) and Luigi Luzzatti (1910-11).

Mussolini's desire to recreate a Fascist "Roman Empire" in Africa changed this scenario. Fascist Italy had inherited colonies in East Africa from the previous century: Eritrea and "Italian" Somaliland. To unite these territories Mussolini saw the independent Kingdom of Abyssinia (Ethiopia) under Emperor Haile Selassie as the convenient target whose conquest would create a united Italian land and coastal empire in East Africa along the Red Sea, one pressing British and French spheres both in the Eastern Horn and the Middle East. With modern military technology, including terror bombing of civilian centers, the first in history, and poison gas (a war crime under International Law), Italy occupied Abyssinia over the course of the war, from 1935-36. King Emmanuel III accepted a new title, Emperor of Ethiopia.

His actions in Ethiopia alienated many European powers, with varying forms of embargo imposed by them. Italy withdrew from the League of Nations. Germany had no such biases against Italy. The regimes spoke a similar, if not identical, language of opposition, to liberalism and socialism. Now it seemed they should ally similarly in action. Most notably, they participated in the Spanish Civil War, coordinating their actions. A military coup composed of the Spanish military, conservative Spanish nationalists, monarchists, right-wing Roman Catholics, and the official Spanish fascist party the Falange, under Generalissimo Franco, defeated the official Republic of Spain.

World War II began on 1 September 1939. The Spanish Civil War ended 1 April 1939. It was World War II in microcosm, a preface. Italy provided perhaps 70,000 volunteers and much material aid and shipping transport to help Franco. Germany provided aircraft with German pilots and intelligence. Stalin's Soviet Union supplied the Republic—not because he believed in the Spanish Republic for its own sake but saw it correctly as a battlefield to accrue more international prestige and support Communism anywhere. Mexico, too, aided the Republic with munitions, and more importantly, offered itself as a refuge for Republican supporters and refugees. Western democracies—including the United States—were officially, emphatically neutral.

In the alliance with Hitler, Mussolini, much to his shame, eventually did have anti-Semite laws passed in Italy in the late 1930s as a condition of continued German allegiance and support. Many Italian Jews were arrested; many were sent to concentration camps.

Spain under Franco did not join the Axis powers, Germany, Italy, and Japan, in World War II. Franco recognized that Spain was too exhausted by its own civil war to take on another and much broader, continentwide conflict, one that might threaten her remaining overseas colonies. Great Britain, with her long-term interests on the Iberian Peninsula, namely ownership of Gibraltar, the strategic threshold between the Mediterranean Sea and the Atlantic Ocean, made clear in nearly ultimatum form this threat to the colonies of Spain, one she could carry through given the Royal Navy's global reach. General Franco acquiesced and survived World War II and beyond, ruling Spain until his death in 1975.

The Spanish preface to World War II was Mussolini and Italy's last notable success. World War II was a disaster for both, a primary cause being their increasing belief in their own propaganda, following doctrine instead of practically adjusting it to circumstance.

Italian, *Fascist*, military prowess was a lie. Before Germany's invasion of Poland, Italy did succeed in annexing Albania in 1939; King Emmanuel of Italy accepted another title, King of Albania. Everywhere else, the Italian military failed: The invasions of Egypt, a British protectorate, in September 1940, and Greece, in October 1940, were disasters that required Germany assistance.

With the Allied invasion of Italy, Mussolini was deposed by his own self-created Fascist party; rescued by Hitler, he was set up as a puppet in Northern Italy. When that front, too, collapsed, he tried to escape across the Italian border into Switzerland. He was caught by anti-Fascist Italian partisans and executed.

Thus ended Mussolini and, with the end of the war, Italian Fascism. What of small "f" fascism? As stated in its introduction, this chapter will leave this an open question for readers to decide with the evidence of their own observations.

However, consider the following: As one can find photographs of Generalissimo Franco with Mussolini and Hitler, one can also find American presidents in cozy poses with Generalissimo Franco: Presidents Eisenhower, Nixon, Ford, and the, at the time, California governor and future president, Ronald Reagan.

This chapter is not claiming that these Americans are fascists. However, small fascism, "f"ascism, can be permissive, even friendly in association, based on the fear of a mutual enemy, e.g., communism with a resulting "Cold War" and an enemy that is seemingly everywhere: the USSR, Cuba, Vietnam, and Hollywood.

The Cold War is presumably over, but new enemies can create new fears that facilitate "fascist" reactions. The circumstances of Italy's embrace of Fascism are repeatable elsewhere. Such reactions foment certain tendencies, a certain state of mind leading to certain methods, and to a certain style of political discourse. In such discourse, advertising the image of the politician, with her or his proclaimed cures for fear, is more important than the content of the message, especially when that message is swathed and clouded by *mythic* hopes and *mythological* history. Erik Erikson reminds us:

> But a myth, old or modern, is not a lie. It is useless to try to show that it has no basis in fact, nor to claim that its fiction is fake and nonsense. A myth blends historical fact and significant fiction in such a way that it "rings" true to an area or an era, causing pious wonderment and burning ambition. The people affected will not question truth or logic; the few who cannot help doubting will find their reason paralyzed (1963, pp. 327-28).

This kind of discourse is always potentially alive; it is both obvious *and* stealthy, a new normal that does not need to be, or even can be, seen as different. Is it now a basic component of contemporary politics, in campaigning, but also in governance itself? This chapter leaves those answers to the reader to decide.

John McClain, PhD, teaches in the Humanities Program at the University of North Carolina at Asheville. His doctorate in political theory is from the University of North Carolina at Chapel Hill; his MA thesis was on Thucydides and his PhD dissertation on Michel Foucault. He was co-editor for *The Asheville Reader: The Medieval and Renaissance World* (Copely). He is currently at work on a book, *Sacred Views of St. Francis: The Sacro Monte di Orta* (Punctum Books).

References

Erikson, Erik H. (1963). *Childhood and Society.* (2nd edition). New York, NY: W. W. Norton and Company, Inc.

Gentile, Giovanni. (2002). *Origins and Doctrine of Fascism: With Selections from Other Works.* (A. James Gregor, Trans.). New Brunswick, CT: Transaction Publishers. (Originally published in 1929)

Jung, C. G. (1989). *Essays on Contemporary Events: The Psychology of Nazism.* (R. F. C. Hull, Trans.). Princeton, NJ: Bollingen Series, Princeton University Press.

Michaelis, Meir. (1978). *Mussolini and the Jews: German-Italian Relations and the Jewish Question in Italy 1922-1945*. Oxford, England: Institute of Jewish Affairs, The Clarendon Press.

Mussolini, Benito. (1935). *The Doctrine of Fascism*. (? Trans.). Rome: Ardita.

Mussolini, Benito. (1975). *The Corporate State*. New York, NY: Howard Fertig. (Originally published in 1936)

Waking Up! Malignant Narcissism
How Bluebeard and Hitler Came To Power

BY CLARISSA PINKOLA ESTÉS, PhD

My father's family fought to stay alive during an era of world dictators who were besotted with malignant narcissism and ambitions to divide, damage and murder countless souls they found to be "life not worthy of life." Bluebeard was a folktale the family knew well, but Hitler and Stalin became their horrific Bluebeardian realities. I was their young witness.

Born mestizo Latino, I was adopted as an older child into a fragmented Eastern European refugee/ immigrant family who survived WWII. My immigrant father worked tirelessly to bring wounded kin, village neighbors to Ah-mare-ee-kah, even though he himself could not read nor write, and his heavily accented English was rarely understood by most. How hard he struggled to tell the stories of his missing kin to whomever would listen, in order to gain the helps needed. Then one day, our war refugee relatives began to be found, one by one, two by two, in slave labor camps and refugee work camps. They fell into our arms, and we held them as they came to live with us for a long time in our tiny boondocks home.

Our broken kin brought their stories with them, both folktales, and real life horror tales from living under *politicians* who had not even a modicum of conscience. As your family stories have come with your kin also, any who survived any conflagration, any slaughter, any takeover, often trying to meet superior firepower, raping aggression, with words, hands, or a planting stick.

So isolated in forests, they spoke a 17th century version of their own natal language, our refugee kin were not only a deep storytelling people in oral tradition, they were a people who knew plants, animals and farming— the dark and shining aspects of human nature too—for these jewels of, and for life, had been handed down in their stories for centuries.

Now, harmed so in body, spirit and soul, stripped literally of peaceful sleep for life, calm body reactions to sounds and smells, their civil rights, their bountiful little farmland they worked as serfs, their forest, their hand-made cottages, their river, their beloved horses, dogs, cats and songbirds, and many family members and village friends—who did not survive the killing war—and yet even so, all their blessings of stories, knowing land, animals, crafts and trades of the hands, loving soulful ceremonies, rituals, healing remedies, remained. All beautiful blessings remained inherent, even through curtains of tears that often came for the men as well as the women.

Folktales evolve over time, such as when persons previously unknown to each other are abruptly thrown together. During and after WWII, those marched to slave labor camps often came from different language groups. Some knew or were able to learn quickly the languages of others. In stolen moments, stories told and folktales shared, took loan passages from one another's tales. These were sometimes shared in each teller's home language after. Our family's Bluebeard tale accordingly, held him as *vámpír*, cutthroat drainer of others' blood, for he could not sustain his own energy without living off others' energies. Thus, he sought acclaim and dominance. The family carried many Bluebeard stories. This is one briefly summarized along with remnants of their remembered commentaries interspersed, as was our family storytelling tradition:

> Bluebeard was a man with an unusual *tell*—the hair of his head and beard, so abundantly coifed, were most definitely and oddly colored blue. His skin reflected also a blue-milk hue. This was because he cannot keep enough of his own blood for himself. He *leaks* because of his self-indulgences, high-energy rages and planning of cunning schemes. Thus, he is a more than *half-hidden* vampire-in-need.

> Bluebeard seeks a village where there is temporary discord, where headsmen and headswomen are temporarily at odds, the people no longer led in spiritual works—work in the fields has come to a stop. Precisely there Bluebeard ensconces himself, begins to seduce naïve, needy women, men, girls and boys, old people, with empty sugar-candy promises, with bravado claims of what he will do in future heroic deeds to be their *beloved* leader over *the uncaring fools* who are their headspeople now...

> He plays upon the unfulfilled dreams of small groups. The people do not remember a liar can also *tell truths* and *repeat the challenges*, but only to ensnare a cohort to be used in nefarious ways... later. The small group forgets in their ongoing thrall that an honest, visionary person of good intent for the people, can not only tell the same truths and challenges, but bring humane solutions to them also. But, Bluebeard fails to mention this, as part of his intended *enchantment* through rousing words and empty promises.

Bluebeard with his dark strategy, wines and dines his prey, praises them, cheers them, telling them he will take them to/ restore them to a higher place. He purposely mocks any truth-seekers and non-divisive truth tellers as, the group's enemies. Bluebeard plants 'gossip' about his many *antics*, for he knows the village gossips will publicize him greatly. And they do, for they do not realize, just as he wishes, the gossip about his antics disarms the suspicious and makes everyone think he is just a harmless fool. But then he, and his vampire cohort lure ten young women [in some versions males and females] to his dark castle on pretense of marriage/granting *a better life*. Bluebeard and his fellow vampires give the maidens the keys to the many doors of the storerooms, saying they may open and enjoy all sights behind all doors, except...

This one tiny key, do not use that. Bluebeard and his fellow vampires have forbidden the naive to enter *the one small door*, for there lay the corpses of other trusting young ones who believed Bluebeard's pack of vampiric lies, thereby falling under his spell. They became unwilling blood donors for his endlessly hollow needs for blood slashing excitement to use to empower and validate [to himself] his ill actions, to make him feel even vaguely alive.

The naïve visitors to the mold-ridden castle of Bluebeard, by asking a critical question while Bluebeard is away, decide to use the small key to open the forbidden door. The question is: What is being hidden here? Thus, the key/ question is used; the forbidden door swings open to the deceits, cheatings, lies and horrors of Bluebeard's actual life. When Bluebeard returns, seeing 'the bleeding question' has been asked and answered, seeing the tiny key is weeping blood and will not cease—in other words, Bluebeard's targets cannot unsee what deleterious acts they now know he and his pack of vampires have done. Now Bluebeard rises bellowing, arm waving, screeching to punish them, to kill them all, same as the others, to live off their blood... and... to set up his next round of prey, without revealing himself a death maker, not a bringer of new life.

But, the wise in heart and mind, rise to oppose him: They call from the castle parapets for their brothers to come help them. And horses pounding like fury, come their brothers—in flank after flank of riders. In the end, they corner Bluebeard the liar, Bluebeard the cheat, Bluebeard

> the vampire who takes from others what is not his to take...
> and they cut him down *into right size.* They cut Bluebeard
> down, and as it is said, *his blood watered the roses.* In the
> end, the village headswomen, headsmen and the people
> were chastened to meet, and speak of ways to amend the
> ill atmospheres that had made ripe ground for a vampire
> to appear to begin with.

This is one of many family tales told in a cycle, about new life coming not from rounding up, inflating, then taking the lives of innocents, but rather from struggling in dark times, to preserve, in sanctity, all Life within one's reach. Though some might call this a family compensation in attempting to survive horrendous circumstances, as a post-trauma recovery specialist for forty-seven years, and a psychoanalyst since 1984, I'd call the many souls throughout the world who tell survivor stories that carry life-giving and life-sparing intent—their *blessed and moral necessity to warn others.* Through the humble story.

Following, I offer you a chart of central tactical similarities between a war-survivors' story of the folktale Bluebeard, and Adolf Hitler. We see Bluebeard [called by the family *karizmatikus gyilkos,* "the charismatic killer"] and his vampiric tactics: to first seek a vulnerable populace; then purposely deceive them by thrilling them with claims he can bring back their dreams; then using their savior-izing energy to attain malicious power over others; then with a cohort of like-kind thugs, sending the innocent to their deaths. We see the trajectory of Adolf Hitler [called by the family, *hulla alkotója,* "the corpse-creator"] who eerily followed the same death-psychology tactics as Bluebeard. Except for Hitler and his murderous thugs, there was no redemptive ending. Instead, over 55 million souls, including within Germany and worldwide, were taken to their deaths, most all being in many ways, innocents.

Steps	Bluebeard	Adolf Hitler
1. **Modus** **Operandi**	Bluebeard mobilizes in relative secrecy and suddenly shows up in what is meant to be *a lightning strike* modus operandi—before people barely know what hit them, have little time to think, evaluate, analyze, see Bluebeard for who he really is, which is a malignant being who has no conscience, no reliable heart, faux words of compassion, no self account-	Hitler mobilizes in relative secrecy and suddenly shows up in what is meant to be *a lightning strike* modus operandi—before people barely know what hit them, have little time to think, evaluate, analyze, see Hitler for who he really is, which is a malignant being who has no conscience, no reliable heart, faux words of compassion, no self accountability, no sense of truth telling versus

Steps	Bluebeard	Adolf Hitler
	ability, no sense of truth telling versus his own prevarications, and who is bloated with needy self-importance and a need to be thanked and touted constantly, to be *right* in all matters, and to be worshipped unequivocally.	his own prevarications, and who is bloated with needy self- importance and a need to be thanked and touted constantly, be *right* in all matters, and to be worshipped unequivocally.[1]
2. **Target**	In our refugee family story of Bluebeard, he is a vampire who ensconces himself in villages wherein people are poor in wages, and where the headsmen of the village are fighting with one another, thereby leaving the health of the village in disarray. Bluebeard exploits the disarray to present himself as *the answer* to all that has gone wrong. But Bluebeard's eyes are only on the blood pulse at people's throats.	Hitler bides his time until the hierarchy of his own nation is teetering and thereby begins to destabilize the peace between the different cultures within that nation. Hitler then springs in to make himself suddenly appear as *the salvific answer* to all ills of *the best of the nation,* [meaning a small portion of the nation] by affecting the garb and stentorian talk of *the strong man* archetype. [2]
3. **Tactic**	Proclaiming faux empathy: Bluebeard proclaims, "You have been neglected by those who said they would help you. I am here to court you, and save you from the utter ruin I am certain you are headed toward. Look to me only."	Hitler will proclaim faux outrage for the sad state of *my beloved people*[3] [people only of a certain kind]. Hitler will decry their diminished circumstances from having lost a devastating war, being stranded by changing borders, deep inflation in the economy. But instead of bringing prosperity and peace, he will bring mayhem and murder.
4. **Tactic**	Bluebeard will urge others to give him their most naïve, unsuspecting children who are hungry, who hope to improve their lot in life by investing in Bluebeard's sham *castles in the air.*	Hitler will target the most naïve, unsuspecting people who have lost status, are hungry for honor, understandably wanting to be lifted from the humiliation of having lost so much [a world war that fractured the empire and took away from it huge land masses of resources and jobs, not to mention sending its own young to be wiped out via outdated military tactics.][4]

Steps	Bluebeard	Adolf Hitler
5. **Tactic**	Bluebeard says, he will court everyone's kith and kin, treat them to treats, give everyone tastes of *his luxurious lifestyle*, feasts of food and drink [very strong lure for the hungry, those with food scarcity ongoing], music, horses, gatherings and gaiety beyond their ability to gain by themselves … and he shall win them over.	Hitler will court the needy and disappointed, the shunned, those who feel they fell or are blocked by others in power, from their personally deserved entitlement. He will attempt to raise national pride through xenophobia, and he will attempt to do so via giant rallies, tables groaning with food, alcohol, singing of sentimental songs, rants about *what's wrong with Germany, and how Germany will rise in utter superiority again*. That Hitler will make Germany great again![5]
6. **Tactic**	Bluebeard in a wily way, encourages all the gossips of the village to speak his name, and tell about his strangeness and his prowess—far and wide. He wants them to laud his oddness of blue hair, blue beard, and connives essentially—planting the gossip he most wants to hear repeated, so the *word of mouth* will help even more people to *come and see his wonderful oddities*. That is, come to stay long enough to hear *the visionary and flattering iron man spiel* and be captured by "Yes, this fellow really knows what he is talking about. We are downtrodden. He really will help us wherein no one else has." Bluebeard knows some who come will stay, for he has all his life, cast a spell of fraudulent promises to hold forth the undoable idea that dead and broken dreams of the past can walk again. He has taken many in at the front door, but kills their spirits and bodies at the back door—in part for blood lust, but also so they cannot testify against him, revealing his virulent conceits.	Hitler will use the press and film-makers, to gloss over his rotting and ulterior hopes, to be entertaining and also to be feared, for his condemnations of others are many and so severe. The more the press proclaims him, the more many new persons are duped, but also many citizens become increasingly alarmed. Hitler will use the press, heroic music and puff piece films to aggrandize himself, attempting to transform himself into *most noble being* who *loves his people* so utterly, that he will also use or suspend the press to attempt to beat down all naysayers in the most vicious manner—out of love for *his people*—and so as to lure more devotees to himself. Thus Hitler uses mainstream media propaganda to indoctrinate and also to lie boldly to the people of his times. He will falsify news stories, as when a battle went badly, his media would be charged to say, "the battle went very successfully."[6]

Steps	Bluebeard	Adolf Hitler
7. **Tactic**	Bluebeard draws to himself the girls, the boys who need/want daddies, the fatherless of any age, those who do not have a powerful enough father/mother to make things happen for them to the better. Symbolically, in folk tales, often the father figure, that is, the one who sets the accepted values and tones of the greater culture, big or small, is missing—thereby making the children and their new bright ideations vulnerable to being extinguished. Bluebeard relies on proselytization of the very young to carry his water for him, to proclaim him far and wide. He gives them new clothing, beautiful gowns, fine suits. Bluebeard believes if he can capture the young he will have the entire next generation in his pocket for additional nefarious uses, even if their parents, grandparents, neighbors or friends see through him. He is the deadly pied piper leading the young to be poisoned of mind and into granting unflinching loyalty in return for faux promises given. Thus, the innocents lose energy and will, becoming deader than dead in more ways than one.	Hitler attempts to draw to himself those who feel *righteously wronged,* disenfranchised—those who often remember a day when they were able to sit in the sun, had ideas and dreams. He promises a better life, but many will be taken to their deaths. But first, he will give them *new clothing,* dress them, praise them, make both young girls and young boys seem like an elite platoon with uniforms, insignia, bright colors—[or the colors of the dead] badges and code words—and worse, give authority to the inexperienced young to harm and to kill for der Führer, in order that the Führer be proud of them and reward them. He poisons the innocent hearts of the young and attempts to make them into what he is, a blood lust subhuman, by promising them membership in the inner circle, ability to have power over others far older than they are, and to stop with a threat or a bullet any parent, grandparent, neighbor of friend who sees through Hitler and tries to edge the young person away from Hitler's web of falsehoods and deceits.
8. **Feasting on harming others**	At his first vampiric feast, joined by his thug comrade vampires, Bluebeard murders all ten young people whom he has invited to a feast at his castle. Bluebeard and his ill cohort feast on the blood of the young, and drag the bodies into a small room to hide the evidence of their true natures. Everywhere Bluebeard goes, he draws to himself fellow bloodshed-sadists who remain loyal as any such sadist would, if allowed to share in feasts of others' blood continually.	His first wholesale blood feast: Hitler murders 70,273 German children before he ever gasses 6M Jews, 1.5M gypsies, gay people, 3m Russian prisoners of war, other groups he finds 'disgusting' [one of his favorite words to dehumanize others]. He orders in 1939 the slaughter of *life unworthy of life,* that is, children who are intellectually challenged, ill, paralyzed, having Down syndrome, cerebral palsy, birth challenges of hearing, sight, accidental injuries, *halfbreeds,* and more. Physicians are

Steps	Bluebeard	Adolf Hitler
		to murder the babies and children immediately. A cost saving measure and to *rid of* blight. The German public, physicians and churches rise up, protest loudly and refuse cooperation. Many doctors help families bring their serious ill and disabled children, babies and old people home to hide them. [Hitler extended his murder order to nursing homes] But some doctors and helpers carried out Hitler's malignant lust for literal *bloodshed power over* innocents. Murder gave Hitler uncanny energy he definitively appeared to not have on his own.[7] He drew to himself, like-kind, who killed the innocent by gassing, injection and starvation.
9. **Wea-seling through confron-tation**	When the more wise and insightful amongst the populace question Bluebeard, he says he knows nothing of the disappearance of the ten young souls, why are they picking on him, he's a good fellow, that young people of the village disappear every day, that he loves the young people [but secretly only in one way, for their life's blood energy].	When confronted about his blatant excesses, Hitler hears this as *disloyalty* to himself; he hears *they think I am not perfected*, which is disabling to his sense of self—for being held accountable for his own actions/words, is his weakness. Thin beyond thin of skin, Hitler removed whomever dared to question or criticize. Once a judge refused to follow Hitler's sudden personal order that contravened German law, saying Hitler had not created yet a formal legal declaration. One of Hitler's top assistants, besotted with his own self-importance, said the judge was not worthy of being a judge, if he could not *be loyal to any order of der Führer* no questions asked.[8]
10. **Unveiled at last**	There is only one problem: his hair and beard are blue, In symbolism, this odd color of hair [and cast to Bluebeard's skin] is also a symbol of a seemingly cyanotic state, that points to Bluebeard's own blood-	There is only one problem with all these strategies and tactics that Hitler uses to pretend, presume and attempt to become the shamanic wonder of the modern world, mixing mysticism with bad science, a 2+2=5

Steps	Bluebeard	Adolf Hitler

Bluebeard

lessness, blood oxygen starvation,[9] and his bloodthirstiness, his blood hunger, giving away his true intents—which are, to live on the worshipful, then pleading energies of human beings, as many as possible. As vampire, in his reality, unlike his persona and claims, he lives inside a black rotting castle in a woods that is dying all round him [and in family version of the story] has a slew of slaves to paint the dead leaves green to give the appearance of life. He has no verifiable evidences that equal his bragging about his great status, for the bragging is used only to snare new devotees. He has no colleagues other than *thug buddy* vampires, who likewise lie to the naive, break promises, punish with death for same reasons Bluebeard carries: to get rid of wiser persons who can actually *see* into the utterly self-centered heart of Bluebeard. Those who hold *the key* to the room—and open it... who see the contents—corpses for as far as one can see... cannot unsee the actual reality of Bluebeards life and motives, and Bluebeards driving intent to climb others' bones into a malignant form of power over all, He is filled with *friends* he has bought with feasts, promises, bragging about what he has, will do, has done, but without plans or proofs he has ever done them. He is a murderer of souls. He is the grasping greed-bloated thing that attempts to wear *the crown not yet given.*

Adolf Hitler

propositions of falsity. Throughout, by his writings, speeches and orders to others, Hitler is unmasked as a malignant narcissist—without conscience, without compassion for humanity, and like the vampire, his ghost-pale complexion turns livid red when he bellows with rage during his staged gatherings of the masses. In films, we see he appears to feast on the excitement of the people's life's blood which has been pledged to him, to be his, those who promise to be his *pretty* until they are not *his pretty* anymore. And when any human or group becomes *his ugly* because they won't adore him properly, thereby they are exiled immediately by him, torn from their homes, snatched right out of their seats at a meeting with him, and taken to their deaths via a shot to the back of the head... not only because they finally saw through him to the dead heart he truly was, but also because once seeing, they refused to worship him, refused to not have a mind of their own. It is pertinent to mention that he was dry dust empty of even the merest compassion. That some say he is said to have loved dogs—this will never be near enough evidence to acquit him of having the eerie lustre of not being intact as a *ser humano*, true human being. As sometimes is found in psychopathic behavior, there was a truly sad ending for the dogs too. As told by those who found his body—before he committed suicide, Hitler first killed his dogs, [Blondi and her pups] ordering them to be forced to bite into the cyanide capsules meant for himself. Thus his *beloved* dogs, who could have lived long lives with others of kindness, were sent to their deaths.

Steps	Bluebeard	Adolf Hitler
11. **Nemesis**	The brothers ride in to save their sisters, brothers, parents, comrades, whomsoever has been lured to Bluebeard's castle. They have used the key to unlock the forbidden door. [Using the key in symbology can represent this question, What does Bluebeard not want me to see that he locks this one room so tightly?] To open the door to the killing room, thereby knowing Bluebeard's true nature of malignant intent and desire to wound and feed off the energy/blood of others— has caused the final crises. The brothers hear their family/friends calling them in desperation, and they ride hard. But instead of politely entering the courtyard of Bluebeard's castle, they drive their huge powerful horses right up the stairs of the castle, shaking the mortar from the stone walls. Finally they engage Bluebeard who attempts to stab them with his sword, hoping to draw their blood to drink. But, the brothers are stronger, more in number, and with their daggers and swords, they give Bluebeard the death of a thousand cuts. Thus they take him down, dismember him with the sharpness of their sight, the sharpness of their daggers... and as they say in my family at the end of the story, *and Bluebeard's blood then waters the roses.* In other words, given that all energy has been leached from Bluebeard, that he has been effectively dragged off the stage of performance he so loved, exposed now as a liar, thief, conceited self-centered, criminal mind—with merely a charming exterior—that the energy released now goes toward growing of goodness truly, instead of acting as though the artificial	Hitler gained power through his tactics of feasting and faux praising persons he deemed in need. Many were happy he *told the truth.* But persons of conscience could also tell the truth. *The truth* can also be bandied about for self gain by a pathological liar. The problem was Hitler as *truthteller* grasped an obvious set of truths to lure people in, and then gave faux promises; literally crying he was going to make return Germany to her *right* place again. One without certain kinds of people. But, many people began to wake up, to break the net of enchantment he had tried to cast over them. They began to speak up, even as Hitler silenced them, literally *to death.* The people were standing up, acting up. But... because Hitler was not stopped in time, because he commanded an entire army he could unleash and did, at will—to burn, assault, kill ... because he moved quickly to strike against others, because "it was barely two decades since the last world war and surely some fool wouldn't start that up again..." and because most people, when things *get bad* or even become quite bad, often take a *wait and see* attitude, many underestimated the speed with which their doom was being planned by others. As in the Bluebeard story, the ending, the denouement, comes eventually to Hitler too. His armies are torn asunder, and his infested will is dismembered, and finally and again so oddly, he dies as many of his victims died; gunshot to the head, then his body burnt. There has to be a better/deeper word for Hitler's end, than *irony.*

Steps	Bluebeard	Adolf Hitler
	is substantive, as though mere words are effective methodology to bring goodness to the world.	
12. Better and best outcomes for now and the future	The people of our many cultures, tell folktales for many reasons. One of the central reasons in my family was to warn and re-warn one another, to remember that evil ever dresses in sympathetic words and tries to act the role of *hero*, but without the deep street creds, without verifiable and transparent proofs. That story is used to keep the aspects of evil above the waterline so the tactics of evil intents can be seen and dealt with effectively and in a timely manner, to reveal the universal perils to the next generation and the next. Story teaches whatever horror or good occurred, it might happen again, and here are the signs to know it is coming. And if evil, to prepare to resist utterly, and more to push it back strongly. And if goodness, to make a place of welcome for what is goodness. To say story exists so that people ought remain ever awake and vigilant, may be too much to ask of every last person on earth. But the stories people can stay awake with, carrying the stories of their own kin, the stories that are often like a tiny master's class in psychology, teaching about brutish aspects of human nature that are to be contained by the village, as well as the beauties of human nature to be thoroughly savored by all. These stories are essential to the peace, knowledge, and well being of all.	Some say, people are stupid, that time after time as the historical records of holocausts and slaughters of innocents record, that many people will not pay attention, are too busy with whatever to see a malignant smiling version of Death personified coming toward themselves and others—a thing that appears to have a human head but a missing heart. Some believe it is beyond many humans to learn from the past. That some are deficient in thinking function, or are *born* not able to be truth seekers and instead thinking they are better than other groups, rant and rave about such, pretty much showing they are not *better than* but also thereby, derailing truly useful negotiation for better for all. I think often of the Spanish philosopher Jorge Agustín Nicolás Ruiz de Santayana y Borrás /also known as George Santayana. He has many bellwether warnings that can be put to good effect to stop a dictator in the making... long before the *too late to do anything*. One is how to recognize the first sign of a pretender, a narcissist "The highest form of vanity is love of fame." Remaining observant of human nature, to not overanalyze in error, nor to cover over a wasp nest with a velvet doily, but to see with acute vision, both the past and ahead—this often brings better choices for all.

Another poignant saying by Santayana is this one which will be familiar to many: *"Those who cannot remember the past are condemned to repeat it"*[10]

I'd gently remind that some forget Santayana's thoughts surrounding that sentence. Santayana is saying that when previous experiences [personal or about the world], that is stories, are not retained, the person is signing on for a perpetual infancy. I'd paraphrase it this way: Grow in wisdom, and remain alert by retaining in clearest memory—stories of how to, when to, why to—about both good and evil. This is the way of the insightful and leaderly adult.

Keep stories of actual past and present and potential future close, then act to mediate one's world as needed. In courage. With clear vision, with wise courtesies, firm resolve, and no mealy mouthing around. Winston Churchill said about Joe Stalin, *He's an S.O.B., but he's our SOB*, and in so saying minimized Stalin's murderous heart—and consigned murder and mayhem onto good and innocent people of Eastern Europe and beyond for the next near forty-five years. Colluding for temporary advantage makes no sense, when it causes the people to suffer long term.

As we say in our family, it is the stories we carry that allow us to be fully lit *memorial candles* for those of our own and others who suffered so. We as the children of, the grandchildren of, the great-grandchildren of... can watch over and carry memory of great good and great evil—and how to proceed in good faith and effective action with it all—if only we *remember the past* and tell the stories, [and there are literally millions of stories.] If only we tell them and remember their life-giving, life sparing instructions to live out and to pass on to others. Amen.

Clarissa Pinkola Estés, PhD, [doctorate in ethno-clinical psychology: thought processes/life choices within diverse groups] is a Mestiza Latina poet, award-winning storyteller in the old traditions, a senior Jungian training analyst, and post-trauma recovery specialist who began working with war veterans at Hines VA Hospital in 1965. Her Post-Trauma Recovery Protocol is used worldwide to help train citizens in post-trauma recovery work following tragedies and disasters. Her books, *Women Who Run with the Wolves*, about the wild woman archetype, and *Untie the Strong Woman*, about the mercies of La Señora, Our Lady of Guadalupe, are published in 37 languages.

(Table Endnotes)

1. Suggested reading: I wish in such a brief letter, I could cover in a few pages an entire era, but it is not possible. However, to help point interested persons toward more topics to read about in the books of their choices, I add here for you some topics to study as you wish, and I hope you will.

Mein Kampf, My Struggle, by Adolf Hitler, written while he was in gentleman's prison with many visitors. He was there for his role in a failed takeover of the government and he was found guilty of treason, and sentenced to ten years but oddly released after only nine months. What he learned in prison, and during his 24 days trial which was covered in great fanfare by the breathless press, was the power he could harness of the press to take his propaganda out to the world in ways his mere publishing of his writings could not match. His book Mein Kampf, is in part a rant against those he perceives as *not loyal* to himself and to his ideals: Gypsies, Jews, the infirm, Catholics, teachers, freethinkers, non-Nazis, persons without German citizenship.

His book can be found in many editions and many languages. The first time I read it, I found it a striking document in one way only: what Hitler projected onto the Jews he took upon himself to enact precisely. What he accused others of, he turned to do himself, want only, that is... "waiting for the princes to topple before the self-assigned *strong man* steps in, rewriting law by fiat to suit oneself, crying *my beloved people* of his constituency, two-facing all the way home, deceiving and impoverishing, gaining unpatrolled coverage by the press, but then taking over control of the free press... etc." In probably the most coldblooded agenda ever seen, Hitler turned to do exactly what he projected onto others. He waited until the powers *that be* were in disarray with one another. Then Hitler stepped in as der Führer, *the strong man*, smiling and bedecking himself in flowers for and with his *beloved people*, taking control of the press to laud himself, then attempting to silence the press, then hiring the filmmaker Leni Riefenstahl, to God-ize himself, and more.

2. An archetype is not a stereotype, but rather a universal idea that has existed often across the world, inherited from earliest human thought, being transmitted without cross-cultural transmission overtly, and holding a special meaning that is often a bit to a great deal more than merely human. Archetype of *father* is not the same as personal father. Archetype carries vast ideas about what *the idea of father means*, often divine and well as mundane.

3. Hitler's *my people*: I found in my studies useful to remember, *his people* were not the majority. The majority of Germans did not belong to nor endorse the Nazi party. Hitler's Nazi party is said to have held 33-44% of voters in Germany, depending on the early years when voting still took place. Hitler was not the leader of *the people* as he proclaimed loudly. He was *the leader of a minority*... but through terror tactics like Kristallnacht [*The night of the shattering glass* assaulting Jews, their shops, their places of worship, and evilly requiring afterward that Jews pay for all the thugs' damages to their shops, land, people and dwellings] and other wholly horrific planned out and unprovoked unleashings, Hitler dominated through fear, and the claim that people would be better off, and that he would just get rid of *the vermin*. As it turned out, enormous numbers of German people suffered, were left behind, starved literally and perished because of Hitler's policies.

4.   For this point, one might review Hitler's pre WWII actions in suddenly *annexing* Sude-tenland, pouncing and warring with Czechoslovakia, the complicated multi-national deci-sions made by other nations, oddly often without the Czech people's leaders' presences] re fanning divisiveness between ethnic groups, breakup of their nation made of those several ethnic groups, and break up and redistribution of empires after WWI, and later, invasion of Poland, etc.

5.   Referenced from Mein Kampf, My Struggle, by Adolf Hitler.

6.   See the highly staged filmmaking of Leni Reifenstahl, Hitler's *personal filmmaker* hired, paid to create and—to inflate with music and images and grand scale staging, [to rival *The Ten Commandments* film in scope,] to prove to the public domestically and abroad, how im-portant a personage was Hitler, how powerful the preening, need-glutted dictator. Hitler's love of the limelight for seduction of the masses, were central to his self-aggrandizement and grandiosity, these all being deep evidences of what is called in psychology, narcissistic personality disorder, and character disorder.

7.   There is a saying in my deeply ethnic, refugee family—a saying I teach when persons ask, "How could such evil have ever happened?"—and they are speaking of some proximate unspeakable evil unleashed here and now, or *back then*. I tell them of my father Jozsef and our family survivors of slave-labor camp imprisonment, those who said in many ways that evil is not understandable. The way I'd word it, is this: "You cannot understand evil unless you are..." [are yourself evil... for to the usual person, it is beyond the pale to try to understand the dastardly, the insensible, for most persons are neither of those in action]. Though some have said they will take the time to confront *the evil of/in their own shadows*, and once done, that is somehow enough... in our family, that would not salve nor bless. Self-reflection could be first step for many, but the most needed steps are in the Bluebeard story: being bold; fitting the key to the forbidden door; swinging it open to admit broad daylight so that one and all can see what naïve or even cunning backing of a monster truly brings... so all can see the cheap seductions of being feasted and fattened and flattered—are really only meant to disarm, so as to more easily bring new blood to feed the hungry ghost that can never be satiated.

Using the key [questions] to see clearly, then to speak clearly the underlying truths revealed, to speak in the ways of dignity, to aver that just because a monster can display a modicum of intelligence, that one ought not close one's eyes to that that person's largest driving force is to be a seductive candy-thrower without substance on one hand, and on the other, filled with contempt and mocking of others who see him as he really is, and call him not names, but call out the truths.

In the old psychological tales, there is nothing a vampire hates more than daylight. By seeing the monster's hidden agenda, one can speak up, saying some version of, "There's something wrong with that Bluebeard, starting with that "his beard is just too blue". Noting the factual truths to others who have the eyes to see, the ears to hear, that Bluebeard hunts for prey to daily re-inflate his constantly deflating ego, along with his repetitive claims that he is *the only one*, and no one can exceed him, nor succeed him. To note that he is far too quick to self-adore, being unable to rein in his extreme impulsiveness whenever he senses fresh energy in others, fresh blood...to score. And thus, the ones who see his true nature, [symbolized by first the sisters, family and friends in the tale, then the equally awakened brave brothers,] after seeing what the dictator forbade to be seen, move to right action—to speak, to condemn, to break the spell Bluebeard casts with false promises by exposing the falseness of them with *sharp edged, well honed* facts.

To then speak the contravening facts, thereby exposing to the bone the evil intents. Thus is the malignant agenda interrupted and routed, that of Bluebeard, as well as the thugs who've enjoined him with like-kind hungry ghost, sick and desperately grasping ego schemes. In the tale, the bloodsucking avenues to the innocents, are severed. The better and deeply *sighted persons* take up the opportunities to prevent evil from dominating... preventing the one who knowingly enacts multiple deceits, exposing Bluebeard as an over-reaching, self-anointing cold colossus who is not for life, but only for death By cutting Bluebeard down to size one might say—life's energy is freed to be used in far more reasoned ways that take humanity into account, that is, as right conduct, in which virtue and the visionary, rather than virulence and violence, are the ultimate goals, the penultimate prizes. My grandmother Katerín, who was in "perpetual little old lady bent over knitting in the corner" mode, had her old country squinty-eyed, finger-raised insights too. One was a warning from the old gods, old school style: *"He who attempts to be like the Gods will be punished by the Gods, not for conceit, but for falsifying the truly Godly."*

8.   For this point, as interested, see the issues regarding the breaking off of Sudetenland from Czechoslovakia.

9.   This cyanotic oddity in the Bluebeard tale, his hair, beard, skin having a blue cast, was not lost on the old women of the family. They were elderly and had borne witness in the village to many conditions in newborns, including what in the west were called *blue babies*, a life threatening crisis of blood-oxygen starvation. [In time interventions were developed.] Amongst our elderly women, there was the idea that oxygen starvation in the blood at any age could cause the skin to turn blue—and thereby cause the brain to also die in certain ways. On another note, given his deep need to "hunt human beings and kill them over and over again," the old woman also thought that persons like Hitler may have been assaulted regularly as a child, thereby addling/injuring his brain so that whatever brain center that governed and lit conscience—went dark. Thereby they speculated that one might become a heartless person because of brain damage or head injury when young, or at any age, if the injury was repetitive and severe, and not mediated.

10.   *The Life of Reason: Reason in Common Sense* by George Santayana. Scribner's, 1905.

The Trump Phenomena

BY THOMAS PATRICK LAVIN, PhD

History says, Don't hope
On this side of the grave,
But then once in a lifetime
the longed for tidal wave
of justice can rise up
And hope and history rhyme.
 So hope for a great sea-change
On the far side of revenge.
Believe that a farther shore
Is reachable from here
Believe in miracles
And cures and healing wells
___Seamus Heaney, *The Cure at Troy*

How Could This Be Happening?

The upcoming presidential election of 2016 is creating mayhem and confusion among the country's top political theorists. Donald Trump started as an unbelievable figure on the road to the White House. Initially, few Republicans and Democrats took his candidacy seriously. Other potential Republican candidates have dropped out of the race. Before Donald J. Trump was the *presumptive nominee* of the Republican Party, he was still funny, but he was no longer a joke. There have to be methods other than humor to deal with these phenomena. We, as Americans, have to ask ourselves some serious questions.

So, how did a candidate who was viewed as a reality TV star become a serious contender for the presidency of the United States? How did the man described by billionaire media mogul Haim Sabin described as *"a dangerous clown"* become an aristocratic contender? How did the Trump

Phenomena possess America? "So what would happen if Donald Trump, a clinical narcissist with a thin skin, touchy temperament, and a taste for flattery, got into the Oval Office?" (*New York Times*, Maureen Dowd, 2016, January 31)

When we refer to the *phenomenon* of Donald Trump, we are referring to a singular person. When discussing the Trump Phenomena, we are referring to the many images, behaviors, and emotions that surround the person of Donald Trump. The word *phenomena* points to a plurality of meanings.

Donald J. Trump is an emotionally evocative person. Usually, when his name is mentioned, people respond emotionally. They either like him or dislike him. The main reason for this primary gut response is that Donald Trump himself seems to deal primarily with life in an emotional way. He seems to be long on emotion and short on reason. He often responds more with one-liners than reasoned statements.

He is a controversial figure in America today because he taps into our culture's complexes as well as our own personal complexes.

He seems as if he should come out of the pages of *Grimm's Fairy Tales*. Mr. Trump reminds us of a vaguely familiar archetypal pattern. Haven't we experienced the likes of Donald Trump in our stories before?

The Fairy Tale

Once upon a time in the 1930s, there was a very sad and depressed country. The people were very angry and frustrated because they knew they had been misled. They realized that some people in their military had been sent to countries in which they did not belong and some had died there. They realized that new borders were proposed. They felt lost and did not feel they belonged anymore. They no longer felt they were a part of something bigger. They realized their pride and their trust were gone.

Then came a man out of nowhere. He had never served in an elected office. He said he would make the country great again. Huge crowds came to hear him speak of renewed greatness. He promised to employ the unemployed. He promised to build new roads and repair roads that were impassable. People who did not belong were to be expelled, and walls would be erected to keep undesirables out of that country striving so hard to be great again. The man's name was Adolf Hitler, nicknamed "Der Fuehrer" (the leader).

Today in America, we have many people who feel ashamed, angry, and powerless. Our cultural consciousness seems to be less than or diminished. What is this Trump Phenomena, this cultural complex of ours? In order to avoid the tragic madness of Germany in the 1930s, we in America would do well to go back to the theories of C.G. Jung about psychological complexes and look at how archetypal patterns can possess a person, a people, and a country. "Possession" is the key experience we must keep in mind, if we are to understand the deeper meaning of the Trump Phenomena.

Today, the Trump name is on so many lips because he has touched a cultural complex. Sometimes we have complexes; sometimes complexes possess us. As Dr. Tom Singer mentions in *Jungian Psychoanalysis,*_"The cultural complex can possess the psyche and soma of an individual or a group, causing them to think and feel in ways that might be quite different from what they think they should feel or think and it can be defined as emotionally charged aggregates of ideas and images that tend to cluster around an archetypal core and are shared by individuals within an identified collective."

For some of us, Trump constellates feelings of fear or hope from a deep place inside of us. His rhetoric is a source of personal fragmentation in our culture. Many Americans are divided in their reactions to the statements of Mr. Trump, especially his one-liners on Twitter and his statements to and about women. There is also anxiety on the other side of the Atlantic, "Europe, the soil on which Fascism took root, is watching the rise of Donald Trump with dismay. Contempt for the excesses of America is a European reflex, but when the United States seems tempted by a latter-day Mussolini, smugness in London, Paris, and Berlin gives way to alarm. Europe knows that democracies can collapse." (*New York Times*, Roger Cohen, 2016, February 29).

Jung Experiences Wotan

In the spring of 1937, C.G. Jung's body shook with fear on a Berlin street when he and Adolf Hitler met eye-to-eye. Jung was in Berlin to speak to a group interested in his psychology. Both Mussolini and Hitler were in a parade that Jung witnessed. Hitler and Jung were less than 10 feet away from one another when they looked into one another's eyes. After Hitler passed, Jung turned to his assistant, C.A. Meier, and said: "Go to the Hauptbahnhof immediately and get us train tickets on the first train back to Zurich. This man is psychotic; he is possessed; we have to get out of Berlin right away!" Meier, who personally told me this story, said that he had never ever seen Jung so overcome with fear. Jung had a complex reaction to Hitler from a very deep place inside. In Hitler's eyes, Jung saw and felt the German god of fury and war, Wotan. Meier and Jung left for Zurich the next day.

According to John Toland in his book *Adolf Hitler* (p. 64), Wotan worship was no stranger to Hitler. When he was fighting as a corporal in the German army on the Western Front in 1915, Hitler wrote the following autobiographical poem:

> I often go on bitter nights
> To Wotan's oak in the quiet glade

With dark powers to weave a union-
The runic letter the moon makes with its magic spell
And all who are full of impudence during the day
Are made small by magic formula!

This written history of Hitler's mystical union with Wotan is very significant. For at the center of every psychological complex is an archetype. Archetypes are known by and through images that are often seen as divinities. Wotan's myth, which can be seen and heard in Wagner's *Ring of the Nibelung*, was a primal conscious force in Hitler's life. "Hitler was fascinated by the *Ring Cycle* and identified with it in some way. I knew that he was a major patron, that he insisted that SS officers attend, and required that schoolchildren be exposed to these operas." (Bolen, p.39)

The Complex Reaction/Possession

What happens to us when a deeply felt positive or negative emotion takes our breath away? We experience what Jung called a complex reaction. A group of feeling-toned images and ideas in the unconscious jumps up into our awareness and possesses us. We act in ways that are atypical for us. Often, we are driven to do and say things that are outside of our ordinary behavior, ways that are abnormal.

Jung said in his *Tavistock Lectures* (C.W. 18, para. 149) that complexes behave like partial personalities. "It behaves like a partial personality. For instance, when you want to say or do something and unfortunately a complex interferes with this intention, then you say or do something different from what you intended."

Getting caught up in a powerful collective emotion can lead to mob behavior, as we saw recently at a Trump campaign event at the University of Illinois in Chicago and elsewhere around the country. The constellation of cultural complexes can lead to mob behavior in which a person acts atypically because she/he is possessed by a powerful archetype coming up from the cultural unconscious. The Republican Party grew frightened of mob behavior as its convention in Cleveland approached, a concern Mr. Trump seemed to confirm when he stated on CNN, "I think you'd have riots."

It is also important for us to distinguish between personal and cultural complexes. A personal complex is an emotionally charged idea or image, with an archetypal core, that I have personally experienced. For example, we all have complexes about our fathers and mothers because they have been major emotional influences in our lives. Sometimes we are still possessed by our parental complexes, and they bring us into therapy.

Cultural complexes are emotionally charged ideas or images that can possess the psyche of a group and/or possess the psyche of an individual within the group. Persons within an identified collective share them. A personal recollection illustrates my being swept up in a cultural complex. I was in Chicago's Grant Park in the fall of 2008, and I watched a black couple come out onto the stage, and I began to feel tears coming down my cheeks. I felt overjoyed and very privileged to experience a newly elected African-American man and his wife being thunderously applauded as the next First Couple. Was it my ego or my cultural complexes about black persons in places of authority and honor that brought tears to my eyes and joy and a great release to my heart? An anti-black cultural complex, to which I had been exposed and had experienced as a child in my south side of Chicago neighborhood was being powerfully overcome, and I was extraordinarily happy. We all have culture-based complexes and we can grow out of them.

A third and last example of the clash between personal and cultural complexes comes from my family. One day, when I was about seven years old, I came into the house and made an anti-Semitic comment about another kid on our block. I said that he was a "cheap Jew, like all the other cheap Jews." My father jumped up from his chair in the living room and began a half-hour lecture at our kitchen table. He told me about the Feldman family, who were Jewish and who took my father into their home and hearts, gave him a job at their stables at the Chicago Stockyards, and made a permanent place for him at their family dinner table. During the Depression Era, the Feldman family rescued my father from daily hunger. I was told very strongly that I was never, ever to say anything negative about Jewish people in our home again. Of course, I never did.

Whether positive or negative, sometimes we have personal and cultural complexes, and sometimes those complexes can and do possess us. That's just the way we live our lives. We are indeed a very complex people and we are filled with emotional images and complexes waiting to be brought up to the surface from our personal and cultural depths.

The Wotan Archetype

Do we Americans need to become conscious of a god of war energy behind Donald Trump just as Jung saw Wotan behind Hitler? "Jung used the god Wotan as the Ergrifer (one who seizes) to make a direct attack on Hitler as the Ergriffener (one who is seized) (Bair, p. 455). Hitler, who was possessed by the archetypal image of Wotan, a national German divinity, possessed the German people. National gods are a class of guardian divinities whose main concern is the safety and well-being of an ethnic group or nation.

Jung thought, "The most impressive thing about the 'furor teutonicus' was that one man, who is obviously possessed, has infected a whole nation to such an extent that everything is set in motion and has started rolling on its course to perdition." (Jung, C.W. 10, para 388). Can a man who is furious infuriate a whole country? Could this "state of possession" take place again?

Here? As Trump wins elections state by state, are we witnessing a similar underlying, archetypal pattern as Jung saw on the streets of Berlin in 1937?

The Trump Phenomena possession by the Germanic god Wotan has many characteristics. Wotan has been archetypally described (ibid para 393) as the berserker (crazy and crazy-making), the god of storm, the trickster, the wanderer, the warrior, the lord of the dead, the master of secret knowledge, the magician, and the god of poets. Wotan uses his gifts to instigate rage and frenzy.

We must remember that Trump's windiness can be put to a good purpose to uplift the culturally oppressed. As the god of wind he is, like Hermes, able to stir up a crowd. He is, in his positive side, like the wind/Spirit at Pentecost who inspires crowds to speak in tongues. The experience of the archetypal image of Wotan is an experience of overwhelming power, which can and often does possess us for good or for evil.

When Wotan appears initially, we don't always know how to understand his presence. Is this tremendous power positive or negative for my culture and me?

According to Deirdre Bair in her biography of Jung, Winston Churchill wrote about Hitler in 1935:

> "We cannot tell whether Hitler will be the man who will once again loose upon the world another war in which civilization will irretrievably succumb, or whether he will go down in history as the man who restored honor and peace of mind to the great Germanic nation and brought it back serene, helpful and strong, to the forefront of the European family circle." (Bair, 2003, p. 453)

Jung too was ambivalent about Adolf Hitler in the early 1930s. He had a wait-and-see attitude about the events in Germany. "The contents of the collective unconscious, the archetypes, with which we are concerned in any occurrence of psychic mass-phenomena, are always bi-polar: they have both a positive and a negative side. Whenever an archetype appears, things become critical and it is impossible to foresee what turn they will take. As a rule this depends on the way consciousness reacts to a situation." (C.W. 10 para 461) By 1936, Jung was convinced the psychic mass-phenomena surrounding Hitler was indeed so negative that he published his monograph, *Wotan*, in which he wrote that the ancient god of storm and frenzy had erupted like an extinct volcano, the unleasher of passions, and the lust of battle was energized again in Germany and also in most of Europe.

Five months prior to the beginning of World War II on April 5, 1939, Jung gave a talk in London to the Guild of Pastoral Psychology. Jung said:

> "Everything is banal, everything is 'nothing but'; and that is the reason why people are neurotic. They are simply sick

of the whole thing, sick of that banal life, that therefore
they want sensation. They even want a <u>war</u>; they all want a
war. They are all glad when there is a war: they say, 'Thank
heaven, now something is going to happen-something
bigger than ourselves!'" (C.W. 18, para 627)

Is the spring of 2016 like the spring of 1939? Has our need to be a part
of something bigger again forced us to be possessed by a stormy trickster who tells us we can again be great? Are we so devoid of an authentic
symbolic life that we, in our banal materialism, allow ourselves to be
conned by this incarnation of The Trickster Archetype? These are questions America must ask itself at this juncture in history. Our history stands
proud with memories of the John and Jacqueline Kennedy era. The early
1960s brought up romantic images of Camelot, and we embodied hope for
a brighter future. It was a time when hope and history rhymed. This was a
time when we were told not to ask what our country was doing for us, but
rather to ask what we were doing for our country. We were called to move
out of a narrow narcissism and into a dynamic and open altruism. "Life is
too rational, there is no symbolic existence in which I am something else,
in which I am fulfilling my role as one of the actors in the divine drama of
life." (C.W. 18, para 628) How can life be meaningful if we are not invited to
become actors in a divine drama? What if the TV and computer are so loud,
we can't even hear the invitation?

An Oppurtunistic Infection

It is also possible to look at the Trump Phenomena from a medical perspective. My wife, Mary Ellen, and I have a good friend, Bob Magrisso, M.D., who
wrote about Donald Trump as an "Opportunistic Infection". He likens the
Trump Phenomena to a skin rash rising from a systemic, deeper pathology.
When the body is terminally weakened through a long-term illness, it can
become vulnerable to a bacteria or virus that it would normally be able to
fight off. That lethal bacteria or virus is called an "Opportunistic Infection."
Magrisso sees Donald Trump as bacteria in a terminally ill Republican body.
The Republican Party, having become a weakened body, became susceptible to an opportunistic pathogen, bacteria that never would have been
taken seriously at another time. "He is a self-promoting businessman of
questionable success, an entertainer, an insult artist, a narcissistic joke
actually. But now, he is dangerous to the weakened political body and can't
be stopped. Taking his script from the demagogue playbook, he seemingly
has preyed upon the fears, distrust, and betrayal of people." (blog post
Speaking of Jung) If this hypothesis that Donald Trump is an Opportunistic
Infection is correct, does Mr. Trump pose a lethal threat to the Republican
Party, a political party we need to be strong in order to maintain our healthy
tension of political opposites?

The Trickster Archetype

In addition to the presence of the god of war and frenzy lurking in the background of the Trump Phenomena, we have also become painfully aware of the shocking, outlandish Trickster Archetype that is doing all it can to capture our attention—no matter how zany, freaky, and bizarre the attention-getting word or behavior might seem. When we imagine native American medicine men or shaman of any culture, we can get a good idea that the Trickster Archetype appears in a cultural setting as a healer or savior. "I will make American great again!" seems to be trying to sell an audience that the speaker is a savior and healer and that she or he has superhuman powers. "There is something of the trickster in the character of the shaman and medicine man, for he, too, often plays malicious jokes on people only to fall victim in his turn to the vengeance of those whom he has injured." (C.W. 9i, para. 457) As the song says, "When I fool the people I fool, I fool myself as well." A trickster tries to give the impression that the meaningless can be transformed into the meaningful. He doesn't tell people specifics, doesn't tell people how he will make this "deal" happen. He is not selling "how to" deals, but the trickster is rather selling *illusions* of wellness and greatness. He tells a depressed culture that miracles can happen and that "great things" are waiting just around the corner.

Jung calls the incarnation of the trickster as a "faithful reflection of an absolutely undifferentiated human consciousness, corresponding to a psyche that has hardly left the animal level." (C.W. 9i, para 465) To have an undifferentiated consciousness means, in part, to rarely say, "I am sorry," to rarely experience guilt or seldom be ashamed, and not to know what it is to experience remorse. The trickster is so caught up in the "now" of performance and tricking his listeners that there is little time given to reflection about the past effects of one's broken deals or promises. Tricksters just don't own their own shadows; they project their shadows onto Mexicans and Muslims, women and POWs, for example.

Bullying and Blaming

Tricksters are a one-person show. They strive to be in control most of the time. A trait commonly found in tricksters is bullying. It is an attempt to intimidate and tyrannize others. A bully is a person who has a chronic fear of being less than others. Through exaggerated and malicious statements, bullying behaviors and words strive to keep the bully on top and all others below.

Tricksters are experts at using blame. They blame others for the ills of a culture. It's always the other guy's fault, and if we can just get rid of them, America will be great again. Successful demagogues and agitators place blame elsewhere. Owning a shadow has no place in the speeches of tricksters. A shadow is a psychic reality that contains all of the personal qualities which with we refuse to identify. We don't initially accept our shadows as belonging to us. The shadow is plentifully and sometimes viciously projected onto others. Perhaps this is why demagogues are so popular among disenfranchised groups; they blame others for any darkness. When we own our own shadow and do something about it, we put the Trickster Archetype out of business. However, it takes a lot of courage to admit that we are being conned by a superb con man and that we are vulnerable.

A trickster is a person who has the ability to easily deceive others; he's a fast talker who can "take us for a ride." Like the trickster-god, Hermes, he is able to move quickly to trick his mark. He is a con man who knows how to play tricks and defraud or "pull a fast one" on others. If a person is uncovered as a trickster, people become weary of being cheated. Depending on their goals, tricksters can lead others to positive or negative outcomes. They can take us to heaven or hell before we know we have left the earth. Many politicians have a bit of the trickster complex alive and well inside.

Tricksters are at their best when someone is in the throes of some sort of life conflict. Being in an emotional state lowers our defenses and makes us more susceptible to being conned. A country that feels less powerful is ready for a politician who is capable of exaggerating himself into power. "The Trump campaign is employing many of the same political tactics that notorious leaders like Adolf Hitler, Idi Amin, and George Wallace used so effectively in building their own followings over the last century" (*Newsweek*: Emily Cadei 2016, May 10). The support behind Benito Mussolini was more about getting behind a perceived strong leader than a strong political party. Those supporting a trickster are more interested in images than issues. In Jungian terminology, it can be said that a huge persona is necessary to cover up a huge personal and collective shadow. The trickster seems to be constantly trying to cover up shadow aspects of the personal and collective unconscious. "Let's *not* go deeper into the pain you are experiencing" says the trickster. "Let's just know that you are going to feel great again."

America's Shadow

The reality that we as Americans have to face is that we are no longer a superpower. We can no longer identify with the reality of "superpower" because in a nuclear age, we are no longer able to rescue the world from evil, dominating forces alone. America's shadow is that it can no longer identify with the archetype of the Savior. As America faces its collective shadow, it will deal with the reality that it is not the only light in a dark world. We have to let go of that pseudoidentity. We cannot afford to elect a pseudosavior who is promoting a pseudoidentity for our nation.

Our shadow is that we can no longer be for the world what we thought we were, saviors. We are no longer able to come to the aid of a Europe in chaos. It is hard to realize that we can no longer identify with 19th century

Europe's persona wars, when everyone was trying to prove that their king was stronger and better than their neighbor's king. We really don't need another Kaiser Wilhelm II or Hitler to lead us out of our perceived shame. Rather, we must have leaders who can lead us into accepting an opportunity of global, peaceful equality among nations. With the dawning of our nuclear age, all power games must be called to an end.

Jung's commentary on the dangers of our nuclear age is appropriate:

> "The conflagration that broke out in Germany was the outcome of psychic conditions that are universal. The real danger signal is not the fiery sign that hung over Germany, but the unleashing of *atomic energy*, which has given the human race the power to annihilate itself completely. The situation is about the same as if a small boy of six had been given a bag of dynamite for a birthday present. We are not one hundred percent convinced by his assurances that no calamity will happen. Will man be able to give up toying with the idea of another war?" (C.W. 10 para 485)

> Dare we give the little boy a bag of dynamite by electing him? Nukes are not toys to be entrusted to a narcissistic leader.

In a Sea Change

Today we are in a paradigm shift, an Axial Age, and a sea change. We find ourselves reaching for metaphors that will help us better understand what is happening. At the center of a sea change is turbulence, and this turbulence is the result of a clash in values. Older values are sinking deeper into the unconscious and newer values are rising into higher consciousness.

> "The cultural critique—of patriarchy, the legitimacy of war, ecological exploitation and pollution, racism, injustice, religious exclusivism, and imperialism—has arguably never been more pronounced. At the same time, we've begun to explore and even embrace emerging values including non-violent conflict resolution, universal human rights, social and economic justice, ecological sustainability, and interreligious harmony," (Kenney, 2010, p.11)

In this time of exciting and emotionally gripping cultural turbulence, in this time of a profound alteration of cultural values toward a better balancing of current psychic realities, we are called to be present to a richly creative period, the 21st to 26th centuries. Our culture is experiencing what the German philosopher Karl Jaspers called the Axial Age, a time when the destiny of humankind is turning a corner (Armstrong, 2005).

In the First Axial Age, from 800 to 200 B.C.E., new mythologies, new ways of imaging our dialogues with the divine were erupting out of the ground of our being. There was a palpable regenerating force happening in humankind. New religions and philosophical systems sprung into life in China with Confucianism and Taoism, in the Middle East with a Yahweh-centered monotheism, in India with Hinduism and Buddhism and in Europe with Greek rationalism.

The year 2016 is a time of consciously beginning a paradigm shift and a time to wonder about the possibility of a new formation of a global mythology. The Trump Phenomena, in spite of the pain of the possibility of being archetypally supported by a Wotan and/or a Hermes getting out of control, are telling us that something bigger and not yet imagined is going on. Hermes is the spirit of wind that is capable of stirring up a crowd. Our emotions are telling us that strong winds are blowing and that change is in the air. Yet, we have to decide which winds we are to follow at the crossroads. We are like the poet Robert Frost in the woods, and we hope and pray that the path that our culture chooses to take is the road of openness to the hope of possibility and not the narrow road of the blaming bully that leads to cultural brokenness and splitting. Perhaps our grandchildren will recall that in 2016 we took the road not of revenge, but of rebirth, the road less traveled by and "that has made all the difference."

Working on Our Pillars

This essay has to end with a positive story of hope and meaning to balance the stories of great confusion and disorder caused by the gods of war and trickery. Jungian analyst and concentration camp survivor Dr. Max Zeller had studied with Jung before the war and was able to escape Berlin and move to Los Angeles in 1938. He returned to Zurich to consult with Jung in 1949 and he had the following burning question: With all of the horror we have experienced in Europe during the past decade, what are we as analysts doing? Does seeing only one patient at a time have any deeper meaning, any long-lasting effect? Prior to his last session with Jung, Zeller had the following dream:

> "A temple of vast dimensions was being built.
> As far as the eye could see ahead, behind, right and left there were incredible numbers of people building on gigantic pillars.
> I, too, was building on a pillar. The whole building process was in its first beginnings, but the foundation was already there, the rest of the building was starting to go up, and many others and I were working on it."

Max Zeller—*The Dream: The Vision of the Night* p. 2

Jung said: "Ja, you know, that is the temple we all build on. We don't know the people because, believe me, they build in India and China and in Russia and all over the world. That is the new religion. You know how long it will take until it is built?"

I said: "How should I know? Do you know?" He said: "I know." I asked how long will it take. He said: "About six hundred years."

"Where do you know this from?" I asked. He said: "From dreams; from other people's dreams and from my own. This new religion will come together as far as we can see."

And then I could say goodbye. There was the answer to what we as analysts are doing. (Zeller, 1990, p. 3)

The experience of the Trump Phenomena, in all of its personal and cultural complexity, will have been worth our agony and ecstasy, if it brings us to value the pillar we have been given and to keep working on it daily. I must keep open the pathways of dream reflection, active imagination, and reading Jung again and again to find meanings and directions we could not see at first glance. Working on my own pillar and helping others to work on their pillars is the best thing I can do to overcome phenomena of daily chronic fear in and of a violent world.

Number 41 in William Martin's book *The Sage's Tao Te Ching* is the best response I have found to quiet meaningless fears stirred up from inner and outer provocateurs.

> Learning to see things from a different angle
> requires great courage
> Old voices within will seek to kindle
> the fire of fear
> "You're not going to have enough.
> You must hold on!
> You're going to be alone.
> You're going to die."
> This is the truth of the Tao,
> We will always have enough.
> We can let go.
> We are never alone.
> And dying will be like coming home.

May the readers of this essay have an exciting trip home and find the Trump Phenomena to have been an occasion of grace and wisdom.

Thomas Patrick Lavin, PhD, is a Zürich-trained Jungian analyst with a PhD in clinical psychology and theology. He is a founding member of the CG Jung Institute of Chicago. His clinical practice is in Wilmette, Illinois.

References

Armstrong, K. (2005). *A Short History of Myth*. Edinburgh: Canongate Books Ltd.

Bair, D. (2003). *Jung: A Biography*. New York: Little, Brown and Company.

Bolen, J. (1999). *Ring of Power: Symbols and Themes*. Love vs Power in Wagner's Ring Cycle and in Us: A Feminist Perspective. York Beach: Nicholas Hays.

Cadei, E. (2016, May 10). *Cult of Personality: Ho Trump uses the Playbook of Europe's Far Right*. Newsweek.com.

Cohen, R. *Trump's Il Duce Routine*, http:/www.nytimes.com/2016/03/01opinion/donaldtrump-il-duce-routine.html? smidnytcove-ipad-

Dowd, M. (2016, January 31). *Here's the Beauty of Trump*. New York Times.

Heaney, S. (1990). *The Cure at Troy*. Derry N Ireland: Field Day Publishers.

Jung, C.G. (1950). *Symbolic Life Miscellaneous Writings* (Vol 18 CW). New Jersey: Princeton University Press.

Jung, C.G. (1959). *The Archetypes and the Collective Unconscious* (Vol 9 CW). London: Routledge & Kegan Paul, Ltd.

Jung, C.G. (1964). *Civilizations in Transition* (Vol 10 CW). London: Routledge & Kegan Paul, Ltd.

Jung, C.G. (1989). *Memories, Dreams, Reflections*. New York: Vintage Books.

Kenney, J. (2010) *Thriving in the Crosscurrent*. Wheaton: Quest Books.

Lavin, T. (2016, May 3). *Speaking of Jung* – Episode 17: Tom Lavin [Audio podcast]. *The Trump Phenomena*. Retrieved from http://www.speakingofjung.com/pocast 2016/5/3

London, L. (Producer). (2016, May 3). *Speaking of Jung* [Audio podcast]. Retrieved from http://www.speakingofjung.com/podcast/2016/5/3

Magrisso, R. (2016 May 9). *Opportunistic Infection*. Retrieved from www.speakingofjung.com/blog/2016/5/9 an-opportunistic-infection.

Martin, W. (2000). *The Sage's Tao Te Ching: A New Interpretation Ancient Advice for the Second Half of Life*. New York: Marlowe & Company.

Singer, T. Kaplinsky, C. (2010) *Cultural Complexes In Analysis*. In Jungian Psychoanalysis: Working in the Spirit of C. G. Jung, edited by Murray Stein pp. 22-37. Chicago: Open Court Publishers.

Toland, J. (1976). *Adolf Hitler*. New York: Doubleday & Company, Inc.

Zeller, M. (1990). *The Dream: The Vision of the Night*. Boston: Sigo Press.

Section 3
Personal Narcissism

The Hall of Mirrors
Narcissism and Celebrity in the World of Twitter and Reality TV

BY KATHRYN MADDEN, PhD

Everywhere I Look, I See Myself

One of the characteristics common to the narcissistic personality is an inflated self-worth, which creates in the individual a tendency to view all things and all people in terms of themselves and their own needs. The phrase "everywhere I look, I see myself" comes to mind as an apt description of how the narcissist approaches the world.

To illustrate this, an old story—a joke, really—that was making the rounds when I was a working actor comes to mind. The tellers would each put a different spin on the tale, but the *punch line* was always pretty much the same. As the story goes, two actors—a male and a female—meet each other on a street corner in Manhattan. She asks how he has been doing. He launches into a long litany of successes and accomplishments that have occurred since the last time the two met. After about 10 minutes of this blather, he asks the woman, "Well, that's enough about me. What do you have to say about me?" (End of story.)

In their book, *The Narcissistic Epidemic: Living in the Age of Entitlement*, Drs. Jean Twenge and Keith Campbell echo precisely the same theme in the following passage:

> One journalist wrote in our online survey, "I interviewed hundreds of well-known actors and actresses over a 10-year period, and this, basically is how the interview went: 'I think . . . I believe . . . I am . . . My passion is . . . I'd like to think what I do makes a difference to the world . . . Me . . . Me . . . More Me . . . Major Me . . . did I mention Me? I am a role model to so many . . . I am, in fact, God incarnate.' [They], and not only the mega-stars, were so self-absorbed, so self-obsessed, that my attendance at the interview wasn't totally necessary. They blurted out their Me-ness unprompted." (2013, pp. 92-93)

This observation is not to disparage performing artists as a whole, but to isolate and focus on a specific tendency that appears in many a performer's life. It is a cliché that many actors, singers, and other entertainers—especially those who are driven by a strong desire for stardom and celebrity—can be unusually, even annoyingly, self-absorbed. And, while it is certainly true that narcissists frequent career paths other than entertainment, such as politics, I will focus primarily on the phenomenon of narcissism, in its inflated-grandiose form, in the context of the recent emergence of social media and in the world of the celebrity culture that has grown up around the entertainment industry and social media.

Celebrities in this universe are usually drawn from the subset of those actors, singers, or entertainers who have reached a level of fame that seems to come only through incessant exposure on television and the covers of magazines that scream at you from newsstands and supermarkets everywhere. But, a new category of celebrity has been formed in the past couple of decades with the birth of the phenomenon of *reality television shows*. Here *instant celebrities* are born.

But, before delving further into the contemporary world of television and social media as both broadcaster and enabler of narcissistic behavior, let us take a quick step back and consider a symbol from a much earlier time that captured the essence of self-absorption and promotion in myth, fairy tales, and literature.

The myth of Narcissus is so well-known that I will not retell it here, except in the briefest of overviews. A handsome young lad was walking alone in the woods. He stops by a pool of water in a forest for a drink, sees his reflection in the still water, admires the beauty that he sees reflected back to him, and never moves away from the pool again until he pines away and dies. The once-removed symbol derived from the Narcissus myth on which I would like to focus in the following pages is that of *mirror*. Although the term itself does not appear in the myth, the clear pool of water serves the function of a mirror. It is that function of *mirroring* that occurs both in many retellings or reinterpretations of the myth as well as in psychological studies of the nature of the development of the narcissistic personality. Let's start with the retellings.

From the Grimm Brothers' fairy tale, *Schneewittchen* or *Snow White*, first published in 1812, appears the famous scene in which the *evil Queen* demands of her magic mirror: "Mirror, mirror on the wall, who in this land is fairest of all?" Comes the mirror's response: "You, my queen, are fairest of them all." All is then well with Her Highness, that is, until Snow White grows up and supplants the Queen as the fairest in the land. The magic mirror—apparently unable to lie, fudge, or spin in order to protect the Queen's vanity—tells the Queen the revised truth when asked again. The Queen's (dare we say?) *narcissistic* rage at being demoted from her lofty self-image as the most beautiful one in the kingdom is what propels the rest of the narrative, resulting ultimately in her own destruction.

The self-admiring evil Queen and the eventual dénouement of the story takes a page from the Narcissus myth. As with Narcissus, the story of Snow White ends, not with the elevation but, rather, with the fall and demise of the self-admirer. And this, of course, is the moral of the story for all us would-be self-admirers. There are many more iterations of the myth of Narcissus and stories that have been influenced or inspired by it. As the late Mario Jacoby, Jungian analyst and former director of the Jung Institute in Zurich, explains:

> At the end of the eighteenth century the development of the Narcissus theme was lent new impetus by Herder and the Romantics. The mirror symbol became very important and was frequently used. One of the prominent themes of the period was that of genius, the glorification of the great individual's creative power. The soul of the artist was seen as a mirror of the world, thus justifying artistic subjectivism despite the attendant danger of self-admiration. The artist-as-Narcissus motif cropped up first in the works of W.A. Schlegel..., who said, "Artists are always Narcissi!" The more that attention was focused on Narcissus and his reflection, the more the story as a whole receded into the background. This narrowed view is often blamed on the psychoanalytic concept of narcissism, but in fact it goes back to the Romantic tradition, which also revived the neo-Platonic interpretation. In the work of F. Creuzer...the searching soul finds mere illusion instead of existence, and Eros, insulted by overweening pride and egoism demands expiation. Much is made, too, of the narcissus flower, seen as a symbol of the artist who has lost his real self and can find it again only in the dream world of poetry. (1990, p. 15)

Schlegel's quote in the above passage is interesting in that it reveals the fact that, for more than two centuries—and probably for much longer—artists have been thought of as being narcissists—and that is even without any reference to the contributing factor of celebrity. It was during the German Romantic era that sprang from the ideas of Schlegel and his contemporaries, however, that two such performing celebrities and crowd sensations appeared on the European scene. They were Niccolò Paganini (known as the Devil's Violinist) and pianist and composer Franz Liszt. Paganini virtually single-handedly invented the concept of the solo recital in a large hall, as opposed to the early 19th-century Viennese salons played in by Ludwig von Beethoven, Franz Schubert, and Robert Schumann. More significantly, Paganini drove audiences wild when he performed. Liszt, attending a Paganini 1832 charity concert to help victims of a cholera epidemic in Paris, was so impressed with the Italian's virtuosity as well as the enthusiastic impact his playing had on audiences that he vowed to become the *Paganini of the keyboard*. Liszt achieved this goal and much more. In fact, one of his concerts in Berlin produced such hysteria in the audience, a reaction that was to become so commonplace with successive solo appearances, that the German poet and critic Heinrich Heine eventually dubbed the effect *Lisztomania!*

Celebrities are often more complex, however, than contemporaneous media and popular opinion would make it out to be. Paganini and Liszt, narcissists though they may have been, were also great contributors to charity, for example. In fact, Liszt had earned so much money at the end of eight years of touring Europe and performing to sold-out houses, that after 1857 he gave away virtually all of his earnings from concerts to charity and humanitarian causes. He also moved to Weimar, at the time a cultural backwater of Germany, where he graciously gave away his time, teaching and mentoring piano students for no fee.

Jacoby continues with the theme of the mirror as a symbol of Narcissism when he speaks of "the theme of a man in love with his own mirror image" as exhibited in Oscar Wilde's 1890 book, *The Picture of Dorian Gray*. Borrowing from the Faust story, Wilde has his protagonist "give up his soul so that his portrait will grow older instead of his physical body." When Gray can no longer stand to look at the portrait, which "mercilessly records the traces of his excessive, unscrupulous life style," he takes a knife to his "mirror, mirror on the wall," destroying both it and himself in the process (1990, p. 15).

The Mirror Effect

Anyone who attended an amusement park as a child, or who has taken his or her children to one, has surely experienced what is often called the "maze of mirrors." This room, generally located in a structure known as a "Fun House," is usually decked out with curved and/or strategically placed mirrors offering such optical illusions as seeing distorted reflections of oneself or an endless array of one's reflection from all directions. A perfect visual metaphor for the narcissist's point of view, the mirror maze in the amusement park Fun House has a much loftier ancestry, however, that dates back to the second half of the 17th century in France.

The original *mirror effect* was experienced in the *Hall of Mirrors*, which was constructed at the direction of King Louis XIV, also known as the "Sun King," for no fun house, but rather for the French court's grand palace in Versailles. As described on the official website that accompanies the PBS special called *Marie Antoinette and the French Revolution*:

The Hall of Mirrors was completed in 1686, and features breathtaking garden views through seventeen ornate windows. Mirrors hang on the walls opposite the windows, strategically placed to reflect the natural light ...

... The room's 578 mirrors, which were of exceptional size at the time, were produced at Saint Gobain, the Royal Glassworks established by Louis XIV in the seventeenth century. Like Lyons silks and Gobelin tapestries, the mirrors made in this Paris factory represented the royal effort to establish monopolies on the production of luxury goods ...

... The main purpose was to keep French wealth within France and to attract wealth from abroad, but the more lasting significance was to establish France, and Paris in particular, as the worldwide capital of taste and fashion, a reputation it continues to hold today. The Hall of Mirrors thus reflected the economic and cultural power of France, even as it reflected those who held it.

The Hall of Mirrors also represents the society of the royal court, in which seeing and being seen were crucial. In the Hall of Mirrors, *every movement, every nod, every glance was reflected hundreds of times. The dazzle was amazing, but the stakes were high: one stumble, one awkward step, would be magnified for all to see.* (2006)

A great believer in and beneficiary from the concept and ideology of *The Divine Right of Kings*, Louis XIV was a monarch who unabashedly had concentrated *absolute power* into the throne and who organized a support system to enable him to rule France as only he saw fit.

[W]ith a great system of well provisioned clerks, residents, heralds, ambassadors, and spies, French statecraft was to become Louis' own instrument: a great *narcissistic* engine—fueled and sated only by war. Backed by a colossal army (some 450,000 troops at its height), and a treasury never too depleted to find huge sums to subsidize and suborn, Louis' agents worked tirelessly for his advance. (Nathan, J. 1993, np).

With his Hall of Mirrors—his *galerie des glaces*—at the Palace of Versailles, Louis XIV—who just happened to be quite enamored with his royal personage—had created the perfect setting to glorify his radiance and rule as *Le Roi Soleil* to friend and foe alike, and, perhaps as significantly, to himself.

The Electronic Hall of Mirrors

In the 1960s, the Canadian media and social critic Marshall McLuhan mused that, thanks to the growing pervasiveness of television, we could all now expect to have our very own *15 minutes of fame*. But, even that seemingly bold statement sounds quaint now. Remember, that was a time when there were only three national networks (NBC, CBS and ABC) and a smattering of local stations around the country. None of them ran all night long.

Now, however, with hundreds of TV channels available on cable and satellite networks (24/7/365), and with the meteoric rise of Facebook, YouTube, Twitter and other social media, there are so many more opportunities for even so-called regular people to have their *15 minutes* over and over again that it is like a *mirror effect* on steroids! Let us call it the *electronic mirror effect*.

We can all now literally broadcast *ad infinitum* our music, our opinions, our rants, or whatever it was we had for breakfast to our heart's content at no, or very little cost to us, through a multitude of electronic media to anyone in the world who will deign to *friend* or *follow* us. It is surely no great secret that many users of social media derive some sense of pride in the number of Facebook friends and Twitter followers they have amassed, as if the sheer quantity of eyes and ears paying attention to their every posted opinion, comment, photo, or video clip is the measure of their self-worth. Our virtual self becomes a constant reflection of what we've done today, what we think today, what we've seen today, and what other people think about what we've done, what we think, and about what we've seen. In other words, it is very easy for us to use social media as an electronic embodiment of the Narcissus myth, or—if you will—an electronic hall of mirrors.

In their book *The Narcissism Epidemic*, Twenge and Campbell reveal the results of a study that surveyed the Narcissistic Personality Inventory Scores of 16,275 students from 31 colleges across the U.S. during the years 1982-2006. They found that: 1) a significant upswing in NPI Scores has occurred over the two decades surveyed; and 2) this upswing really picks up steam in the years spanning 2000-06. They observe that:

> [c]ollege students in the 2000s were significantly more narcissistic than Gen Xers and Baby Boomers.... The Boomers, a generation famous for being self-absorbed, were outdone by their children. By 2006, two-thirds of college students scored above the scales original 1979-85 sample, a 30% increase in only two decades.

And what is more they discovered that:

> [a]lthough Boomers rebelled against their straightlaced parents in the 1960s, their own offspring are more than

happy to continue their parents' focus on the self.... In addition—we can't stress this enough—young people didn't
raise themselves. They got these narcissistic values from
somewhere, often from their parents or media messages
created by older people. (2013, pp. 32, 34)

This study and others that Twenge and Campbell present in *The Narcissism Epidemic* go a long way to explaining the effect of the adoption of and the belief in certain personal qualities or values extolled by contemporary popular culture: i.e., popularity, fame, wealth, and power. There are basically two ways to achieve these goals: the hard way and the easy way. Some celebrities have attained their status through honest, hard work. Certain come to mind such as Steve Jobs, Bill Gates, Robin Williams, Tom Cruise, Philip Seymour Hoffman, Charlie Sheen, Michael Jackson, Madonna, Miley Cyrus, and Lady Gaga, regardless of our personal appraisal of their talents. Few, I think, would doubt that they got where they are (or were) in their careers by a lot of hard work and probably more than a *little bit of luck*. Neither would there be much disagreement that many of these celebrities would probably score high on the NPI; others, probably not as much.

Others have achieved their fame—or appeared to—by taking advantage of the communication tools and other benefits that our contemporary culture hands them and all but demands that they employ at an earlier and earlier age. Therefore, with these celebrity wannabees, 1) *popularity*—or the appearance of it—can be measured by how many Facebook friends or Twitter followers one has managed to acquire; 2) *fame*—however fleeting—can be attained by many through appearing on reality television shows or in videos gone viral on YouTube; even 3) *wealth*—or the appearance of it—can be attained through the buying of expensive homes, cars, and various adult *toys* on relatively cheap credit; and, finally, 4) real *power* is admittedly harder to achieve but not beyond the grasp of those willing to sacrifice ethics and *do whatever it takes* to attain it. This fourth *quality or possession* is probably as it has always been, but having easier access to the other three may just put this one within the grasp of more, especially those undeserving of it or who would possibly misuse it. Thankfully, not everyone in this category craves or seeks power. But beware those who do.

I offer as examples of reality TV *celebrities* such *luminaries* as Donald Trump (*The Apprentice* and the 2016 presidential election and his very prolific Twitter account), Kim Kardashian, et al. (*Keeping Up with the Kardashians*), Spencer Pratt and Heidi Montag (*The Hills*), Honey Boo Boo (*Toddlers and Tiaras*), Alexis Bellino (*The Real Housewives of Orange County*), and last, but not least, Mike "The Situation" Sorrentino, Jenny "JWOWW" Farley, and Nicole "Snooki" Polizzi, et al. (*The Jersey Shore*). While I have met only one of this group, and then just briefly at a fund-raiser for a nonprofit for which I was CEO, I have a very strong gut feeling (not a psychological term of art, mind you) that ALL of this crowd would score high on the Narcissistic Personality Inventory!

(In the interest of full disclosure, the only reality television shows I have ever watched were one or two episodes of Season One of *The Apprentice* and this year's seemingly interminable presidential election *circus*. However, since I was only marginally aware of some of the other shows, I had to create the above list from scratch with the results of a Google search for "Reality TV Show Stars." There were many more, but I thought this was plenty enough to illustrate the point!)

One thing that many celebrities have in common—well, at least those of the narcissistic variety—is the tendency to engage in risky, sometimes even self-destructive behavior. It is another cliché that celebrities, especially young ones, have a way of getting themselves into trouble with the law or have harmed themselves, sometimes fatally, by consuming large amounts of alcohol, narcotics, or prescription opioids, or sometimes by mixing categories of intoxicants. This can also lead to the death of others, if one is in such a condition and attempting to drive a vehicle with passengers. And, although the thin-skinned narcissistic personality can become unruly or combative in public with no assistance from intoxicants if he or she thinks that someone has said or done something to slight them, adding intoxicants into this mix can be a harmful or lethal combination.

For examples of celebrities arrested for behaving badly one need only think of Mel Gibson *(DUI)*, Winona Ryder *(shoplifting)*, Bill Cosby *(aggravated indecent assault)*, Lindsay Lohan *(DUI)*, Sean "Diddy" Combs *(assault with a deadly weapon)*, and probably the most infamous of all, O.J. Simpson (tried and acquitted for *double murder*). Others' actions have, either intentionally or unintentionally, resulted in their own deaths. Here are a few names from that list: Heath Ledger, Whitney Houston, Philip Seymour Hoffman, Robin Williams, Mark Balelo (star of the reality TV show, *Storage Wars*), Kurt Cobain, Keith Emerson, Spalding Gray, and on, and on...

Spending time, as I have earlier in my life, in the performing arts gave me an opportunity to meet and/or work with many celebrities, and I have observed many more, as have all of us, in film, on television, on talk shows, and in newspapers and magazines. While I am fortunate not to have known any celebrities who have self-destructed, I have often wondered what is going on in the lives of those who have that causes them to do so. Is it the pressure of living life continually in the public eye? Could it be an inability to resist the temptations that come from achieving too much wealth way too fast? Is it easy access to illicit drugs and prescription opioids along with the overindulgence in the same that comes from becoming a part of a partying culture that encourages such behavior? All of these factors, and others, appear likely to contribute to the problem, but the more I have reflected on it, the more I have come to believe that these problems are more likely derivative of the underlying cause of an extremely unhealthy narcissism and its roots in the psyche.

It can manifest as a grandiose belief that such people are so special and entitled that nothing so bad can happen to them that they (or their lawyer) can't talk their way out of regardless of the trouble they have gotten themselves into. It also can come from not listening to one's friends, family, and/or advisors if and when they are told that they are heading down a dangerous path, whatever that may be. In other words, the celebrities may reason that they have become successful by being themselves and see no reason to change. Or maybe they have tried to change and failed at it. How many celebrities have gone into and out of rehab over and over again, until one day we read that they have finally overdosed on pills and booze and died?

So, yes, the successes of the self-destructive narcissist may very well stem from an overblown volcanic burst of energy—an insatiable need to be seen and admired—that launches them into the celebrity universe in the first place. But, does this need stem from a deep-seated wounding from an imperfect mirroring of the infant by the mother who is too distracted or preoccupied to give the child the attention it needed at that critical time of life? Or does it result from oversolicitous parents who inflate the child's ego with the belief that the world revolves about them, thereby inculcating in the individual a grandiose sense of specialness or entitlement? Finally, how much does the current culture of *me first-ness*, spurred on and nurtured by reality television and social media, contribute to a self-perpetuation of this need? The fact that scores in the Narcissistic Personality Inventory have been accelerating upward for the past two decades suggests that, whatever the underlying cause of the narcissistic personality adaptation, popular culture and modern technology have been having a multiplier effect. It appears that a new normal in incivility, acquisitiveness, aggrandizement, and otherwise just plain bullying is upon us.

Depth Psychology, the Narcissism Epidemic and Its Implications

What is it about the mirror and its reflection that have been so important in both the interior world of myth and the exterior world of ego identity over the ages? What is this so-called *mirror effect* or *electronic mirror effect*? Are we now beginning to witness the effects of a *narcissism epidemic* run amok? Will this era become known in hindsight as *the age of entitlement*? Or could it signal that something far worse may be on the horizon if we, as individuals and a civilization, do not find a way to compensate for and alter the course we seem to be on?

Part of the answers we seek, may be found in depth psychology. Since its beginnings with Sigmund Freud and his followers, modern depth psychology has been trying to make sense of the causes and effects of narcissism. Dr. Freud and his close associate, Otto Rank, were the first to introduce the myth of Narcissus into the original Viennese school of psychoanalysis that was founded by Freud and, thereby, helped to give the phenomenon of the self-absorbed personality an imaginatively descriptive diagnostic name. Some decades later, self-psychologist Heinz Kohut expanded on the theoretical basis for the diagnosis and identified the condition as a definable and official *disorder,* i.e., "Narcissistic Personality Disorder." Some 10 years after this designation, NPD was to be included in the Diagnostic and Statistical Manual of Mental Disorders (DSM) III.

The term *mirror transference* was coined by Kohut to explain his observations that "certain patients experience the analyst as if he were nothing but a mirror of their own self." He further comments that the patient, "[b]eing in a mirror transference...will expect from his analyst empathic resonance to the slightest of his utterances. But he also expects...that the analyst will be *there* only and exclusively for him and for no-one else" (Jacoby, 1990, p. 201).

Child psychologist and object relations theorist Donald Winnicott continues the metaphor of reflection in his analysis of the significance of the mother-infant bond in the following passage from his book *Playing and Reality* (1971).

> What does the baby see when he or she looks at the mother's face? I am suggesting that, ordinarily, what the baby sees is himself or herself. In other words, the mother is looking at the baby and what she looks like is related to what she sees there. (p. 112)

Other than the obvious connection to vanity and self-absorption, how does the symbol of the mirror come into play in helping us to understand the phenomenon of the narcissistic personality? Jacoby, again, tells us that:

> People with narcissistic problems normally have a more-or-less distorted *mirror image.* It is as if their true person is never properly reflected by the environment. This distorted reflection was formed in early childhood and influences unconsciously the way they feel about themselves. (1990, p. 201)

In other words, the imperfect mirroring of itself that the narcissistically wounded child experiences from its parents, but more importantly the mother, creates a need and a drive to find this reflection elsewhere. The adult who has not resolved this deficit in mirroring becomes the narcissistic personality in constant and sometimes desperate search for the perfect reflection of itself in the outside world but is doomed to finding only images akin to those found in one of the distorted mirror rooms of a modern-day *fun house.*

I find it fascinating that Carl Jung—who sought in the myths of our culture and others the keys to truths emanating from the collective unconscious—didn't seem to have much use for the terms *narcissism* or *narcissist.* He did, however, write about an inflation that can occur when the individual's ego identifies with archetypal material coming from the unconscious, especially with the Self archetype—which is the archetype of wholeness, containing all opposites. Rather than conflating the ego with the Self, however, the process of individuation is designed to, as Jungian analyst Edward Edinger says, get the ego in alignment with the Self in what he termed the *Ego-Self Axis* (1972). For Jung, the ancient art of alchemy or the *Magnum Opus* was a symbolic representation of the individuation process, but for him the steps leading to individuation are psychological in nature not chemical. A grandiose ego through inflation is not the desired outcome in psychological alchemy any more than a bigger quantity of lead or base metals was the goal of the ancient alchemy. The journey involves a number of steps that lead through a sort of death and rebirth. The individuated person is found to view himself or herslef differently, acting not only from the ego position but from the ego in relation to the Self archetype. In other words, an individuated person will have left no vestiges of grandiose ego inflation behind in his or her journey. Individuated people are not narcissistic because they no longer operate from the illusion that their ego is equated to the Self. At least, that is the theory.

In his lifetime, Jung saw that this identification with the archetype could be a potentially lethal byproduct of the individuation process gone offtrack. He knew by experience of the danger that world leaders with overinflated, grandiose egos could be to their own countries, their neighbors, and the world at large. At least three such individuals were very influential in global politics during the height of Jung's career and embodied this danger: Adolf Hitler, Benito Mussolini, and Joseph Stalin. Many of today's world leaders and would-be world leaders, both home and abroad, demonstrate some of the same personality traits of inflation and grandiosity to varying degrees. They are also experts at manipulating and transmitting their image or their *brand* through the use of television and/or social media. Let us hope that we have learned our lesson from World War II and more recent episodes with Middle Eastern dictators, strongmen and terrorist networks, to stop or contain such leaders before they have the chance to amass the power to achieve their malevolent goals.

Maybe it is no paradox that those who are called to political leadership on a global scale—and who are able to survive the weeding-out process that occurs along the way to achieving their position and status—are not necessarily very *nice people,* but, at least here in the U.S., we want our leaders to appear to be friendly folks with whom we would feel comfortable sharing a meal. However different their policies have been over the past 30 years, the presidents we have chosen to represent our country appear to be—or have been—affable, relatively socially adept, and just plain likable individuals.

I find it fascinating and dismaying, then, that unless something radical occurs in the next couple of months, the two candidates with the highest unfavorable ratings according to the most recent polling are going to be pronounced the nominees of their parties in the 2016 race for the president of the United States. What has changed? Has the new normal of the collective discourse that we have with each other and as a nation descended to the level and absence of nuance of a text message or a 140-character tweet? We might as well communicate by throwing slogans and bumper stickers at each other. The ones with the loudest voices—the ones who can shout down and belittle their opposition—at least at the time of this writing seem to be the best-suited to win. Hopefully, as the saying goes, clearer heads will prevail before the race is over. At this point, though, it seems that the bullies have a chance at winning and/or dividing the country even further than it is now.

It is at times like this that I take some comfort in recalling such stories as the myth of *Narcissus*, *Snow White*, or *The Picture of Dorian Gray*. For in all of these narratives, there has always been a self-destruct *button* within the narcissistic personality. A president of the United States cannot be all about *me*, nor should presidents be allowed to think that they are *are above the law*. The position is too powerful and important for that. At the time this was written, we had a few months to find out whether these candidates could find a way to convince us that they truly have the interests of the American people in mind, instead of merely advancing their own, and whether they have the character to fill the office. Or, rather, will their character—like Narcissus or the Evil Queen or Dorian Gray—betray a flaw that will lead to one or the other of them imploding along the way to the finish line?

For the future, we as a society must find a way to balance the individual with the collective. The United States Constitution was written by individuals who knew very well the dangers of concentrating power into the hands of a grandiose, narcissistic ruler. The checks and balances on power of the three houses of government that were written into the document, and continue to be refined and reinterpreted for our modern world, are there to prevent any one person or group from gaining irreversible control. We have seen how an imperial presidency can *get around* Congress by executive order. We may never again see a king, queen or tyrant in control of this country—though it is not an impossible proposition—but we need to find a better way to encourage and enable balanced and wise leaders, who have, both in mind and at heart, the interests of the nation and to discourage the power-hungry, self-enthralled narcissist.

Kathryn Madden, PhD, is Editor of *The Unconscious Roots of Creativity*, and has been the Editor-in-Chief of *Quadrant: The Journal of the C. G. Jung Foundation for Analytical Psychology* for 12 years. She is a licensed psychoanalyst of Jungian and psychodynamic focus in private practice in NYC. She is the author of *The Dark Light of the Soul* (Lindisfarne), and was co-editor of *The Encyclopedia of Psychology & Religion* (Springer). She teaches as Associate Faculty at UTS/Columbia University and at Pacifica Graduate Institute in CA.

References

(2006) *The Hall of Mirrors.* In *Marie Antoinette and the French Revolution.* David Grubin Productions Inc. Accessed online at: http://www.pbs.org/marieantoinette/life/mirrors.html

Edinger, E. (1972). *Ego and Archetype.* Boston: Shambhala Publications, Inc.

Jacoby, M. (1990). *Individuation and Narcissism: The Psychology of Self in Jung and Kohut.* London: Routledge

Nathan, J. (1993). *Force, Order, and Diplomacy in the Age of Louis XIV.* In *The Virginia Quarterly Review.* Vol. 69. No. 4. Accessed online at: http://www.vqronline.org/essay/force-order-and-diplomacy-age-louis-xiv

Twenge, J.M. and Campbell, W.K. (2013). *The Narcissistic Epidemic: Living in the Age of Entitlement.* New York: Atria Books

Winnicott, D. (1971). *Playing and Reality.* London: Tavistock Publications

Narcissism and the Masculine

BY JAMES WYLY, PsyD

When Len Cruz asked me to contribute an essay on *Narcissism and the Masculine* to this collection, I have to confess my first inclination was to thank him graciously and turn him down. I closed my analytic practice 13 years ago, and since then I have devoted myself mainly to painting, music making, and keeping up with the arts in general. I wondered, do I still have anything to say in the language of Jungian psychology? But then I thought, perhaps I can do this with the language that's current for me, the language of the arts. Narcissus has, after all, been painted quite a few times over the past half millennium, and some of those painters thought profoundly about the deeper implications of their subject matter. And Narcissus was a young man, so maybe the paintings say something about the connections between his mythic destiny and masculinity—*the Masculine*. I looked at some paintings, I read some Ovid. I was encouraged by the ready availability on the internet of images of important paintings from museums and collections all over the world. I began to have some ideas, which grew into the following meditation.

I had to start, though, with the most basic of questions. If I am going to discuss psychology with a vocabulary other than its own, I have to answer in the language I'm using: What does my assigned topic, "Narcissism and the Masculine," refer to? *Narcissism* and *the Masculine* are discussed everywhere among us these days, but once we step outside the precisely delineated clinical categories of the American Psychiatric Association's *Diagnostic and Statistical Manual of Mental Disorders*, they can easily fall among those *Through the Looking Glass* concepts that we often use, like Humpty Dumpty when he says, "...[that] means just what I choose it to mean—neither more nor less;" and, though it usually is not too difficult to get the drift of what's being implied when we hear about someone's terminally narcissistic ex-spouse or the masculine pleasures of contact sports, if I am going to develop an essay on the connection, implied by the *and*, between the two terms, I'm going to have to pin them down from the beginning.

So I decided to accept the proposal and start my essay Humpty Dumpty style, with a couple of definitions of my own. By "narcissism," I mean everything that happened to Narcissus, and by "the Masculine"—a construction of somewhat shaky pedigree, arrived at by converting an adjective to a noun by means of attaching a "the" to it—I mean the sum total of everything that most people in our culture would associate with the adjective.

To be a little more specific, Ovid gives us the most complete ancient version of Narcissus' story in his *Metamorphoses*. (I'm using the 1955 translation by Rolfe Humphries, Indiana University Press, pp. 67–73.) Three things happen to Narcissus, an unusually beautiful youth of 16. First, when his mother asks Tiresias if her son will live to old age, the prophet answers, "Yes, if he never knows himself." Second, Narcissus is totally immune to the many girls and boys who fall in love with him, even including Echo, who repeats Narcissus' exact words. (A device which, artfully deployed with a beloved, can be one of the more effective weapons in the armamentarium of seduction.) It seems he's well defended against self-knowledge, then, for he can't hear what anyone says of him, even when it comes back in his own words. But, thirdly and fatally, one day he spots his own reflection in a pool and falls hopelessly in love with it. Here, it would seem, starts something like self-knowledge; but unfortunately Narcissus can't get beyond his initial bedazzlement to carry his new self-knowledge with him away from the pool and into his life, so he pines away while gazing at it and dies. Meanwhile, Echo fades into the earth until only her voice remains. Narcissus can't integrate an accurate perception of himself. (Evidently, Tiresias diagnosed this ultimately fatal flaw in Narcissus' personality by talking with his mother. I suspect some of the other contributors to this anthology will have something to say about the connection between certain kinds of parenting and narcissistic personalities.) So what I mean by narcissism is inability to register self-knowledge; and given the outcome Tiresias foresaw, it's apparent that Narcissus' resistance to self-knowledge was, in a sense, well-founded.

This, of course, is mythology, and we have to realize that in the everyday world narcissism comes in degrees, and it occurs, more or less, in all of us. The achievement of complete self-knowledge is not easy, probably about as difficult to maintain as is Narcissus' mythic level of resistance to it. Most of us fall somewhere between the two extremes.

To say a little more about "the Masculine," I'm imagining it as the sum of everything that our culture would ordinarily describe as masculine. It includes physical characteristics, behaviors, styles of speech, styles of dress, and so on. The sum of all the adjectives equals the noun. It isn't quite the same thing as *masculinity*, which seems something people can have in greater or lesser degree, or not at all, while "the Masculine" is a concept independent of human possession or identification. I always assumed it was a new construction but the *Oxford English Dictionary*, which defines "the Masculine" as *that which is of the male sex*, finds it has been in occasional use since the mid-16th century. For the OED, *masculinity* isn't quite the same thing: it's "The quality or condition of being masculine." Most of the time we probably don't need to distinguish between "the Masculine" and "masculinity." But it's important to be conscious of our language here because the nouns "man," "masculinity," "femininity," and "woman" have recently become blurred with one another's characteristics. Imagining one's self as a man or a woman, masculine or feminine, used to be fixed forever, some time before birth; now it's becoming a matter of self-examination and choice. In the earlier years of the 20th century acceptable styles of being a man or a woman were firmly defined in the public consciousness; but recently (and thankfully) those rigid categories, which never worked as well as was claimed, have been devastatingly challenged by the LGBTQ movement and have begun to bleed into each other so that individual freedom of self-identity, behavior, dress, and so on (we might say the possibility of integrating self-knowledge into one's life) has increased. What this finally demonstrates is that the ideas of "man," "woman," "masculine," and "feminine," are no longer givens but for us are mutable and relatively superficial. One can decide whether one is a woman, a man, or something else, and can aspire to live one's life accordingly. Other cultures, less invested than ours in inflexible binaries of sex, sexuality and gender, have known about this for a long time and at last ours seems to be catching up.

Hence "the Masculine" and "the Feminine" as nouns that seem to me to denote the impersonal characteristics against which individuals compare themselves in order to determine what, if any, gender-, sex-, and sexuality-identity they feel most authentic identifying themselves with. They look at the Masculine and the Feminine in order to determine their own personal renditions of masculinity and/or femininity. When we come to examine specific paintings, I am going to treat their female subjects as representatives of the Feminine and the male subjects as representatives of the Masculine.

Up to this point, it seems that what we are calling narcissism can be found as well in men as in women, or, better said, as well associated with the Masculine as with the Feminine. So our next project is to see if there is some connection between narcissism and the Masculine that is different from narcissism's relationship to the Feminine. I think there is, and that it can be most easily grasped if we look at some paintings that are concerned with narcissism, or, in a broader sense, with mirroring. (The reader should note that excellent digital reproductions of all the paintings I mention can be easily viewed by searching their titles and artists' names in Google Image Search.)

When we think of painting and mirroring, one of the first things that occurs is self-portraiture, so at the outset I need to say that unfortunately, the vast number of self-portraits that artists have made over the past many hundreds of years will not serve our purpose here. We are interested in the painted subject's (Narcissus') response to the mirrored image. In the case of self-portraiture the subject is the painter, and we don't have access to how the painters felt about these works. So we are confined to a much smaller group of paintings, those that show a subject with a mirrored image, for here we can legitimately analyze the painted subject's reaction to the reflection. It is, after all, our projection, our own.

It will be easiest for the reader to follow our path through the paintings if I state its end point in advance. The conclusion to which we shall be led is that in Western painting the Feminine, represented by female figures, can usually contemplate her mirrored image with equanimity, while in the relatively rare paintings of men looking in mirrors, the Masculine's reflected image generally evokes anxiety, rejection, or some other disturbing response, such as Narcissus' own fatal obsession. The rarity of this kind of painting by itself testifies to the unease that surrounds the image of men looking in mirrors. And naturally we need to understand from the beginning that the equanimity, anxiety, rejection, unease, or whatever aren't in the painted men and women; they are in us, the viewers, emotions we find ourselves feeling when we look at the works of art. Thus, art leads us to discover things that our accumulated experiences of our culture have constructed for us; and when we discover them, we can decide how we feel about them and whether we want to keep them as they are or question them.

Paintings of women looking in mirrors occur throughout Western art. All have something in common with two of the first, and perhaps the greatest: Diego Velázquez's (1599–1660) *Venus and Cupid*, also known as the *Rokeby Venus*, and Titian's (Tiziano Vecelli, c. 1485–1576) *Toilet of Venus*. In both, a beautiful nude Venus looks at her image in a mirror held by Cupid. Our associations with sexual attraction and love are activated; after all, this is Venus, Olympus' most beautiful and irresistible goddess; Cupid, her mischievous emissary, is present; there can be nothing disturbing or threatening to Venus about having her essential identity confirmed by Cupid's mirror. Similar kinds of associations come up when we look at almost any of the many paintings involving women and mirrors, whether painted by men or women. I might mention Georges de la Tour's (1593–1652) two *Penitent Magdalenes with Mirrors*, Jean-Auguste-Dominique Ingres' (1780–1867) female portraits, which include mirrored images, Pablo Picasso' (1881–1973) many women with mirrors, Balthus' (Balthasar Klossowski de Rola, 1908–2001), and so on, down to the 2015 *Woman at the Mirror* by Nicola Pucci (1966 —). Not all those women react with pleasure to the images they see, but in all cases they appear to accept what they see as a reflection of something fundamental about themselves. They do not turn away or flee their reflections, and we experience the painted situations as natural, as having clear connections to what we understand to be the Feminine.

In contrast, paintings of men looking in mirrors are rare (except for self-portraits in which the mirror is part of the composition). The prototypical male figure looking at his reflection is, of course, Narcissus himself. The anxiety he evokes in us is undeniable, for we know the story; Narcissus dies as a result of his fixation. Thus Michelangelo Merisi da Caravaggio's (1573–1610) Narcissus makes us a little uncomfortable, and Nicolas Poussin's (1594–1665) makes us more so, for there Narcissus is already dead, and Echo is visibly turning to stone while Cupid, torch burning brightly and spear at hand, stands, seemingly in triumph, over the desolate scene. (We shall return to this work in more detail later.) And while we find many paintings of women and mirrors that show women other than Venus, we find very few with men and mirrors when we look beyond representations of Narcissus—and even where paintings of Narcissus himself are concerned, Poussin's staggering 17th-century rendition of the story left very little more for his successors to say.

We also find a very few paintings of men other than Narcissus looking into mirrors. Let's consider what are possibly the three most widely known ones. First, René Magritte's (1898–1967) *La Reproduction Interdite*, in which we see a man from the back who is looking in a mirror; but the mirror reflects not his face, but the same back view that is shown standing before the mirror, as though the reflection has turned away from its subject. The title tells us there is something forbidden here, as though that were not already clear from the painting itself.

Second is Paul Delvaux's (1897–1994) *The Sabbath*, which shows nine variously undressed female figures engaged with one another in what might be arcane and sexually tinged ritual activities while a rather strange-looking man, totally isolated from the action, gestures anxiously at his reflection in a tall mirror. He is so involved with his reflection that he is oblivious to the activities of the nymphlike creatures all around him, and we worry that he's trapped in a fixation that will end like Narcissus'.

And third is Sylvia Sleigh's (1916–2010) *Philip Golub Reclining*. Here we see a naked young man from the back, looking at his image in a mirror, which also reflects the painter. His pose is identical to that of Velázquez's *Venus* and, changes in fashion notwithstanding, his full, long hair remains a feminizing marker in our culture. At first glance we are inclined to see him as a woman, and when we realize he is not, we are forced to examine our culturally predetermined assumption in a not altogether pleasant way. The painting reminds us that it isn't as easy for us to see a man engaged with his own image like this as it would be if he were a woman. Like the others, it is a disturbing painting, though probably less so in our own time of relative gender fluidity than when it was painted in 1971.

I think these examples confirm our proposition, that in Western art, paintings of women (the Feminine) contemplating their reflected images do not involve the disquieting emotions that we encounter in similar paintings of men—the rarity of which seems to confirm this subject's disquieting influence. It remains for us to think a little more deeply about why this should be so, and for this I would like to return to one of our painters, Balthus, and a painting that occupied a large part of 1925, his 17th year.

This is Balthus' copy, painted in the Louvre and now lost, of Poussin's *Narcissus, Echo, and Cupid*, which we have already mentioned. Balthus intended it as a birthday gift for his mentor and his mother's lover, the poet Rainier Maria Rilke (1875–1926). (The following material about Balthus' *Narcissus* is taken from Chapter Five, titled "Narcissus," of Nicholas Fox Weber's *Balthus: a Biography*, Dalkey Archive edition, 2013, pp. 95–106.)

As we know, a number of artists have painted Narcissus over the years, but perhaps Poussin's rendition most forcefully communicates the most of the story. It clearly communicated deeply with Balthus, for as Weber tells us:

> The seventeenth-century painting offered an exquisite, melancholy rendition of a dead, sexy young man—whose exact position Balthus would repeat, albeit on women, in his own work for years to come. Poussin's half-dead Echo is the prototype of even more of Balthus's women: those modern Parisians mimicking the mythical creature's dream state in their way of being somewhere between this world and the next. (p. 99)

So it would be fair for us to see in Balthus' copy a reflection of something of importance to his psychological makeup; Narcissus' isolation from himself, followed by his obsessive and fatal encounter with his own image, must have echoed something in Balthus' youthful experience, evidently an important awareness in which Balthus must have felt that Rilke had a hand. For "...in January 1925 Rilke had written his poem "Narcisse," which he dedicated to Balthus." (p. 102) Balthus' painting, then, was his gift in response.

Some observations about Balthus's life and reputation will help us to understand this. Balthus was famously reclusive and is regarded by some as one of the two greatest painters of the 20th century, the other being Picasso. He defied his century's fascinations with abstract painting on the one hand and surrealism on the other, and his work remained steadfastly representational, though in an immediately recognizable and highly personal style. His paintings of pubescent girls in overtly erotic poses scandalized the art world, and his lifestyle, which involved divorce from the mother of his sons, teenaged mistresses, and a later marriage to a young woman 35 years his junior, did little to redeem him in the eyes of the public. Through it all, Balthus remained grandly silent as his fame as a painter grew, permitting only the rarest, most strictly controlled interviews with selected journalists who would breathlessly convey his cryptic pronouncements to the world. Then in extreme old age he dictated his memoirs to Alain Vircondelet. (*Vanished Splendors—a Memoir*. HarperCollins, 2002.) The volume was published posthumously.

Balthus steadfastly maintained that his paintings of young girls had nothing whatsoever to do with pederastic fixations, or with sexuality of any kind—a claim at which many openly scoffed and few found easy to take entirely at face value. But Balthus was totally serious about his art, and if we examine what he himself said about it, we see that he found in it a process of profound self-reflection; and it becomes obvious that he neither rejected nor judged what he saw of himself there. The themes of mirrors and Narcissus run through both Balthus' painting and the critical commentary on it, leading us to the idea that Balthus may have outdone Narcissus himself: he gazed deep into his reflection, assimilated what it showed him without fear or obsession, and lived to tell the story in his work. Balthus would have us believe that the superficially semipornographic images that emerged from his brush were involuntary products of his self-explorations, and therefore demanded neither judgment and censorship on the one hand nor acting-out in the real world on the other. Balthus' models confirm this. Some have written at length about their youthful experiences with him, and others have been interviewed by journalists hoping to expose any hint of pederastic scandal. The women are unanimous in saying that Balthus behaved with absolute propriety with them at all times.

Here is Balthus on his girls (These and the following quotes are from *Vanished Splendors*, cited above):

> Some have claimed that my undressed girls are erotic. I never painted them with that intent, which would have made them anecdotal, mere objects of gossips. I aimed at precisely the opposite, to surround them with a halo of silence and depth, as if creating vertigo around them. That's why I think of them as angels, beings from elsewhere, whether heaven, or another ideal place that suddenly opened and passed through time, leaving traces of wonderment, enchantment, or just as icons. (p. 37)

Or again:

> ...I completely reject the erotic interpretations that critics and other people have usually made of my paintings. I've accomplished my work, paintings and drawings, in which undressed young girls abound, not by exploiting an erotic vision in which I'm a voyeur and surrender unknowingly (above all, unknowingly) to some maniacal or shameful tendencies, but by examining a reality whose profound, risky, and unpredictable unreadability might be shed, revealing a fabulous nature and mythological dimension, a dream world that admits to its own machinery. (p. 115)

And lastly:

> There is nothing to interpret in what the canvas says.
> Nothing to be said about it, after all. It can get along by
> itself perfectly well. No codex or dictionary required.
> Dreams continue stories that are lived in the daytime. In
> the studio. They reach the canvas's reality and command
> attention by their disturbing strangeness, without the help
> of any analysis whatsoever. (p. 92)

Here, as in many other places, Balthus tells us he simply painted what
he encountered in an inner reality to which Rilke felt he was gifted with
access and which, while he found it magical and spiritually enlightening,
he refused to interpret or judge. He achieved his indisputable status as an
artist by painting it. There, for him, the story ended.

Balthus understood the "mirroring" function that we are finding to be
at work here. He said,

> One of my art's main motifs is the mirror....my young girls
> often hold them, not only to look at themselves, which
> would be a mere sign of frivolity—and my young girls are
> not shameless Lolitas—but to plumb the furthest depths
> of their underlying beings....Some of my young girls have
> mirrors; they gaze at them, and the painting takes off
> unpredictably. It's up to viewers to rediscover the diverse
> strands that are unconsciously and obscurely gathered
> therein. (pp. 175–76)

"To plumb the furthest depths of their underlying beings": Is that not what
Balthus implies he spent his entire life attempting, guided by Rilke's tute-
lage and furthered in his painting? And is it not the project at which Tiresias
predicted Narcissus would fail?

And if this is so, then this is the very project symbolized in all the paintings we have discussed here: paintings in which women, the Feminine, can
gaze unabashedly into whatever "depths of their underlying beings" the
mirror reflects, but in which Narcissus and a few other painted men—the
Masculine—find in their mirrors obsession, rejection, confusion, and the
risk of death, with the result that they turn away from the deepest aspects
of their beings.

In the early 1970s the psychoanalyst Heinz Kohut revolutionized the
psychoanalytic concept of narcissism when he published his realization
that the so-called narcissistic personality in all its grandiosity and self-cen-
teredness is in fact an elaborate construction designed as cover for an
intractable inner sense of shame, inadequacy and self-loathing. (Heinz

Kohut. *The Analysis of the Self: A Systematic Approach to the Psycholog-ical Treatment of Narcissistic Personality Disorders.* Hogarth Press. 1971) We are now in a position to say that mythology and painting have known about this for rather longer.

It remains for us to ask why it is that our culture should attribute what we might call healthy (but risky!) narcissism, or self-acceptance, more to the Feminine and pathological narcissism, or turning away from the self toward a grandiose socially determined construction, more to the Masculine. The answer that occurs is that masculinity is for us a more rigid, externally defined concept than is femininity. Masculinity is relatively easy to talk about, while femininity is often described as mysterious and inscrutable. The Masculine appears to be made up of a series of standards or tests rooted in culture and often related to size, power, performance, and endurance, the violation of enough of which calls into question one's status as a man and can even redefine one as effeminate or a woman. Femininity doesn't seem to have a set of external rules comparable to masculinity's, but instead, at least in men, is often imagined very simply, as absence of masculinity.

("You throw like a girl!" Classically humiliating for a boy to hear. But girls aren't shamed for throwing like boys; they are usually praised, though for them, girly throws are acceptable as well. So the Throw Rule states that masculine-looking throws are better than feminine-looking ones, and feminine-looking throws are never executed by fully certified males. That's an external, societally constructed criterion with little or nothing to do with one's inner self or identity, and living under its judgment risks an ongoing sense of shame and self-rejection. Thus the way is opened for inauthentic conformity to a social norm, or construction of a fragment of a narcissistic persona.)

Thankfully, these rules are being widely questioned as I write, but we can't forget that when the men in our paintings look within, we are not encouraged to feel at ease with what they find. The women look within and seem able to consider what they see. We may well suspect that the painted men and the painted women are in fact encountering in their mirrors similar kinds of things and that they are not necessarily innate determinants of sex or gender. Then the issue becomes not so much what they find as what they do with it. The Masculine's path has been one of either obsession or of anxiety, avoidance, and turning outward, while the Feminine path seems more accepting of the inner experience. Balthus seems to have followed the Feminine's path; and after all is said and done, there seems no reason why either path should continue to be thought inherently more character-istic of one sex or gender than another.

Here it seems appropriate to quote from Paul Lombard's beautiful and poetic foreword to *Vanished Splendors*, appropriately titled "The Painter at the Mirror."

After Masaccio and Piero della Francesca, whom he loved above all others, [Balthus] became the painter of the soul.

The great Italian painters represented the link between mysterious immateriality and the body's fragility, their spiritual lucidity and blind senses, through portraits of heavenly creatures who, tormented by Lucifer, sprang up from the void.

Instead of them, Balthus preferred budding young girls, victims of puberty's agonies and delicious torments. (p. xii)

....

[Balthus's] art is a religion where sin is never impious, and he reminds us that the sacred message must not be left within the reach of children. The Father so esteemed flesh, its desires, temptations, and failures, that he shaped His Son with them, bringing them to mankind. Desire is the soul's inspiration, the internal and external quality that Balthus revealed in his models' gaze. (pp. xii–xiii)

....

[Balthus's] wise, pensive canvases eschewed premeditation. They didn't seek to dazzle; they bewitched. Not to disturb; but to disrupt. Not to provoke; to enchant. Making grace into a mirror of shamelessness, he offered each day its reformulated light, in colors of earth and skin....He makes eroticism into a hymn, to the disappointment of voyeurs and idlers. (p. xiv)

I don't want to suggest too much about our understanding of Balthus' character here, for it is clear from Weber's biography that in many aspects of his life Balthus behaved in ways that could justifiably be called narcissistic. For example, he maintained with no known supporting evidence that he was a descendant of titled Polish nobility and insisted upon being called the Count Klossowski de Rola (Balthus was the childhood nickname with which he always signed his works), a claim many of his friends found incomprehensible; and, more seriously, he denied his well-documented Jewish ancestry while maintaining he was in no way anti-Semitic. But in relation to painting, which he regarded as the sole reason for his being, Lombard, who knew him well, believed he operated on what looks like a very high plane. Balthus would never claim that he had arrived at superior spiritual or artistic awareness, but only that he was seeking something ineffable that he could sometimes glimpse through meditation and painting. Here he turned back from nothing and he refused to judge what he found.

It simply was, and if he thought it beautiful, he painted it. That was the apparent extent of his involvement and of his curiosity.

Meanwhile, we found the opposite position in Narcissus, who can assimilate nothing beyond his solipsistic adolescent preconception of himself, not even when it comes to him in echoes of his own words; and when at last his own accurately reflected image penetrates his awareness, he becomes obsessed with it to the exclusion of all else, which proves fatal.

I think the phrase "obsession with one's own image" is as useful a way as any to describe the kind of narcissism we encounter daily, and it should help us conclude by bringing this meditation down to earth. In daily life, when we encounter politicians, executives, heads of state, reality show stars, or people of any sex or gender who seem obsessed with the image they project, the fashionable word to use for them is "narcissistic." To describe the issue from its other side, most of us know we are flawed human beings; we have limitations, quirks, fetishes and faults that we meet in our fantasies, our fears, our dreams, our sleepless nights and our bathroom mirrors every morning. We are inclined to keep these things to ourselves. But our daily encounters with the world around us can touch them off and then we suffer—awkwardness, misunderstanding, embarrassment, loss, humiliation, all the negative results of human intercourse become open possibilities. In fact, they are communicated in the voice of Echo, feedback from the inner and outer worlds that tells us who we are, and, difficult though it may be to integrate what Echo tells us, to ignore or contradict her is to substitute something external for some essential part of ourselves.

What do we do with these perceptions? Narcissus tried two solutions. First, he ignored them. Then, in a burst of recognition, he became obsessed with them: at last he saw who he was. But he couldn't take the next step, which would have been to accept himself fully and go on to live out his life among his companions and within his imagination.

There is where the people we ordinarily call narcissistic seem to get caught. Unable to integrate their perceptions of flaws, limitations and quirks, with which their closest associates probably reconciled themselves long ago, they become preoccupied with maintaining what they see as a presentable public image. Inevitably it is too much: it is too perfect, too big, too rich, too powerful, too successful, too kind, too generous, too smart, too blond, too elaborately coiffed, and ultimately too fragile to be real, and the persons' demand that others relate not to them but to the image they try to project causes all kinds of complications and ruptures in their lives. And after a while the narcissist's companions become tired of having to prop up the idealized image; understandably, they want something more genuine, and the narcissist, now sensing the possible rejection and isolation that were always feared to be the inevitable consequences of an imperfect inner life, exaggerates the façade even more.

There is nothing gender- or sex-specific about any of this, but there is one complication that makes a gender-based difference in how it plays out. As we have seen, the Masculine in our culture is largely defined by an external construction founded in specific criteria, some possibly useful and others ridiculous, the fulfillment of which qualifies one as a man. In addition, ours has been a culture that has historically assumed masculine superiority in many aspects of life. For example, only recently have our historians of art and music begun to recognize the well-documented achievements of the many generations of brilliant women painters and musicians, simply because the oft-repeated cultural assumption was that men do these things better.

So when men who can't stand what they find in their mirrors look around for ways to go on living, they have a whole set of culturally prescribed external tasks they can undertake to demonstrate to themselves that they are, after all, men enough to merit the love and admiration they require. Women probably encounter the same problem just as frequently; but Femininity isn't offered as elaborate a set of programs, so the construction of a perceived-as-worthy-of-love-and-admiration façade for her involves a more creative and individualized effort. Furthermore, society's traditional feminine program of domesticity and motherhood has lost much of its luster over the past several generations, and today it finds little favor outside the imaginations of socially conservative male politicians and clergy. The surviving feminine program involves emulating Venus, that is, cultivating beauty and sexual desirability. Some women pull it off for a few youthful years and others manage to convince themselves that they do, but the majority seem to decide it's beyond them and turn their attention elsewhere. If they are to find a workable externally determined program for their lives they have to assemble it themselves. It's a more painful solution than the one taken by men, but probably healthier and almost certainly more difficult in the long run. Here may be the reason that some of Picasso's women with mirrors (notably some of those painted in the mid-1930s) look so desolate. They are profoundly distressed by what their mirrors show them but they can't turn away, for they find no supposedly redemptive program of external tasks to turn to.

But we haven't yet discussed the presence of Cupid in Poussin's painting; and here, I think, Poussin renders the story both darker than Ovid's version and more relevant to our present preoccupation with narcissism. Cupid, let us remember, is Venus' executor; she is the goddess of love, and he, her son by Mars, creates the obsessive demand that makes the need for love so powerful. When someone offends Venus, she sends Cupid to impel them into some calamitous love affair. In Poussin's painting, Cupid clearly triumphs, and his victory has accomplished the deaths of the two protagonists in the story. His painted torch is burning brightly, and his spear (not the toy bow and arrow with which he is so often depicted, but his inheritance from his warrior father) remains sharp and at the ready. I find him profoundly disturbing, for he is a 17th-century portrayal of an increasingly frequent 21st-century nightmare: the three-year-old who kills while playing with the loaded firearms his or her parents, in their narcissistic need to display external demands for respect, insist on carrying everywhere ready for use. Poussin is telling us that Narcissus' need for love has deadly consequences, not only for himself but for those around him.

And here we need to pause and reflect for a moment on Poussin's warning. How far does a committed narcissist's need for love and respect go? Given the opportunity, how much will they sacrifice of the family, institutions, and people around them in order to maintain their carefully and expensively constructed images of themselves? And how subtly seductive and manipulative can they become of the people around them, their well-paid enablers and yes-men, in order to maintain the constant stream of adulation that they require? Some of them go to tremendous lengths, as we realize when we reflect upon the many ruthless dictators in recent history who have steadfastly maintained "my people love me" while sacrificing all around them to their personal needs for glory—straight up to the moment in which they are taken down in bloody coups that reduce entire cultures to ruins. We can read Poussin's inclusion of Cupid in his painting as a sobering elaboration on Ovid's story, as though Poussin realized Ovid didn't fully grasp the frightening implications of Narcissus' inability to know and accept himself completely.

The current edition of the American Psychiatric Association's *Diagnostic and Statistical Manual of Mental Disorders (DSM-5)* describes 14 "Personality Disorders." Of the 14, only Narcissistic Personality Disorder is named for a character in classical mythology; all the others are named with clinical terms from psychiatry's diagnostic vocabulary. To me this suggests that narcissism is something apart from that dreary catalog of contemporary psychopathologies; it obviously has a history that stretches far back in time and the survival of its mythology for so long suggests that recognizing it has always been a part of humanity's effort to understand itself; while trivializing, enabling, or ignoring it can lead to disastrous large-scale results. Perhaps it would be useful to declassify narcissism altogether and remove it from our ever-expanding list of psychopathologies. We could think about ceasing to regard it as a "disorder" that merely needs to be "ordered"; instead, we might place it among the seriously problematic mysteries and catastrophic failures of love that confront all of us in our lifelong project of knowing ourselves and growing up human in the midst of our long-established and demanding culture. That seems closer to how artists who paint encounters with the soul's mirror have regarded it for centuries; and, as we have demonstrated, their works offer us important insights as we try to understand the full implications of this elemental aspect of ourselves.

James Wyly, PsyD, is a painter and musician. He holds doctorates in music and psychology, and practiced Jungian Analysis in Chicago for many years. His publications include *The Phallic Quest: Priapus and Masculine Inflation*, articles on Jungian psychology and the arts, The Brebos Organs at El Escorial (with Susan Tattershall) and articles on Iberian and Ibero-american baroque pipe organs. He lives in southern Mexico with his wife and dog.

Narcissism in the Home

BY NANCY SWIFT FURLOTTI, PhD

This paper is dedicated to all those women who find themselves in narcissistic relationships with men and have a hard time getting out of them, as I did. I want to tell you this story of one woman's experience living with narcissism. It could just as easily be a man's story so it may be helpful for them, too. After many years of living in a dysfunctional marriage with a narcissist, I finally left. It was during my divorce that I had an experience that made me think about speaking out about it, breaking the silence and discussing the shameful secret I had lived with.

During the divorce I was interviewed under oath by his side's hired psychologist, told to answer honestly and in detail about my experiences growing up, my relationship with him, emotional abuse and what that was like, my ex-husband's drinking problem, and his abuse of the children, etc. It was a very hard interview for me. When it ended I looked over at the court reporter to see that she was crying. She had huge tears rolling down her cheeks. She said to me, "Oh my god, if only so many women I know could hear you talk about this, it would help them so much because they are in similar situations and they don't know what to do." I was so touched by her, we cried together. One friend of hers, in particular, was going through just what I described but of course, being a court reporter mandated to maintain 100% confidentiality, she couldn't say a word about what she had heard. I thought the best thing I could do would be to write about my experience in the hope that it could help even one woman gain some clarity about her difficult situation.

It is important for me to point out that everyone's experience will be different, none of us are identical, only similar in certain respects. Our historical experiences are different, we each have a unique nature that we bring to our lives, and our reactions to those same differences in our partners will be our own. I am not going to define narcissism as it is clinically delineated because one can look that up in the DSM-V (the Diagnostic and Statistical Manual V is a book that codifies and delineates diagnostic criteria for mental illnesses). My experience was not a diagnostic code but a living reality that took many shapes, defying my own understanding and morphing beyond any container attempting to describe it. I can only examine my ex-husband's behavior and its "collateral damage" on me, my children and others around us. What makes it difficult to pin down into diagnostic terminology is that with narcissism there are so many other so called pathologies that feed into it and overlap. We are humans and our souls defy definition.

We all hear a lot about narcissism these days, the word is thrown around casually, and we certainly have an idea of what it is. Yet, there is a big difference between having narcissistic traits, which we all do to one degree or another, and the actual diagnosis of narcissistic personality disorder. Narcissism is a normal early developmental stage. You see its manifestation when the young child asks to be watched or applauded for some action or glances at the loving parent wanting that loving glance returned. During this very important stage. the child begins to develop a healthy sense of his or her own agency. He or she also experiences a sense of being appreciated. The child also begins the differentiation between ego and Self. The healthy adult then retains a positive narcissism that enables him or her to take pride in work well done and to appreciate others, as well.

When this early need is not mirrored properly, the child does not develop the sense of being a good enough person, capable of love and admiration. Mirroring, the child's need to be seen in an accurate and supportive way, is essential for the child's growth and development. In the absence of mirroring, the child 's ego instead becomes fused with the Self, in other words, taken over by the archetypal realm and led away from harsh reality where the child is left with the task of mirroring the parent. It is not uncommon for the narcissistic parent to see the child as a little clone of himself or herself and expect the child to behave, think, and act as the parent deems correct. There is no emotional development because there is no independent mind. All thoughts are put into the child's mind by the parent, all behaviors, all actions, all desires are transplants.

The child can be overidealized, referred to as the "shining prince or princess" until he or she finally strives to separate from the parent, and then the game is over. The dark shadow side of the narcissistic parent is projected onto the child, and a split can develop between the admirable, competent half, which remains with the parent, and its opposite, all that is inadequate and unlovable, is attributed to the child. Of course, the child strives to remain the cherished one and will do whatever it can to regain its special status by giving up its own strivings in favor of compliance to the will of the parent. One way or another it is a loss for the child. Either the child is abandoned or is molded to serve the needs of another.

Without adequate mirroring and appreciation for the developing personality/psyche, the child grows up with a hole that will need to be filled just as the hole in the parent's psyche was temporarily filled by the required mirroring from the child and others. To survive, the child has to ensure the parent is "good enough". This means that even though the parent does not have perfect parenting skills he or she has normal sound instincts that support the healthy development of the child. In the case of narcissistic parents, as well as borderline and sociopathic, the parent is frequently a withdrawing "bad" parent. The child then learns to split the good from the bad, the parent is either good or bad but not simply good enough. We describe the child in this situation as having a lack of *object constancy*, and it results in black-and-white thinking that endures throughout the child's life unless the hole is healed in the personality enabling him or her to see that all humans are both good and not so good. Frequently with narcissists you have other psychological issues such as those mentioned above, as well as alcoholism, substance abuse, and sexual addiction. Depression and anxiety are ever-present, also. It is well and good to describe this condition but it is another thing entirely to step into the living reality of it. What does it mean to live with someone who is narcissistic? I can describe it in one word—it's nothing less than an absolute nightmare.

Frequently women get into relationships with narcissistic men because they have been narcissistically wounded themselves having grown up in families with narcissists, borderlines, or sociopaths. I certainly know that one personally. My mother was quite narcissistic. She, as an only child, was her father's daughter, adored him, while she strongly disliked her mother. She was a woman who loved men and disparaged women. I was the only girl out of five children. She wanted me to mirror her, to be a little mirror image of herself. It started very early. Having boys was different but having a little girl made me a prisoner of her own need for constant mirroring. I had to be her perfect identical twin, she would dress us alike, expect me to behave like her: She would control my every move as she knew best in all things, and I should not outgrow her, even physically.

I remember telling my therapist that I felt as if my mother's blood ran through my veins. There was no independent me—I was the vessel that contained all that she disliked about herself and tried to change by re-working me. One example of this occurred when I was 12 and she found a doctor to put me on estrogen to stunt my growth because she was afraid I would grow to be too tall and unsightly. Naturally, my psyche had a reaction to this, which was tremendous rage and envy for being filled up with what was not me. It mostly remained subdued in my unconscious, imprisoned by stern inner figures. If my rage had come out against my mother, I would have been emotionally beaten into submission. It was not safe to express those angry emotions overtly so instead I held the emotions inside me, falling into a deep depression, walling myself off from the world. I was alone with my inner brutal monsters, prison guards, and scary ghosts haunting my inner rooms. My Bi-Polar father was kind and helpful, mirroring me as much as he was able to until he committed suicide when I was 7.

It is known that narcissism is fueled by rage and envy, rage at not being mirrored, not being seen as adequate and lovable, and envy at not receiving what the child needs and sees what other children have—much more positive, caring relationships. The parent may idealize the child at times but easily switches to rejection. Having a narcissistic parent sets the child up for having future narcissistic relationships. She is used to this behavior; it is the norm for her to be the caretaker and mirror for others. The doors to her inner self are tightly locked, as she fortifies herself behind the thick wall to keep all the emotions and demons at bay and to keep others out.

A narcissistic man may target the vulnerable woman who he unconsciously believes will be the perfect mirror for him. Overtly, he looks for status, a good family, financial security—all those things that he does not have but wants to satisfy his hungry grandiosity. For a narcissist, the ego is fused with the persona, so he remains superficial but seemingly powerful and strong. Lacking real depth of character, he is more like a chameleon, able to change on a dime to adjust to his audience. This attribute helps him find the most mirroring. His inner wound remains a hole that hungers for the idealizing projection that was perhaps at first overgiven and then withdrawn, or emerged from the unconscious as compensation for feeling inadequate. These men will often find the needed mirrors in sexual relationships. A compulsive sense of "doing" helps to distract from the constant pressure from the unconscious that threatens to inundate the fragile ego. Everything must by definition remain quite superficial, since whatever interest there is serves to attract attention as compensation for the lack of "being." His rage and envy necessitate an inner need to be so supported, leaving little or no reserve for compassion or empathy for others.

I met my husband when I was 14 years old and he was 18. I was immediately taken by his charm and the attention he paid to me. It was like receiving a few drops of water in a parched and dry desert. I began dating this man when I was a senior in college. We dated off and on for three years. He had been married right out of college but it only lasted for two years. I heard later that his first wife left him because of his infidelities, and much later heard gossip that he may have physically abused her. By the time I began dating him he was working with a psychiatrist at UCLA. I never quite understood why but he said it was because of his divorce, I suppose his being in therapy could have had something to do with how he treated his first wife.

From the time I was 14, he never lost contact with me—it was as if he was keeping an eye on me. I seemingly had everything this only child of elderly immigrants wanted—a large friendly family, social status, and stability. I represented the wholesome America he longed for. In retrospect, I was able to offer him the mirroring he demanded and also credibility for his growing grandiosity. Early on, I had an uncanny intuition that I would end up marrying this guy. It seems my unconscious was aware even then that I had complexes that needed to be worked through and that he would be the challenge I needed to begin to differentiate and heal myself. I was charmed by him, never having had attention focused on me, and it was certainly a new and exciting experience. He was charismatic, intelligent, well-educated, the life of the party, and interested in many things. He was all those things I felt I was not. Everyone was charmed by him—at first. My mother sniffed him out, though, the way one narcissist can sniff out another. She was not happy with my dating him or much less marrying him. Even his father wondered why I was marrying him, and asked me if I was sure about that decision. I did not see beyond the charm and attention, and after three years was truly captivated, in the same sense that heroines in fairytales are caught in spells.

What is frequently the case in early relationships with narcissists is that narcissists are very charming and exuberant, winning you over with their focused attention, and then after you get married or are in the relationship long enough, the projection shifts, becoming negative, and all hell breaks loose. The negative, unstable, inadequate side of their personalities then gets projected, and the partner is the easiest target. Almost over night, I went from feeling adored to despised.

I didn't have any substantial sense of self at that time and was basically taken along by the course of my life without a say in what I wanted. Being mindless I just didn't know. My mother had my mind and had made all decisions for me. My only decision was to shift from her to him, feeling clear about one thing, and that was that he would be able to stand up to her where most men would not. I knew I needed to separate from her and find myself but felt I could not do it alone. He did not like my mother, either, and aptly described her as "tub of war." What I later understood was that I shifted the inner work I needed to do on my mother complex to my husband, and it was within that new toxic container that I was forced to find myself and come to terms with both my mother and with him. We carry our complexes with us into relationships, unconsciously attracting the perfect matches for them. I was repeating the pattern I had grown up with, and while I was given the opportunity to heal myself from that original narcissistic wound, life's irony had me replace her with another narcissist. This one was not as invasive as the former, as a mother can be, but in many ways was far worse. Jumping from one narcissist to another is not a solution but unfortunately is very common, the same way that unresolved complexes often replace each other, or move from one object to the next.

I knew almost right away after we got married that something was wrong, I should have seen the clues beforehand. He drank way too much alcohol. Through the alcohol came tremendous rage and envy, the two calling cards for narcissism. Thankfully, I was not physically abused even though there were threats, but the emotional abuse was corrosive. He was always pleasant outside of the family and could be calm, cheerful, and humorous at home but would switch on a dime for no reason, from being charming to being hateful, shifting from the personality of a Dr. Jekyll to a Mr. Hyde. Alcohol would definitely cause this shift while many other things would, as well. His mood shift was unpredictable and unexpected. He became an unpredictable monster to me and then to the children.

I grew up with these shifts in mood in my mother, so unfortunately it seemed quite normal to me, as that was all I knew. But when the anger was directed toward my children, I changed and began to see it more clearly for what it was—destructive rage. I got my two sons into therapy quite early on because of their competitiveness with each other and was told that I was the one who needed therapy, not them. This was a very important turning point for me. For the next 20 years, I was in therapy working on myself, which my ex described as narcissistic, self-focused behavior.

What emerged because of attacks on my children was a strong maternal instinct to protect them, which I did not have for myself. I didn't have a sense of myself as a feminine being, nor did I have a sense of my own masculinity. I had internalized the negative self-descriptions first from my mother and then my husband. Growing up I felt passive and helpless, rudderless, unlikable, useless, depressed but I also had a shadow rage that was huge and expressed itself in my competitiveness in sports. What developed in therapy was consciousness of this rage. All I wanted to do was to scream because I never counted, what I wanted never mattered. I felt I was brought into this world to serve others. As my rage burned, it of course was felt in my relationship as a negative animus, my negative inner masculine, and my ex-husband never forgave me for going into therapy. He accused me of changing, and indeed I did! I began to speak up and talk back to him.

Before I was able to give voice to my true self, I lived a life of dissociation. He would talk in long monologues then ask why I didn't say anything, telling me that I was stupid and un-educated. When I did speak, he would tell me to shut up and stop interrupting him. The safest place to be was in my imagination, dissociated from the unbearable situation. I escaped into the archetypal world and found it to be life-saving early on as I was buffeted about by my mother's instability, and consequently developed a very rich, imaginary inner life, including an imaginary friend with whom I played for years. He grew up along side me acting as one of my consistently helpful inner figures.

Conversations with my ex were always double-edged swords. Trying to stop one of his monologues was dangerous, as he might fly into a rage that would last for hours, sometimes all night. He would follow me from room to room, badgering me. There was no escape. I'd try to calm him down, get him to go to sleep but that never worked, it only made it worse. He would coldly tell me I was an idiot, a horrible mother, a terrible wife and person, I was retarded, that I would end up in a mental institution. There were nights when he would come home late and I was already asleep. He would wake me up and begin his tirade about one thing or another. Not only was this unbelievably wounding but it was severely abusive. Having been exposed to similar behavior growing up, it was sick in a familiar way. I chalked it up to how relationships were. The easiest and safest thing to do was to not speak to him, as I had done with my mother. I locked myself up from her so I was impenetrable and did the same thing once again with my ex. If I said the wrong thing, I was screamed at; if I said the right thing the same happened. I was in for an attack no matter what I did, so it was better to avoid contact as much as possible.

After his night rages, he would frequently apologize the next day, trying to explain what had happened, what offence from me or someone else he was upset about, promising he would not do that again. He would promise to stop drinking and could stop for a few weeks at a time just to impress upon me and himself that he was not an alcoholic, but he could never stop for good. This was a continuing problem and the source of further and further alienation. After these alcoholic bouts, the charming Dr. Jekyll would emerge, seducing me into believing that maybe this time he would really change and remain this kinder person. I wanted to believe it. He did go into therapy but managed to seduce the therapists into believing he did not have an alcohol problem. Nor was there any evidence of addressing the core issues of his deep narcissistic wound to help him transform. He was just too charming and too defended.

As I continued to work on myself in therapy, I expressed my rage, depression, and hopelessness. I had dream after dream of having lost my heart, being captive by a monster, locked up, abused. My inner masculine at the time was like a prison guard who kept me captive, locked away, forgotten and belittled. He was cold and sadistic. It was this inner masculine that needed to be transformed, the anger and rage that befell me from my mother and husband also attacked me from within in the form of this inner masculine. My primary masculine role model, my father, had succumbed to major depression at the hands of the death forces in the unconscious, so it was hard for me to believe I would be able to escape that same fate.

With the support of a very special Jungian analyst I was able to develop a positive transference in which I felt nurturing support, safety and containment. The brew of emerging feelings was held over a very long period of time, helping me tolerate them in an undissociated state. Learning to remain present and clear, making room for my soft and rageful voice to emerge was healing and led to my transformation. The feminine voice that was now present helped transform and soften the masculine. Both sides supported each other. Slowly, I came to realize that my ex-husband's behavior was destructive and that I did not have to tolerate it. My rage, now subdued into just anger, became assertiveness I could communicate with words rather than through destructive behavior. I became less like the prison guard, as the inside me and outside me began to change.

My transformed inner masculine shifted away from collusion with the narcissist to instead direct its creative energies outward into a career. This shift, however, created a split in me. I pursued my interests steadfastly while I remained in this very unhealthy relationship. I had been in this so long, I thought, "Why leave it?" I always felt guilty about living this split life, though, especially as a therapist myself.

Feeling stronger and now residing in reality, I began to look more closely at other significant areas of particular interest to the narcissist—power and money. Money is power, and it buys friendships and a false sense of self-importance. Money was a big issue in my relationship from the beginning. My ex wanted to take control over budgets, investments, accounting, finances, finally removing me completely from any control or oversight, even though most of it was mine. It was too intolerable to argue with him about it so I withdrew. Later I discovered during the divorce that during an economic downturn he lost substantial assets of his own, and to bolster his bottom line he transferred funds belonging to me and the children to himself. He minimized this transaction by describing it as only, "chump change" which it certainly was not, but he didn't take it seriously or think he did anything wrong. This attitude reflects a weak character and an amorality that is common among narcissists. These character flaws result from the intense focus on self-survival and difficulty feeling compassion or empathy for others. People are there to serve the narcissist, so anything goes; everything is theirs for the taking. Because of this attitude, the narcissist lives outside of established norms of morality and ethics, nor is there morality in the ever-changing, self-serving world of the narcissist.

The compulsive drive for bigger and bigger deals, needing to be seemingly more successful than everyone else, was part of the character traits that accompany narcissism. He was convinced that what he did was the best, while everyone else was stupid or inadequate in some way. Some male acquaintances of my ex were put on pedestals temporarily until they too fell into the trash bin. As a lawyer, he made the best deals, was the best negotiator, wrote the best contracts—filled with land mines that would explode if he were ever sued by the holder of the contract. I certainly experienced this first hand when I finally went through the divorce.

One of the most crazy-making aspects of a narcissist' behavior is that they do not live in a rational, concrete reality where facts are facts and events actually happened. Rather, the narcissist's reality may be a distorted magical reality of his own making. The narcissist has his own facts, his own history, his own imagined future and this has a tenuous and malleable connection to the reality everyone else experienced. For me, it was very fluid, a sensation of going back and forth between what we would call reality and his internal fantasy. It shifted depending on the situation or the people spoken to, and served the function of helping him maintain his grandiose sense of self. He was like a chameleon; his behavior easily led to changing the story in whatever way maintained power, putting one over on the other, or created a scenario where he was better than everyone else. Life was created in the moment to maximize the positive mirroring and grandiosity. It was crazy-making when you would try to have a conversation and you never knew where his facts or ideas were coming from. In my personal experience I would be overwhelmed by words, a tsunami of words that went around and around repeatedly and would wipe you out by overtalking.

My ex would frequently have conversations in his own mind, then be convinced that we had agreed on certain things. When he would bring up one of these agreements or conversations and I questioned him about it, he would fly off into a rage. Because he had those conversations in his own mind, he always assumed I was a part of them. I was a part of him, of his narcissistically expanded subjective world, so wouldn't I know what he thought? He would dismiss me by accusing me of having a terrible memory because I didn't remember what he spoke to himself about in his own mind. Living with this caused me eventually to begin to question my own reality. I could see how easy it is in this type of relationship to lose your ballast.

Another manifestation of this magical thinking, which so easily draws one into a folie á deux (a shared delusion) is a fascinating quality worth mentioning that played out in my narcissistic relationships. It has to do with a psychic connection between me and the narcissist. I was so close to both my mother and my ex that there were no boundaries, physically or psychically. For example, I would have definite sensations and "know" when he was thinking of me or about to contact me. I would dream of him or feel great agitation that I knew did not originate with me, and sure enough, I would soon be contacted by him or his lawyer. Over the years I tried to put up an imaginary lead wall to prevent an intrusion into my privacy, but was only marginally successful. The threads of connection, like a narcissistic nervous system, are difficult to disentangle.

It is not easy to remember some of the tougher moments over the years. There were times my ex would attack me with such a destructive force and coldness, it felt like the coldness of evil, that I felt he was attacking my very soul. One important turning point in my relationship was when I was finally able to rise up against this perceived attempt to be eradicated by him, as what I now know is a defense of the Self, and screamed at him, sending all his hatred back to him. All that I had introjected (a process by which we unconsciously take into ourselves the attitudes, voices and characteristics of the other in a whole and complete fashion) from him was blasted back to him by my deep, penetrating feminine voice. At that moment, I thought I would have been capable of killing him. But, of course, I did no such thing. Something shifted in that experience and I realized that he was capable of killing me, which was also a reflection of the depth of his own desperation. All his hatred for himself and the world was projected onto me, acted out against me. I was the horrible negative mother who did not mirror him properly, who abandoned him, who left him to die—as perceived through his eyes as the very young child. I realized there was no way for me to mirror him properly, as much as I tried, mistakenly thinking my love could heal him and wash away the sadistic Mr. Hyde part of him. What is hard for caretakers to accept is that each narcissist has to learn to mirror himself, each alcoholic has to find help himself. Their giving nature and patience make caretakers especially vulnerable to being targeted by narcissists. In this experience, I saw the supreme danger in his behavior, which at base was a need to eradicate something. Out of desperation to not be eradicated, he lashed out at me to be the replacement victim. I refused.

When I saw the movie, *Pan's Labyrinth*, years ago I was immediately captivated by it, and wrote up a paper to present at a number of workshops, exploring the themes of evil, dissociation, attachment wounds, and narcissism. The movie presents in gruesome, graphic detail the challenges and utter craziness of being captive in a narcissist's web. As the young courageous heroine struggled in her real life with an icy cold, evil figure in the form of her new step-father, her inner reality was not much different. She was seductively guided and then pursued by a magical archetypal figure that was equally destructive. Both the inner and outer figures eventually converged to kill her. The story ends with our heroine dying to life but awakening into a fantasy world representing a grandiose identification with the Self. This story hit close to home for me, as I knew the figures and behaviors so well.

So you find yourself in this kind of relationship and you know it is bad, you see both sides, the Dr. Jekyll and Mr. Hyde, the charming persona and the raging, dangerous monster. You want to forget the dark horrible side, so you split off clear consciousness of this side, focusing on what you can live with, the kind, helpful, caring, charming husband. You hope it sticks, that the other is just a nightmare that will go away. At times life at home was calm and pleasant, but it always eventually shifted back to Mr. Hyde. The children and I learned to scurry into our isolated corners when we heard his key in the door. If it was Mr. Hyde who entered, we knew he would find one of us.

The children's place in this drama is complicated. I didn't know what was better, leaving him or staying. I couldn't imagine him having visitation alone with the kids, without my protection even though I didn't feel I was a very successful buffer. For years I felt I didn't have the strength or solidity to even consider leaving. I was so beaten down, so small, so alone. I had no resources available. I felt it was my fate to be unhappy and stuck. I was accustomed to being told I was horrible, useless, and incompetent so how could I manage on my own? By the time the children were teenagers they began acting out and I really didn't feel I could handle all the responsibility of taking care of them on my own. So I stayed and stayed, finally leaving after the children were grown, after I no longer cared whether I stayed or left. I guess it was only when I had resolved my own inner wounds and found myself, when I was able to remain "me" whether I stayed or left, that the door finally opened for me to leave. That was way too long but it is a hard choice for a woman in this situation.

Having a narcissistic father is a special horror for the children, and it was especially so for my daughter, who was a particular target of his shifting moods, moving back and forth between closeness and rejection. Ripped from one side to the other, hoping for the positive but always seeing it shift to the negative left her uncertain and angry. The boys hid but have retained a degree of fragility to this day.

I feel lucky that it was my children who led me into therapy, where I found the inner strength to remain and heal myself. There was no way I could help him heal, though I certainly tried. My ability to mirror him grew dim with the slashing and scratching that obscured the glass surface. He cheated on me from the beginning of our relationship. That was his way of looking for mirroring, needing that constant fix of positive reinforcement. Infidelities are common with narcissism. It got worse as time went on, as he projected more of the negative feminine onto me. I could do no right while strangers could do no wrong. He needed them compulsively to compensate for his own inner prison guard and demeaning attackers.

For him, this stemmed from his narcissistic mother, who treated him with terrible cold withdrawal and little compassion. While still living in Italy, she abandoned him to boarding school in Switzerland at the age of 3, causing terrific pain and suffering. She didn't have friends and severely broke off her relationships with a number of her siblings, leaving her quite alone. She was incredibly critical of him and everyone else around her with her inflated grandiosity, which she certainly could not justify in any way, as she hadn't accomplished a thing in her life. He never had a chance with her. Imagining the scared, little, abandoned child he was, broke my heart. It was knowing this and empathizing with his inner pain that contributed to my remaining in the relationship. This was a hook for me, but one I should have spit out to avoid becoming the sacrificial meal of the day. He hated his mother, and that should have been a warning to me. Unfortunately, I was too young and mindless to notice. As I should have expected, he then turned his hatred for her onto me. Looking back, I can see that the horrible things he spewed at me came to him, to a large extent, from her. His father was cold and dismissive, as well, the ultimate Saturn figure. He had witnessed his own mother's suicide as a child resulting in a severe wound and life-long avoidant attachment. The mother was envious of her son's relationship with his father and sent him away to boarding school for good when he was 12.

For people growing up in families with either mild or severe narcissism, both can be equally devastating, as it was in my case, where I moved from the lesser, my mother, to the greater, my ex. The sad and inevitable outcome is that it tends to get passed on from generation to generation. I know my mother was not the first in our family to be wounded. She passed the effects onto me, and I see how it has challenged my own children. I talk openly about it with them and hope they find their own help to transform and heal. I see the scars left behind, areas that are blocked out, acting out in certain ways, anger that is not addressed. It breaks my heart to know this could have been prevented. I don't want this to continue on to my grandchildren and beyond, contributing to the so-called narcissistic world that is all around us. We need to recognize it, to talk about it, to reveal the secrets we keep of the embarrassment and shame of what we have tolerated for way too many years. We put on a nice face and live under the persona that everything is OK, believing we are strong, that we can take it. This is what I would tell myself along with, "Just don't think about it". That was, by the way, what my mother told me to do when things got tough. Her response to depression was, "Just don't think about it and get on with your life." And yet that was impossible. The pervasive depression was a constant reminder that something needed to change. Depression is, of course, an antidote to narcissism, though, not always a recommended one. While depression led me to change and move away from my captivity in the narcissistic web I was caught in, it can be too frightening for some. In that case, maintaining one's outer persona defense against it and the unconscious is a safer way to be. Depression forces one down into the core of one's being as a way to focus attention on the need to re-balance the personality into a whole that naturally contains both positive and negative expressions. The working through of my depression included consciously accepting my inherent strengths and abilities and transforming what was negative and destructive.

I held things together for the family and gave my ex the containment he needed, as hurtful as it was for the rest of us. I remember thinking, "Well, I guess this is my fate in this lifetime to live in a soulless marriage and to not know love. I hope in my next life it will be different and I will find a partner who cares about me, what I think about, my dreams and viewpoints." After I was finally able to leave this unhealthy relationship, I did find such a partner, and it changed my life. I never imagined that anyone would be curious about me, as all I had previously known were narcissists.

Narcissistic relationships are sick environments but what is quite remarkable in such dire situations is to glimpse the spark of life within, hidden and small but very much present, that grows just like a tree taking root in the crack of a rock and growing misshapen, but tall and strong. We can find our strength to transform but it is not easy. It helps to hear similar stories, to know others made it out. There is a fellowship of survivors of narcissistic relationships.

The narcissist can transform, too, if his own inner spark of light is strong enough to find the right therapist and tolerate being honest. Frequently the wound is too great, the shadow too large and destructive for the fragile ego to go anywhere near it. For the narcissist, giving up identification with the Self may be too high a price to pay for change, the power of identification with it is too seductive. This psychological state of identification with the Self takes shape as the wounded and unprotected child retreats into the world of imagination and finds solace with the archetypal figures in the unconscious. This story is played out in many familiar fairytales where the child finds safety in nature—a symbol for the unconscious. As these children grow up, the door to the unconscious remains ajar, where it is easy for them to retreat from the unsafe world of reality. In this archetypal world they identify with the positive, potent side of the Self and can be whoever they want to be. This leads to inflation and grandiosity. All the feelings of inferiority and inadequacy fall away into the forgotten shadow and are projected or deposited onto others. These poor fools are the inferior ones, while the narcissist is the best in all ways. Over time, though, as one neglects to integrate one's shadow, it becomes increasingly vicious, as seen in dreams filled with scary images that grab our attention. Even then it is not uncommon for the narcissist, initially afraid in a dream, to turn the dream image around to make it appear positive for him. Being associated with what is perceived as negative is intolerable. Power is seductive, and the power of the Self is the ultimate power. Therefore, it is not easy for a narcissist to walk away from this identification into the bleak world of reality. The narcissist instead remains shallow and youthful in his or her own grandiose fantasy world.

The myth of Narcissus tells us that he died at 16, that important age where one can no longer remain unconscious but must grow up. As we age, we are faced with more and more of our limitations. The youthful strivings of the narcissist reflect this mythic condition. Without the ability to accept the shadow side of the personality and reflect on one's limitations, one psychologically dies. When this happens, we are all victims of the narcissist.

To conclude, my desire to step out and talk about narcissism in the home has helped me further digest the experiences of a lifetime. I am hoping it can be helpful for others caught in its web behind closed doors, and ultimately for our entire culture, which seems to have such strong narcissistic leanings.

Narcissism is quite hidden in the shadows and not so easy to pin down with its tricksterish, ever-changing nature. It behooves us to examine the positive and negative sides and all the sides in-between. I would like to open the shut doors to all those women who are stuck in these relationships, so beaten down that they often don't know what to do. Perhaps if they hear others' stories they might take a risk, reveal the secret, break the silence, get some help and know that they are not alone. There is a way out to find one's own fulfilling life and to stop the transmission of this horror to our future generations.

Nancy Swift Furlotti, PhD, is a Jungian Analyst, co-chair of the C.G. Jung Professorial Endowment in Analytical Psychology, UCLA, and board member at Pacifica Graduate Institute. She is a past president of the Los Angeles Jung Institute, and past co-president of the Philemon Foundation. Her longstanding interests include Mesoamerican mythology, the nature of evil, dreams, and the environment. She has written numerous articles, and co-edited *The Dream and its Amplification* with Erel Shalit. Through her publishing imprint, Recollections, she brings into print works by first generation Jungians, such as Erich Neumann.

Narcissism and Social Media
Eros Held Hostage

BY EVE MARAM, PsyD

I was gearing up for a Jungian training on the feminine in Santa Fe, New Mexico, offered by sage analyst Marilyn Matthews. Most of the assigned reading was predictable: Jung, Marion Woodman, and Kerényi. However, Marilyn's email also recommended Nancy Jo Sales's New York Times best-seller, *American Girls: Social Media and the Secret Lives of Teenagers* (2016).

Sales interviewed more than 200 girls, ages 13-19, from across the country (with their parents' permission and sometimes their parents' participation) to explore these girls' relationship with social media. Sales reports some stark facts.

» 73 percent of children have smartphones.

» Teens spend up to 11 hours daily *plugged in*.

» Children begin viewing online porn as young as age 6, and the majority of boys and girls have watched it before they turn 18.

» 92 percent of American children have an online presence before age 2.

» 7 percent of the estimated 50 million users on Tinder, the *dating* (and *hookup*) app, are between ages 13 and 17.

American Girls makes frequent reference to self-promotion in cyberspace. This popular trend includes the rampant exchange of online nudes by young teens and a collective preoccupation with sending carefully Photoshopped *selfies* by people of all ages and lifestyles to gain online *likes*.

The fallout of these instantly accessible electronic means of self-promotion entails the waning potential for viable in-person relationships and may even supersede the need for them. The capacity to communicate directly is compromised or at least challenged. The youths interviewed used impersonal means of sexual and self-expression. Hazards arise from the overzealous pursuit of popularity. Vast cyber audiences post arbitrary responses about other people's physical appearance, values, and feelings that undermine their intrinsic self-worth and ability to develop intimate relationships.

Sales reveals a world of engulfing narcissism: hyperextreme, extraordinary, unabashed (unconscious) self-focus accompanied by tremendously fragile ego development. This narcissism is expressed through a variety of self- and other-inflicted wounds—including breathtakingly thoughtless, overt cruelty toward others, and concomitant increased suicide rates, particularly among teen girls. In Jungian terms, this technology-driven phenomenon reflects a collective persona-dominated worldview that lacks deeply felt individuality. Sales' findings point to an unavoidable social media tsunami that is shaping, defining, and expressing our collective values about self-esteem, sexuality, and relatedness.

I grew up in Berkeley, California, a hotbed of radical philosophy during the emergence of the "free love" era in the late 1960s and early 1970s. Nudity and liberal attitudes toward sex, gender roles, and relationships do not shock me, but this current cultural trend is different. Neither the nudity nor relaxed attitudes toward sex concern me as much as the disconnection from feelings and the blind obsession with persona (the socially acceptable mask worn for the outer world). The sea change ushered in during the 1960s was ostensibly about *love*, rejection of "the establishment," and disavowing conventional collective expectations and values like status, wealth, vanity, and self-consciousness—all of which we now worship via social media. The advent of the Internet introduced a sort of third partner (or a *substitute* for relationships)—an electronic participant—observer that invades and oversees everything in our most private lives. The convenience of the Internet comes with this uninvited electronic companion.

Pornography epitomizes the confusing values that social media and the Internet have produced. In *American Girls*, Sales quotes Harvard Medical School adolescent psychologist John T. Chirban: "With porn, you're not looking at the meaning and value of a whole human being. Girls take away from it the message that their most worthy attribute is their sexual hotness" (p. 17). His first statement is a valuable nutshell description of an obvious, irrefutable current concern. As for his second, pornography certainly did not invent prurient interests, although it may encourage sexual obsession through the amplified, overexposed medium of the Internet. Throughout the ages, we have collectively acknowledged female sexuality as an ultimate asset.

For many individuals of both sexes pornography enters their lives during early formative years when they are just discovering who they are personally, sexually, and in relationships. The pressure to participate, the unprecedented accessibility, and the easy anonymity make for an amplified influence and potentially dangerous distortion in meaning with subsequent ramifications. The horrific statistical increase in human trafficking and underage sex workers may reflect the attitudes fostered by such readily attainable pornography.

This social media phenomenon affects boys as well as girls; they are not represented in their wholeness by a "dick pic" any more than girls are with their "booty pics" and "tit pics." Both are left wondering how to have a date, let alone a satisfying sexual encounter or intimate relationship. I have young-adult male clients who got into legal trouble for viewing underage porn; they are addicted, per se, and while they struggle to have relationships and insist they prefer to have real relationships at least psychologically and emotionally, they often have difficulties. A nearly paralyzing fear blocks their engagement with real-life partners because they are accustomed to achieving sexual arousal and satisfaction by masturbating to two-dimensional "perfect" images they select and control. Along with problems in relating and intimacy deficits, this ubiquitous practice can result in erectile dysfunction when men encounter less than image-perfect actual human counterparts. I have young-adult female clients who are used to consensual "hookups" with male peers but have no clue how to get a boyfriend. As Roberta Flack and Donny Hathaway first sang in 1972, "Where is the love?"

Years ago I wrote about this divide between physical sex and the rest of the mind/body/spirit, and the inevitable misunderstandings when these are divorced.

> Sex . . . can be a good barometer of inner energy level, because it is an area where physical contact can bridge the realms of conscious and unconscious reality and identity. Sexual intercourse taps into the psychic core of the individual, even if it appears lacking in meaning or deep motivation, simply because we are each connected in mind, body, and spirit. . . . The notion of "casual sex" is an oxymoron. . . . As Jung points out, the world of dreams and symbols common to humankind throughout time is evidence of our inner life, as real as our physiological legacy, the common thread that binds us. Therefore, if the sex is empty, it is because the participants are not really present and available for a true meeting. (p. 51, *The Therapist Magazine*, September/October 2004, "How to Use a Jungian Perspective on the Marriage Relationship: The Container and the Contained," Eve Maram, Psy.D., and Steven M. Harris, Ph.D.)

Some of the teenage girls Sales interviewed commented that the increased accessibility of potential sex and dating partners available on social media day and night, whether "out of loneliness or horniness or boredom," has created a culture in which interpersonal connections are inherently shallow and "cheating" is the norm. "There is no trust. . . . In our generation . . . love is just a word, it has no meaning. It's very rare you will ever find someone who really likes you for who you are—for yourself, your originality. And it doesn't matter what you look like, if you have a big butt or whatever. Rarely, ever, do you find someone who really cares" (p. 146).

The Internet is an omnipresent partner in our communication with the world, in most every social interaction. Though in some respects it brings us all closer together, at the same time it can leave our hearts and souls empty. Something is missing. The advent of faster, more robust technologies summons human beings to question how we relate to ourselves and each other. Our extremely polarized politics may be a manifestation of how we are responding to this challenge. There is an increasing chasm between prevailing narcissism and healthy compassion. This great divide can be conceptualized in terms of the increasingly shaky status of *eros*—something I have come to view as a fundamental archetypal energy binding us together in the midst of our tenuous existence.

In Jungian terms, the principle of eros is a form of love (that the Greeks personified as the god of love, Eros), involving psychic relatedness and the spontaneous, deep-rooted urge to connect. Eros conveys tremendous healing potential, evident in the natural human urge for wholeness or the satisfaction of relating with others on a deeply feeling level.

I had just published a book about the absence of this innate desire, the absence of eros (*Psychopathy Within*, 2016), when I attended Marilyn Matthews' training on the feminine. I was being called upon to notice not only the absence of a desire to relate in our collective culture, but a narcissistic perversion of the actual experience, absent eros. Even in our high-speed, high-tech times, people still seek connection. At the same time that connecting with others is ostensibly more accessible than ever, the quality of online "encounters" is in some ways inherently impersonal and often anonymous.

To those actually seeking deep interpersonal connections, the prospects appear less encouraging than ever. In sharp contrast to the continuous availability of a virtual contact that can quickly lead to an in-person (usually sexual) encounter, the quality of the meeting is often as insubstantial as the Photoshopped instant message used to set it up. Stories abound of individuals on such "dates" distractedly scanning their iPhones to shop for and arrange their next conquest even *during* the present one. This makes for an interesting conundrum, in that although it appears easier than ever to meet up with people, even for sex, the resultant expectations and outcomes are less personal than ever. Ironically, the expanded means for connecting at one's disposal become limited to seductively entertaining, instantly gratifying, often desperate mimicry of heartfelt contact.

As a forensic psychologist, I work with clients referred to me because of legal problems. A young woman became a private forensic therapy client after being filmed on a hidden "nanny cam" while babysitting. On the film she was captured baring her breast to a toddler to see if the baby girl would take her breast, ostensibly to breast-feed her (which the baby did not), and that was the end of that incident—but not the consequences. As I became aware of the details of this case, I was convinced that my client's conduct was not primarily sexually driven. However, the story did contain some concerning characteristics that tie in with our theme. My client was a high-functioning, pretty young woman with very large breasts who struggled with cognitive distortions about her attractiveness. She believed that she was "fat," which she associated with being devalued and unlovable. Although I do not perceive her conduct with the toddler to have been sexually driven, I found it fascinating that in that moment, a *narcissistic* moment, her collectively driven poor self-image and low self-esteem, amplified by personal experience, allowed her to *objectify* the baby and commit behavior that brought about her arrest and a personal life crisis.

Given my forensic work with sex offenders, I noticed that while this young woman's case did not bear much resemblance to most of my sex offense cases, there was an eerie common thread: the objectification of the "other," in this case the baby, revealing narcissistic self-focus and poor boundaries. Her admitted oblivion regarding possible consequences of her conduct as it might impact the baby girl—or the parents—was a key factor in this case. This realization was central to her work in therapy and the fact that she committed this offense at all. Her conduct may have been relatively benign, but it was still problematic, and it appeared glaringly out of character for her.

This idea of objectification of the other has two diametrically opposed implications: (1) how we understand "sex offense" conduct that provokes a powerful collective social outrage; and (2) the vastly increased collective exposure and consumption of sexually depersonalizing images on the global Internet. Cyberspace glorifies unreal images of the "perfect" (almost always Photoshopped) nude or seminude body in the absence of any indicators of mind, spirit, or relationship. Instead, users hungrily solicit a parallel form of one-dimensional approval: "likes" posted/tweeted from hordes of strangers.

This lack of boundaries along with prevailing superficiality and objectification of the other is characteristic not only of social media with young girls (and boys) but of a collective cultural problem; this is a *narcissistic* problem. We are engulfed in an extremely image-oriented culture. Consider two very popular public figures. Kim Kardashian is to show business what Donald Trump is to politics: Both are deliberate crowd-pleasers/inciters whose thundering popularity is hugely media-image dependent. In 2014, after years of building her status, Kim had 34 million followers on Twitter (Sales, p. 25). Trump has garnered over 8 million in just the last six months. Both blatantly flaunt wealth, toys, power, and braggadocios appearance, often to the exclusion of any other qualities, or at least dwarfing them. If there is creativity involved in either of their endeavors it mostly appears as the noteworthy capacity to create an uber-popular image driven by motives that are unapologetically self-serving, selfish, racist, and/or sexist. They both evince a strong knack for intuiting the hunger of the masses. They have succeeded in establishing themselves as our modern collective prototypes for physical perfection (Kardashian) and power (Trump) with unabashed inattention to how they accomplish their desires. The Machiavellian "principle" that the end justifies the means seems to underlie much of this behavior—and seemingly precludes any flow of eros.

These representative self-proclaimed cultural icons teach us that being self-involved is a paramount virtue. Young (and not so young) females submit to surgical alteration to appear more like "reality-show" star Kim, while another reality-TV star makes a bid for America's highest office by flagrantly boasting of his wealth and power. Mr. Trump has espoused polarizing opinions by proposing to build a wall along the southern border (paid for by Mexico), excluding all Muslims from entering the country, and reversing hard-won advances in women's rights. These cultural phenomena say something about the collective "us," what we have become, and more importantly, what might be missing.

A 2016 episode of the American political drama television series *Madam Secretary* featured a moving speech from someone representing the "other side," not the prevailing narcissistic collective cultural attitude. Matt Mahoney, a geeky, introverted, behind-the-scenes character is standing in for the secretary of state. He says:

> "In this world of relentless self-promotion, we've all been raised to think that the limelight is the only light worth seeking . . . [but] achievement is often anonymous. I'm one of those people that works in the dark. Some of the greatest things have been done by people you've never heard of, quietly dedicating their lives to improve your own."

The paradox of cyberspace is that despite its impersonal qualities, it also provides instant awareness of events and people from everywhere on the planet. This expanded psychic space makes possible far-reaching, empathic responses of an unprecedented scale and magnitude. Thus, we enjoy a personal lens that is active and turned (projected) outward! Simultaneously, an individual's sense of identity and value are defined by and even merged with collective forces being shaped by the media. This vast, abstract, and impersonal audience populating the Internet becomes an introjected identity, a personal barometer. This state of affairs is epitomized by the ubiquitous *selfies* (in all stages of dress and undress) streaming nonstop through cyberspace and underscored by Kim Kardashian's proclamation at the 2016 Webby Awards, "Nude selfies until I die."

A world, a culture, a personality disconnected from eros inevitably seeks power first and foremost. As prominent Jungian analyst and author

Adolf Guggenbühl-Craig wrote, "Those who cannot love want power" (*The Emptied Soul*, p. 92). Or consider this statement on the topic by C. G. Jung:

> Logically, the opposite of love is hate, and of Eros, Phobos (fear); but psychologically it is the will to power. Where love reigns, there is no will to power; and where the will to power is paramount, love is lacking. The one is but the shadow of the other. . . . (CW Vol. 7, *Two Essays on Analytical Psychology*, 1953, 78, p. 53)

Twitter's figurative exile of eros symbolizes the speed and immediacy of the social media world and its version of human (dis)connection. In some respects our boundaries are expanded tremendously through social media; in other ways that very expansiveness invites confusion and worse.

"The medium is the message," wrote Marshall McLuhan in *Understanding Media: The Extensions of Man*. The statement means that the form of the medium used for communication embeds itself in the message, creating a symbiotic relationship by which the medium influences how the message is perceived. McLuhan proposed that the medium itself, not the content it carries, should be the focus of study. A medium affects the society in which it plays a role not only by the content delivered over the medium, but also by the characteristics of the medium itself. He frequently punned on the word *message*, changing it to *mass age*, *mess age*, and *massage*, all of which could be understood as pertaining to our current cyber-tech media culture.

The anonymity, accessibility, depersonalization, and flatness of the Internet as medium are as fundamental to the meaning and quality of the communication as the actual content delivered. The *medium* of the Internet is a breeding ground for rampant narcissism and the will to power, effectively preempting eros and the potential for relatedness. To return to McLuhan's witty wordplay, we are in an unprecedented *mass age*, which has delivered us into an era of highly sophisticated mass communication that is also a grand-scale *mess*. The *mess* endangering fundamental time-less, universal human values that are critical to our survival as a species will exact a great price. The *massage* to which McLuhan refers might be envisioned today as a huge collective one-dimensional group grope, as we revel in the emotional and psychological manipulation of being "liked" online by a shifting sea of virtual spectators.

What is reflected here is essentially a collective-scale narcissistic wound. Prior to the cyber age, the roots of narcissism were traditionally seen as originating in early childhood experience and attachment breaches. What is happening now collectively, however, suggests that the entire social (and political) fabric is enveloped in a narcissistic, sometimes apoplectic stance of epic proportions. We are engulfed in a world that exudes, requires, and demands at least recognition of this attitude. Even if we are not "of it," we are inevitably "in it." This predominant narcissistic worldview framework predates figures like Donald Trump and Kim Kardashian. Cyberbullying is one dark side of the happy "look-at-me" aspects of social media and has driven some to suicide. The implicit message seems to be, "I'm perfect, but only if all of you tell me I am"; there is no inner compass. It may be naïve to ascribe narcissism solely to attachment issues with the primary caregiver anymore.

Psychopathy is a human characteristic that exists on a gradated scale, not an either-or diagnostic category. It is a trait that may be present to varying degrees (Maram, 2016). As Guggenbühl-Craig posited in *The Emptied Soul*, psychopathy is like a gap in the psyche, an *empty* place where love, eros, cannot enter. Accordingly, eros holds the potential to fill that empty wasteland in the soul. Although narcissism is not equivalent to psychopathy, some characteristics overlap. The entirely self-focused, grandiose narcissist, unable to fully appreciate any other except in self-gratifying terms, is operating without eros.

The current state of our world could be conceptualized as one in which *eros is held hostage*, deactivated by a prevailing collective narcissistic mindset. Accessing the archetypal energy of divine love would involve breaking through the pervasive, disconnected style of pseudorelating to real connection, person-to-person, human-to-human. Any solution must consider the advantages and limitations of our high-speed, high-tech lives, and somehow bridge them.

Occasionally, I spot small signs of individuals seeking more genuine connection.

> "My Mom says to be as close to the way you normally look on dates so a guy falls in love with the woman you're going to be most of the time." (Gina Rodriquez, 31, star of *Jane the Virgin* network TV show, *Us* magazine, Issue 1103, April 4, 2016, p. 57)

Maybe the shift toward a less polarized culture depends upon individuals who choose to listen to the still small voice, the spirit within, prompted by circumstances and inner calling—a whispered invitation to free eros.

Eve Maram, PsyD, is a clinical and forensic psychologist and a Jungian-oriented psychotherapist in private practice in Orange, California. She is currently pursuing Jungian analytic training through the Inter-Regional Society of Jungian Analysts (IRSJA), C.G. Jung Institute of Santa Fe, New Mexico. She is the author of *Psychopathy Within*.

References

Guggenbühl -Craig, A. (1999) *The Emptied Soul: On the Nature of the Psychopath*, Woodstock: Spring Publications.

Maram, E. (2016) *Psychopathy Within*, Asheville: Chiron Publications.

Section 4
Archetypal Narcissism

The Wounded Healer
Transformation through Compassion

BY JEAN SHINODA BOLEN, MD

I begin with a metaphor of the wounded healer. Chiron was a Greek Centaur, an immortal who suffered a wound to his knee that would never heal. How synchronistic that the very publisher of this book, Chiron Publications is named after him.

In Jungian work, unlike the psychoanalytic and psychiatric training that I received as a resident at the University of California San Francisco, there is an emphasis on the therapist's vulnerability and woundedness as a therapeutic tool. Psychiatry grows out of the medical model. The medical profession involves authority, fixing things, and demonstrations of proficiency. There is a doctor who knows and a patient who is worked upon by the doctor. The model in Jungian analysis is different.

As a first-year resident in psychiatry, I was drawn to Jungian work by one of founders of the famous Menninger Clinic. He wrote that the Jungian process was based on a notion of a chemical reaction (later I learned that Jung had used the word *alchemical* not chemical). In order for one element, the patient, to be helped, healed, and treated, the other element in the reaction, the doctor or therapist, would also have to be affected. The reaction brought about healing in both, and the doctor, like the patient, was affected by the process. That model awakened my awareness in ways that continue to this day, that is, my ability to affect the person in my office must leave me open to be affected by the soul and pain of that person—the reaction does, in fact, go both ways.

There is another metaphor that helps me understand what this work is all about, namely the notion of the *descent to the underworld*. This is where the pieces of ourselves that have been cut off, repressed, and unwelcomed in our families or society reside; and the underworld is where we must descend to recover them. Unfortunately, in order to become acceptable to others, we cut ourselves off from those parts. The model for this disconnection from vital aspects of ourselves is the myth of Procrustes.

Procrustes was a rogue metalsmith who lived on the sacred road between Elusis and Athens. For those traveling to Athens, that is, those wishing to find recognition in the world, Procrustes would invite them to spend the night. If the guest was too large, whatever part did not fit in the bed was cut off; and if the guest was not large enough to fill the entire bed, he or she would be stretched to fit. Each and every one of us has taken the road to Athens. In that journey we had to deny, be ashamed of, and cut ourselves off from parts of ourselves that were not welcomed in the world.

So we must make a descent into the underworld to find those cut-off pieces of ourselves that have not seen the light of day. Part of the process of Jungian work involves going into the underworld to retrieve those elements of ourselves. There is Inanna, the one-sided deity goddess of the upper world, who descends into the underworld but must give up a part of her persona at each gate. Inanna gives up a part of her identity in the upper world and goes down to meet her dark sister, Ereshkigal. This is also a metaphor for our work in that each of us has a shadow in the underworld. If we may make a descent, if we are courageous enough to enter this process, we will meet the one who is down there.

The metaphor of the wounded healer, often unfolds toward two possibilities. When we become conscious of our wounds and our pain, we develop compassion and are equipped to guide others into those dark and painful places. Our vulnerabilities, our imperfections, and our suffering help us to bridge, mirror, accept, and be present to the suffering of the people we see, but only if we are conscious of our emotions and what has happened to us. The problem with being a wounded healer lies in the potential for identification with the aggressor or the victim. If, as therapists, we do either of those, we end up wounding the people who turn to us for help.

In every institute, in every clinic, in every place and house of healing, there are terrible stories of betrayal of and damage inflicted on those who came seeking help. It has been a painful process in my institute in San Francisco, to become conscious of such things. In order to address these things, it becomes necessary to recognize that therapists' shadows have the potential to do harm. The stories of therapists who sexually exploited patients or clients, re-enacting what was done to the patients or clients as youngsters, stand out as a major shadow features for any helping profession. What about the stories that are less obvious, however, where there may be no acts that define precisely what was done or what physical boundary was crossed? Here, identification with aggressor or identification with victim takes many different forms. One form of identification with the aggressor originates with the parent who had no capacity to see the child clearly and uniquely. Such a parent has an idea about what the child should be like. The child is supposed to conform to the image the parent holds of the child or the child is expected to take care of the parent's needs. When we have rigid theories about what makes people the way they are and we project our theories onto patients and clients, insisting that our reality is their reality, we do the same thing their parents did. This is the wounding shadow of authority that says, "I know what your story is and I know its meaning," and it robs the person of the opportunity to discover this. This is a risk for anyone in a leadership role.

The wounded shadow of a wounded leader imposes itself upon all who are subject to the leader's authority. This process parallels the wounding shadow of the wounded healer. I wrote of this in *Ring of Power*.

> "When people become obsessed by their quest for power as control, security, or recognition, and when they have power over others, then what they do affects those around them [...] A tyrannical parent or an employer with a narcissistic need to control others has a much smaller sphere of destructive influence but can nonetheless be devastating psychologically to individuals." (P 10-11)

"The patriarchy has a powerful hold on our inner lives, as power dominates the outer world in which we live." *(219)*

The wounding shadow in the leader may take on the appearance of an authoritarian father. When narcissistic leaders become identified with this archetype, they will be insensitive to the feelings, thoughts, and needs of those they lead. Such leaders do not permit their authority to be questioned. In their self-inflation, they do not seek out the opinions of others. The wounded leader is cut off from parts of himself or herself, which gives rise to their wounding shadow. Such leaders establish relationships with their constituencies that bear a striking resemblance to the relationships between parent and child in dysfunctional families. The wounding shadow of the leader equips them to inflict enormous harm. Too often their constituents, like children in a dysfunctional family, provide for the leader's needs to be mirrored and praised.

Another manifestation of the wounding shadow occurs through fostering in our clients' dependency on us. This is often rooted in a mother wound that had been inflicted on the therapist and is now passed on by fostering dependencies or fear in the clients. Parents and therapists have the power to encourage growth or inflict trauma. If we are depressed and feel the world is a bad place, we convey that fearfulness to our patients and clients. If we are unable to see their strengths (just as their parents were unable to see their strengths) and we only acknowledge their pain, then we risk fostering further identification with that pain.

There are also difficulties that result from insisting that our clients meet our needs. For example, to bolster our self-esteem we may require our client to mirror back to us as therapist the mirroring that we ourselves failed to get from our parents. Here, the client with the positive transference finds herself or himself in the position of supplying the narcissistically wounded therapist's needs. Alice Miller's book, *The Drama of the Gifted Child*, shows how that happens and how children who are so dependent on a parent are geared to suppress and deny their own feelings as they strive to provide what the parent asks of them. These dramas can be re-enacted in our work as therapists. For example, a therapist who has been victimized by a parent's anger and deprecation may identify with the victim and allow a client to be abusive to the therapist. This is often evident in my supervision of therapists who were trained by their families of origin to be giving and to be tolerant of any emotion that came their way. Of course, some clients are helped by expressing anger, but there are many others for whom excessive anger was a defense against feeling other emotions in their own families. These clients abuse their therapists, and somehow in the name of doing good therapy, therapists find themselves battered and abused verbally. Such clients identifying with their shadow and being possessed by anger are not helped at all to be so immersed in it. Both parties leave such sessions feeling worse, the therapist because of the "negative transference" and the clients because they were permitted to be too caught up in expressing that degree of negativity. As therapists, we have an enormous power to constellate or evoke what is in the psyche of the people we see.

In a positive sense, at times we invoke a *Pygmalion effect*—that is we see the beauty and the potential in the person we work with and through seeing that potential and loving it, we give it life. Michelangelo said that what he did as a sculptor was to free the figure he saw captive in the stone. This is the positive aspect of what therapists do. However, when the shadow takes over, we may only see a complex in the client. For example, if we are engaged with a person who has been sadistically treated, who now abuses us and we do not intervene, it is tantamount to siding with an underdeveloped aspect of that person.

One way of contending with the shadow qualities of our work is to take a moment with each person, in every session to ask ourselves *what are we seeing and therefore constellating in this person*. What are we focusing on and therefore drawing out, and what are we ignoring or overlooking and therefore not giving credibility to?

We have a model for our work that relies on the *temenos*, or sanctuary. It also represents the uterine experience at the physiological level and the holding environment that a family should provide, but it is too often missing in a dysfunctional family. *Temenos*, a Greek word meaning sanctuary, is a place where a person comes to find safety. There is the boundary of confidentiality that whatever is said in the consulting room to me, whatever is expressed in fact feeling, or fantasy, is safe with me. I will not go out and tell others, especially in a deprecatory way. More than just preserving confidentiality, I will listen without demeaning, judging, or distancing myself from the person. Whatever is brought in will be held in confidence and will not be judged. The *temenos* is a place where we accept that we will not exploit our clients, much like a child born into a family is not meant to be exploited. This does not preclude that in an alchemical way, a child has an enormous effect on the parent and vice versa. Still, there is a sense the child should be safe from exploitation, and the same holds true for the client. No child should be expected to provide for the parent's sexual needs, just as no patient or client should be expected to provide for the therapist's sexual needs.

Another question that arises in our work is the financial exploitation of clients. Unnecessary or prolonged therapy can be undertaken under the cloak of the client's needs when in fact the therapist is acutely anxious about his or her own bills or the size of his or her practice. When do you look out for yourself, and when do you look out for your client? If you find yourself looking out for your own financial needs at the expense of the client, you are living out the shadow of greed and exploitation, and you are harming that person. What about the subtle effects of listening voyeuristically to the client's sexual exploits, or your identification with the client's experience in ways that encourage the client to live out your unlived life? In child psychiatry it is known as a *superego lacunae*, when the parent of a delinquent gives double messages, ostensibly admonishing bad behavior, while secretly living out the repressed shadow elements through the child's behavior.

Other forms of exploitation include the transgression of sexual boundaries or when therapists feel enhanced self-esteem because someone they are seeing is important or a celebrity. When therapists let such information slip out to others, they betray their clients. Those transgressions violate the *temenos*.

The *temenos*, like the womb, is a place where one assumes that growth has its own timing. When is it time to finish the work and to be born out into the world? Is it in response to the growth in the person, or is it something that we impose upon the client? Issues of abandonment come up in this work. Many people limp out of a therapeutic process because their therapists abandoned them. Sometimes there is a termination of therapy with hardly any notice at all, perhaps at a time that was convenient for the therapist but was dreadfully wounding to the client.

Knowledge of the spiral journey in a client's life story instructs us about the client's vulnerabilities to our actions. The more we know of the client's story, the more there is a danger of our re-enacting this story and thereby wounding the client once again. The women whose sexual boundaries are transgressed in therapy almost always suffered the same in childhood. Thus, listening to our clients tell us about their vulnerabilities and teaches us where we have to be even more careful.

The concept of the *dysfunctional family* is enormously helpful for Jungian analysis. The ideas of narcissistic co-dependence in the family and the whole notion of denial is of paramount importance. The elephant in the living room is a phrase often heard in 12-step circles to highlight the resistance to even mentioning the major problem(s) in a family. There are clients who have endured many strange things in a session, like having their therapist fall asleep, arrive drunk, engage in sexual acting out, and yet never reacted by saying there is something terribly wrong here. Growing up, it was better to deny what was happening than to risk being abandoned and on the street. Likewise, clients may think it is better to deny what is happening, better to deny the improper kinds of comments made in therapy than to risk being abandoned again. When these things occur, it is common for the client (like the child) to repress it, forgive it, and come back for more.

Other shadows in our work result when we cut ourselves off from our feelings. This can lead us to further wound the people who come to see us. In a patriarchal culture, men's feelings and their capacity for compassion are stifled. Competition and male bonding discourage displays of vulnerability, so a man cuts himself off from his feelings. This is made worse by the fact that he is rewarded for his capacity to be intellectual and to be accomplished in the world—thus the *Procrustean bed* has done its job. When that happens to a therapist and a client later comes in full of emotion, a defense against experiencing one's own feelings may kick in. Being the strong soldier may mean that when a client opens up from the depths of his or her soul, the therapist inflicts harm by becoming distant and intellectualizing. This subtly conveys that feelings are not welcome.

In *Persuasion and Healing*, Jerome Frank described how much clients learn about the therapist during the first hour of treatment. What begins as an unstructured encounter is shaped by what interests the therapist, what bores the therapist, what is welcomed into the *temenos*, and what is deemed unacceptable. That is part of the wounding aspect of the shadow because those things that are not honored end up disallowed in our clients.

During my training I discovered that I had a difficulty dealing with anger. As a result, I cut it off at the pass before it ever came up. My defensive need to make nice impaired the work I was doing in psychiatry. As a Japanese-American child growing up during World War II, I learned to make no noise, to make no waves, to make nobody angry at me. That was an extension of what women in this culture are taught to do all the time. It may be more comfortable to avoid making people angry at you, but if you are going to do the work of a therapist, you do a great disservice to your people by suppressing anger, since this re-enacts the family's denial.

With patriarchy and patriarchal families, there is a central figure of authority who is entitled to be angry, but no one else is. As a medical student at a general hospital I heard residents telling young teens in labor, who were screaming in pain and fear, "You should have thought about that before you spread your legs." As an intern at Los Angeles County Hospital, following Marilyn Monroe's overdose, countless women arrived with copycat incomplete suicides. Again, I overheard angry residents instructing patients on what they might take the next time they made a suicide attempt to ensure success. That's the kind of training I had. It was part of male initiation that says, "Don't be a sissy, don't be a bleeding heart, and cut yourself off from your own feelings." Later, we are expected to distance ourselves from our feelings in service of objectivity. I am a feeling-type person and I do therapy from a feeling, intuitive place; but if my feeling intuition is not permitted to react to what is going on, I lose touch with my own capacity to be expressive of who I am.

When the shadow of identifying with power appears, we risk fostering dependency. The projection of parental authority that is part of the transference allows us the power to heal. If we react differently from the original authorities in that person's life, change is possible. If, however, we react in the same way as the original authorities by insisting that we are the authority and that we know what their dreams and behaviors mean, or if we foster our clients' dependency, we are wounding them. The Jungian model has more built-in potential for looking out for the shadow than any other school of psychotherapy. Its emphasis on the wounded healer is central to the work. Our clients, not unlike our children, sometimes have intentions to do something or to be someone that makes us uncomfortable. These are moments of truth when we must trust the individuation process and allow their autonomy; otherwise in our authority we harm their growth.

The primary shadow within therapy is the risk of re-enacting the wounds of the dysfunctional family, whether it is through identification with authority or through co-dependence to our clients.

There is also a wounding shadow of the wounded healer that prevents the therapist from fully experiencing the client's suffering. How we see the client shapes who he or she can become. When we feel a person is incapable of hearing what we have to say, it is often a rationalization for what we are unable to say ourselves.

There are voices in the wounded healer's psyche that often get in the way. There are two sides to this dysfunction. Sometimes the narcissistic voices murmur that the client is there to take care of the therapists' financial needs, their need for self-esteem, their need for excitement, or even to provide for the therapists' sexual needs. At other times, these voices urge the therapist to be overly responsible for the client— the other side of the co-dependent problem. In these instances, the therapist loses the ability to help the client stop identifying with a complex and grow.

Being a therapist, like being a parent, is an enormously rewarding, difficult, and perhaps impossible task. Fortunately, where there is compassion, a great deal of forgiveness is also found. What people seek is an honest, true relationship. The therapist need not be perfect, but when a client speaks up, he or she should expect to be validated. Denial is so pronounced in the psyche of everyone. We deny feelings. We deny facts. We hold repression that says don't make waves in the family, don't make waves on the job, don't make waves in society. Deny, deny, deny!

Only when there is a true *temenos* does gradual recovery of feelings come through. All of us who are therapist know that memories and repressed feelings may take years to emerge. When the *temenos* is safe enough for what has been buried in the unconscious to come forth, only then does healing occur. If we are aware of our own fallibilities and wounds, we diminish the chances that the wounding shadow of the wounded healer will be at work. Therapists who are the most defended against their own history and their own feelings often find it very difficult to allow other people to bring those feelings into the consulting room. It's too dangerous; it's contagious. If it was repressed in the therapist's family, it could very well be repressed in the therapist's consultation room.

What I have written in this chapter, I would call circumambulating the shadow. So often in Jungian circles we talk about the gold or the luminous aspects of what we might call circumambulating the *Self*. However, the shadow can be as hard or harder to grasp than the *Self*. At best we get glimpses of the shadow. The task of our work as therapists is to discern what might be the shadow in ourselves or in our clients and to engage it. We are able to do that only if we have undergone our own therapeutic process and recovered the wounded aspects of ourselves and become compassionate toward them.

It is not enough to uncover abuse in dysfunctional families. The person must learn to feel compassion toward the child who was abused. This is because compassion was unfortunately not extended to that child when he or she was beaten, denigrated verbally, psychologically terrorized, or physically hurt. This may have resulted from an adult who was incapable of compassion or who was so narcissistic that they wounded the child.

Psychological healing is like physical healing. The surgeon does not heal. The surgeon excises a problem that is greater than that body could solve on its own. The surgeon leaves a clean wound whose margins are sewn together. The actual healing, however, that closes the skin, that restores the body, is not the surgeon's work to do. The surgeon just provides the possibility of antisepsis and a technique. To visit an operating room where everyone is gowned, masked and purified is to visit a temple, a *temenos*, where holy work is done to restore a person. This is what the soul or psyche experiences in our offices. We provide the *temenos*. If we can provide a space of compassion to the victim, another force gradually comes out of the soul of that person to heal him or her. If we are able to be compassionate to our own wounds, we then are able to be compassionate to the wounds of the people we see, and somehow that forms a healing medium.

Our work consists of tuning ourselves like an instrument to know when we are centered, that is when the ego-self axis is aligned within us, versus when we are in a persona position or when we are in a complex. That it is not too much to ask of ourselves, that we should pay attention to where we are in this process of the therapy work we do.

Jungians inherited a dysfunctional family model. If we remain conscious of what the *temenos* is about, about maintaining boundaries, seeking outside help if we start to feel like those boundaries are getting confused, then we need not pass on the *sins of the fathers*. When I entered my training program, the candidates were never told about the triangle between Carl Jung, Emma Jung, and Toni Wolff —but this is our family history. We must be able to say "in my family, in my Jungian family, this is what happened." This allows us to talk about the consequences when a therapist transgresses the soul of another person. Such transgressions are like abducting Persephone into the underworld. The client feels profound disillusionment and confusion. There is something about the meaning of suffering that this journey is all about. That is a uniquely human question.

I remember when Harry Wilmer presented his work with Vietnam veterans at the 1980 International Congress. He read the paper and he started to talk about what he had heard. He stopped in midsentence and began to cry. He said things happen to people that shouldn't happen to anyone. We hear terrible stories every day and we receive the pain of what was done to the people we work with.

Everyone who has been exposed to narcissism and co-dependency in the family has been both the victim and the aggressor. The healing environment of the *temenos* and our witness to a person's healing journey is the bridge that brings that wounded part of the person back. It brings the person back into community, back into connectedness, back to the feeling world, free from shame and a part of human life again. We are greatly privileged as therapists to perform this work. It is then that we enter *kairos* time; we lose track of time passing and enter a holy moment.

So, yes, there is the wounding shadow of the wounded healer. Our intent matters. We do well to develop compassion for our own mistakes and for what has happened to the people we work with. Perhaps like the centaur Chiron, we must endure a wound that never heals; for that is the way in which we do our work. If we are willing to pay attention to our wounding shadow, we will find gold in the dark places.

Jean Shinoda Bolen, MD, is a psychiatrist, Jungian analyst, author of 13 influential books in 85 foreign translations. She is a Distinguished Life Fellow of the American Psychiatric Association, former clinical professor of psychiatry at UCSF.

Who Was Narcissus?

BY ALDEN JOSEY, PhD

The Silent Majority of the human psyche, Jung's Self or the collective (archetypal) unconscious, is eternally at work creating mythopoeic images that inform, console and inspire nascent ego consciousness as it arises and develops toward its full dimension in an individual life. The process of forming a stable ego complex with a strong sense of personal identity is a foundational structuring dynamic in the contemporary psychic life of human beings.

It was not always so. Understanding the arc of emergence of modern individual identity, rooted some 200,000 years ago, is absolutely critical to understanding the present condition and potential futures of humanity.

What can we say of the slow, gradual accretion of Mind, with its multiple adventures and misadventures? One thing we affirm in this volume is that the behavioral phenomena we now associate with the terms Narcissism and Narcissistic Personality Disorder are deeply rooted in the dynamics of identity formation; this comprises not merely the process of becoming human, but of becoming just <u>this</u> human person –"I".

The depth psychology of C. G. Jung has proven a very powerful instrument for the study of these processes. It allows us to paint a portrait of the developmental process that makes clear our vulnerability in our very earliest days comparable to a sustained trek across new territory where life-anchoring new discoveries as well as terrifying threats appear.

How can and does the process go wrong? And, how did the first modern hominids belonging to the species *homo sapiens* become aware of this tragic miscarriage? How did they begin to generate images at first internally, then externally in the form of dramatic creations that illuminate shape and meaning of this process of identity formation?

The human infant emerges from its cocoon of the Mother after a relatively short gestation as a creature that is a human being but not yet a particular person. It then enters into a period of self-formation that in its first phase extends for about three to four years and culminates in the best situation in an achievement of a personal identity rooted in a relatively stable ego complex.

While crossing this virtual "minefield" of identity formation, the infant is subject to severe wounding from the failure of caregivers to create a stable and safe containment, from broken and ineffective, if not sadistic, withholding of "mirrors of positive reflection" in surrounding faces and from the absence of acceptance and affirmation.

In working with analysands (people in psychoanalysis) coping with narcissistic disorder, I came to describe the psychic destructiveness of such environments as bestowing *existential* wounds to distinguish them from trauma occurring at later stages of development—these I call *circumstantial* wounds. The distinction between these two kinds of developmental obstruction is this: Circumstantial wounds are those related to specific acts you have done and the retributive acts done to you by others, i.e., about behavior and about varieties of negative response in the care field; existential wounds are about who you *are*, i.e., about the very texture of worthiness and acceptability of your identity (further discussion below).

The clinical treatment of existentially wounded persons, is, in my experience, exceptionally demanding. It can be years-long in bearing fruit and involves, *inter alia*, powerful transferences to the analyst as the torn psyche seeks to reform and restore fundamental archetypal forms of energy that lay a firm foundation for personality development.

One can imagine that the self-revelation of the archetypal psyche, as C. G. Jung saw its reparative work, especially in the narcissistic personality, began in the submersion of sleep as the dreams of early modern men. It then took the forms of oral traditions, tales, legends, fairy tales and myths when the creative artists of a culture took them in hand.

In this chapter, we try to trace the origins and evolution of this process toward the genesis of a myth, that of Narcissus the Hunter, that speaks vividly of the individual ego's development toward a stable personal identity and, especially, about the nature and consequences of failure in some measure of that process. No doubt at some point in the distant genetic past of some version of our species, *homo sapiens*, a Plato or an Einstein of that time observed that in their small band of hunting comrades, there was one or two, or more, men who behaved differently from most others, who were erratic and unpredictable and who insisted on certain forms of special behavior that could complicate the dynamics of the hunt. We can imagine also a similar experience among the women of that small community who watched bemused at the curious inattention one of their number toward the recently born unhappy infant slung in an animal skin around her body.

In time, such complications from the observed differences in temperament, dependability, and the nuances of social unity among both men and women would have led to some primitive attempts by members of the band to answer the questions "What is it with Grog?" or ". . . with Ooma?" In time, through the search for a *reasonable* explanation for observed phenomena, a story would emerge. Some such a seed we can imagine giving rise to the Narcissus myth.

The story of Narcissus has had a long gestation on the way to its present form. In its profound psychological depths, it is primarily a story of the vicissitudes of the youth of both genders as they begin to awaken to a personal, ego-based identity based on reflections in the *mirrors* held up to them by their interactions with various caregivers in their *outer world*. An appropriate image is that of the seedling plant set in the earth fully prepared for it by mature and knowing gardeners and nurtured toward the fullest expression of its unique being.

Whatever the origins of the empirical discovery of wounded and dysfunctional humans and the speculations that grew gradually out of such observations—and of these we can have no sure knowledge—it is clear that a coherent mythic account of what we now call narcissistic personality disorder had appeared in the Hellenistic culture of the first century in the eastern Mediterranean area with its roots reaching much further into the past. This was the story of Narcissus the Hunter.

The version of the myth of Narcissus usually cited in our experience is the one given by the Roman poet Ovid in Book III of his *Metamorphoses*, lines 339 et seq. We must imagine that ancient curiosity and speculation had long before begun to work through and generate origin narratives when Mind, in its mythopoeic form, first began to reflect on its experiences in human community.

A critical feature of mythopoesy is that its symbolic products should not, indeed cannot, be judged by standards that are uniquely rational and objective. For instance, Narcissus was the offspring of a union of two minor deities in the Greek pantheon, both of the nature of water. Is he to be understood as a demigod himself, or even as one of the *nephilim* (giants who first populated the earth, took human women as wives and created a race of heroic humans)? Or, because of his watery, i.e. undifferentiated parentage, perhaps he should be understood as a life originating not in the full material ordinariness of a human existence but in its primeval, pleromatic, archetypal form? Or, is he simply an inordinately handsome youth with a problem in forming relationships? Perhaps all of these are true. Let the reader judge where, in this wide spectrum of psychological symbolism around the theme of relationship, we enter and are instructed about the dynamics of human connection that work, or do not work, for contemporary men and women.

Here, in its Ovidian form is the myth of Narcissus with its full *dramatis personae*, and it begins with a rape [all quotations of Ovid herein are from the translation of Brookes More (1922, rev. 1978]. Classical translations are kinder and begin by telling of how the water nymph (Naiad) Liriope was seized in the embrace of the river god Cephissus and *ravished*, whereupon their child Narcissus was conceived. This kind of encounter that implies force or *overcoming*, was not at all uncommon in the annals of the gods and goddesses (think of Zeus, who became a swan before raping Leda and impregnating her).

It remains a question of how we are to integrate the circumstance of Narcissus' origin, if at all, into a contemporary, particularly a Jungian, understanding of disorders of personality. We know little of the relationship of Narcissus to his sire, if indeed there was any to speak of. We first meet the exceptionally beautiful youth in Ovid's account when he is 15 years old. He and his anxious mother, who wants to know whether her child "might attain a ripe old age," call on the seer Tiresias for his opinion. His answer is both cryptic and insightful: "If he but fail to recognize himself, a long life he may have." The text continues:

> . . . so, frivolous the prophet's words appeared; and yet the event, the manner of his death, the strange delusion of his frenzied love, confirmed it.

Some five years passed during which Narcissus became the love object of more than a few young women and men, but "none gained his favor," as Ovid tells us, adding, "And many a youth, and many a damsel sought to gain his love; but such his mood and spirit and his pride, none gained his favor."

The impression given by Ovid to this point suggests Narcissus failed to make relationships with any of his admirers, male and female, and that this derived from an inflation around his spectacular physical beauty such that he found no one worthy of his love and attention. His "mood, spirit and pride" were such as to drive away all who sought his company.

What we know about infant development tells us that figures with such pronounced resistance to intimate relationship rarely have come to love themselves in a genuine and conscious way; on the contrary, they are likely to have just the opposite feeling from an intuitive conviction that they have become objects of unconscious desire for the gratification of others, something to be consumed rather than actively seen for their own qualities. Their separateness from others is based on a sense of unworthiness and unacceptability that reflects their failure to discover a positive self-love via mirroring of their inherent worth by their caregivers or admirers. Any prideful loftiness of spirit then becomes a defense against the desperate pain of being invisible, that is, of not being seen in an active and affirming way.

It is this searing experience of personal invisibility and inadequacy that comprises the nuclear, i.e., existential, wound of the narcissistic personality disorder. Tiresias, as one who knew life both as a male and a female, might well have uttered his strange prophecy out of an awareness that Narcissus would do much better at life if he had no awareness of this profound disability of relationship that he carried.

Ovid continues his story with an account of the meeting of Narcissus with the nymph Echo (another demigod) who one day *"in the pathless woods loved him and followed him with soft and stealthy tread."*

Echo had earlier offended Hera by helping Zeus cover some of his dalliances with various partners. As a punishment, Hera made Echo able to speak only with the words of other people, repeating fragments of what they had said. Wanting to make her passion for Narcissus known, she had to wait for him to speak and then hope her response would draw him close to her. But, it did not happen.

"One day, when [Echo] observed Narcissus wandering in the pathless woods, she loved him and she followed him, with soft and stealthy tread. The more he followed him the hotter did she burn, as when the flame flares upward from the sulfur on the torch. Oh, how she longed to make her passion known! To plead in soft entreaty! To implore his love!"

Perhaps Aphrodite is the energy in her lustful, body-centered spirit that has entered the scene. Or, perhaps it merely feels that way to a young man who has never experienced his beauty except in its exploitation by others. Then begins a serio-comic exchange where Narcissus, feeling himself being stalked cries, *"Who is there?"* and Echo answers, *"Here! Here!"* then: [Narcissus] *Come here! Avoid me not!"* and [Echo] *". . . Avoid me not!";* [Narcissus] *Oh, let us come together!",* then [Echo}. . . *let us come together!"* And, with that invitation Echo bounds from the woods and races to throw her arms around his neck. Narcissus cringed back: *"Take off your hands! You shall not fold your arms around me. Better death than such a one should ever caress me!"* [Echo} *". . . "Caress me!"*

There is to be no such consummation.

Narcissus flees the nymph's embrace; Echo runs away in sorrow and shame. Echo languishes in grief and *"all her lovely features melt, as if dissolved upon the wafting winds . . . she lies concealed in the wild woods, nor is she ever seen on lonely mountain range; for, though we hear her calling in the hills, 'tis but a voice, a voice that lives, that lives among the hills . . . Thus he deceived the Nymph, and many more, sprung from the mountains or the sparkling waves; and thus he slighted many an amorous youth."* One of the potential lovers so "slighted" lifted his hands in a raging prayer to the Gods that *"So may he himself love, and not gain the thing he loves!"* There is an addendum to the original story that describes this disappointed would-be lover as Ameinias to whom Narcissus gave a sword after rejecting his attentions. Ameinias uttered a prayer for vengeance upon Narcissus then killed himself with the "gift."

This bitter cry was heard by Nemesis, who granted her approval. The full measure of divine retribution for his hubris was about to be poured out upon the beautiful young man. The story pauses, as in the end of a movement in a tragic symphony, with a sustained minor chord breathing a sigh of grief before passing on to its sad denouement.

Nemesis, an avenging divine figure in ancient Greek religion, was also called *Adrasteia* (the "inescapable") or *Rhamnousia* at her sanctuary at Rhamnous, a coastal city in Attica near Marathon. She was the agent of the Gods against those who succumb to hubris (arrogance before the gods). It was she who in her time saw to it that "what goes around comes around." Divine retribution is a major theme in the Hellenic worldview, providing the unifying theme of the tragedies of Sophocles and many other literary works.

The final act of this profound and tragic drama is so poignant and prescient in Ovid's hands that his account is here presented in excerpted form in the translation of Brookes More.

[Line 407] *There was a fountain silver-clear and bright, which neither shepherds nor the wild she-goats, that range the hills, nor any cattle's mouth had touched—its waters were unsullied—birds disturbed it not; nor animals, nor boughs that fall so often from the trees.(...)Here Narcissus, tired of hunting and the heated noon, lay down, attracted by the peaceful solitudes and by the glassy spring. There as he stooped to quench his thirst another thirst increased. While he is drinking he beholds himself reflected in the mirrored pool—and loves; loves an imagined body which contains no substance, for he deems the mirrored shade a thing of life to love. He cannot move, for so he marvels at himself, and lies with countenance unchanged, as if indeed a statue carved of Parian marble. ... All that is lovely in himself he loves, and in his witless way he wants himself(...) And how he kisses the deceitful fount; and how he thrusts his arms to catch the neck that's pictured in the middle of the stream! Yet never may he wreathe his arms around that image of himself. He knows not what he there beholds, but what he sees inflames his longing, and the error that deceives allures his eyes. But why, O foolish boy, so vainly catching at this flitting form? (...) Avert your gaze and you will lose your love, for this that holds your eyes is nothing save the image of yourself reflected back to you. (...)*

Now with his gaze fixed on his mirrored image, not even hunger diverts him. He then beckons to the murmuring forest.

[Line 435] *"Oh, ye aisled wood was ever man in love more fatally than I? (...)Alas, this fatal image wins my love, as I behold it. But I cannot press my arms around the form I see(...)*

Narcissus is puzzled that the image seems to lean toward his embrace but eludes him. *It seems that I could touch him. 'Tis a strange delusion that is keeping us apart. (...)When I extend my loving arms to thee thine also are extended me—thy smiles return my own. When I was weeping, I have seen thy tears, and every sign I make thou dost return; (...) I perceive 'Tis I in thee—I love myself—the flame arises in my breast and burns my heart— what shall I do? ... (...) Grief saps my strength, the sands of life are run, (...)*

but death is not my bane—it ends my woe.—I would not death for this that is my love, as two united in a single soul would die as one."

[Line 474] He spoke; and crazed with love, returned to view the same face in the pool; and as he grieved his tears disturbed the stream, and ripples on the surface, glassy clear, defaced his mirrored form. And thus the youth, when he beheld that lovely shadow go; "Ah whither dost thou fly? Oh, I entreat thee leave me not. Alas, thou cruel boy thus to forsake thy lover(...)"

Narcissus begins to wither away as he cannot disengage from the object of his love.

No vermeil bloom now mingled in the white of his complexion fair; no strength has he, no vigor, nor the comeliness that wrought for love so long: alas, that handsome form by Echo fondly loved may please no more.

[Line 494] But when she saw him in his hapless plight, though angry at his scorn, she only grieved.(...) And as he gazed upon the mirrored pool he said at last, "Ah, youth beloved in vain!" "In vain, in vain!" the spot returned his words; and when he breathed a sad "farewell!" "Farewell!" sighed Echo too. He laid his wearied head, and rested on the verdant grass; and those bright eyes, which had so loved to gaze, entranced, on their own master's beauty, sad Night closed. ...The legend recounts that various mythological creatures mourned the death of Narcissus and on the spot where he died a sweet, golden and white flower grew.

In the version of the tale by Pausanias, a travel writer who lived in the early second century, about 150 years after Ovid wrote in 4 Cd.E., Narcissus is made to fall into a passionate love of his twin sister, introducing into the pathology of the tale the notion of incest. Pausanias thought it "foolish" to think that anyone could fall in love with his own reflection and not be immediately aware, a rather rationalistic unraveling of the oddities of Ovid's tale in the guise of "fixing" it with the figure of a sister in place of the mirroring pool.

I have already noted above that the life story of Narcissus in the tale begins with a rape. This is rarely mentioned in the literature save for the notice also taken by Schwartz-Salant in his deeply illuminating treatment of the Narcissus story [Schwartz Salant, Nathan, *Narcissism and Character Transformation*, Inner City Books, Toronto, 1982, p, 76]. Both these phenomena involve highly disturbed enactments of critical failures in a personality to construct healthy self- and other-affirming relationships, which is strongly indicative of narcissistic character distortions. The body of the Narcissus myth, of course, confirms this connection in its central character.

To follow this idea a bit further, it is valuable to read Jung on the archetype of incest in his 1946 book *The Psychology of the Transference* (now published in CW 16, p. 218). There he writes: "*Incest symbolizes union with one's own being, it means individuation or becoming a self, and, because* this is so vitally important, it exerts an unholy fascination—not, perhaps as a crude reality, but certainly as a psychic process controlled by the unconscious . . . **Incest is simply the union of like with like** (emphasis added), which is the next stage in the development of the primitive idea of self-fertilization."

In speaking of the image of the King and Queen in Figure 2 of the **Rosarium Philosophorum**, Jung writes: . . . (CW 16, p. 217) *the crucial contact of left hands points to something "sinister," illegitimate, morganatic, emotionally instinctive, i.e., the fatal touch of incest and its perverse" fascination. At the same time the intervention of the Holy Ghost reveals the hidden meaning of the incest, whether of brother and sister or of mother and son as a repulsive symbol for the* **unio mystica** *(emphasis added).*

The child or youth who is subject to what I have labeled "colonization"—that is, a process of neurotic predation by parents or other adults who fail to provide healthy mirroring for the child, but use the child for their own gratification and emotional sustenance—experiences growing feelings of envy and hatred now directed at himself or herself. Schwartz-Salant (loc.cit., p. 48) remarks that *"It is against this feeling of being envied and hated that the narcissistic character erects defenses. The resultant ego-Self structure can be characterized as both a regressive fusion product and as developmentally retarded."*

To return to the Narcissus myth, the psychodynamics of incest as well as the psychic "theft of goods" in the personality constitute devastating wounds in the psyche of the child. We see all the more sharply outlined the meaning in the exaggerated admiration of the beauty of Narcissus. It is as if all who see him cannot wait, or forbear, to get for the dry wells of their own needy souls some nourishment from his own overflowing store.

The classic myth of Narcissus has proven to be an influential and enduring source of resonant themes and images in Western culture. It has shown such durability through the way it portrays the unique human process of attempting to achieve an identity through a sense of *personal Being* in a complex world, coming to grips with the acute pain of having failed to do so, and gaining some understanding of what things obstruct this task. The creative artists of every period have returned to beautiful Narcissus and his tragic fate again and again in mythopoeic imagery rich in visions of pain and transformation. We look at some of these in the next Section.

The Narcissus Myth in Western Culture Through Time

Creative artists of every ilk have been fascinated by the Narcissus myth, probably from the moment when Ovid laid it down with such power and grace in the first century C.E. Within relatively modern times, the myth has had a well-developed iconography in painting and sculpture as well as in various forms of literature. Only a few of these are presented here. A significant source in this general subject area is the work of the Scandinavian author Louise Vinge in the book *The Narcissus Theme in Western European Literature Up to the Early 19th Century*, 1967, Lund: Gleerups.

The Italian humanist, author, artist, architect, and poet Leon Battista Alberti (1404-72), a genuine Renaissance man remarked: *"... I say among my friends that Narcissus who was changed into a flower, according to the poets, was the inventor of painting. Since painting is already the flower of every art, the story of Narcissus is most to the point. What else can you call painting but a similar embracing with art of what is presented on the surface of the water in the fountain?"*

> ~ *Leon Battista Alberti (1404-72) [On Painting.*
> Penguin Classics. 1972. ISBN 978-0-14-043331-9.]

Other painters of note who found inspiration in the story of Narcissus include Caravaggio, whose 1599 painting "Narcissus" showed the youth in a darkly dramatic pose bending over the surface of the pool, eye rapt in its depths. His contemporary Nicolas Poussin, (1594-1665) produced a work, "Echo and Narcissus" (c. 1630) much more traditional and classicizing than Caravaggio's. In continuing to explore the archetypal theme, J.M.W. Turner (1775-1851) produced a new work in 1804, "Narcissus and Echo," that showed human figures dwarfed in a dark landscape around a pool under a looming mountain range.

Revealing a new vision of the myth, Salvador Dali exhibited his "Metamorphosis of Narcissus" in 1937 (fig. below). Narcissus was pictured kneeling at the pool somewhat as in the painting of Caravaggio but in surrealistic fashion with symbolic objects in a landscape. This surrealistic image was Dali's first painting to be made entirely in accordance with the paranoiac critical method, which the artist described as a "spontaneous method of irrational knowledge, based on the critical-interpretative association of the phenomena of delirium" (*The Conquest of the Irrational*, in *The Secret Life of Salvador Dalí*, New York 1942).

Dalí used a meticulous technique that he described as hand-painted color photography to represent with hallucinatory effect the transformation of Narcissus, kneeling in the pool, into the hand holding the egg and flower. Narcissus as he was before his transformation is seen posing in the background. The play with "double images" came from Dalí's fascination with hallucination and delusion. The painting is now in the collection of the Tate Museum in London. The image can be seen on the Internet, **The Metamorphosis of Narcissus** (Salvador Dali, 1937) www.tate.org.uk/art/artworks/dali-metamorphosis-of-narcissus-t02343

In describing the history of this work, the Tate Museum includes this remark: *When he met Sigmund Freud in London in 1938, Dalí took this* picture with him as an example of his work, as well as a magazine containing an article he had written on paranoia. Freud wrote the following day to Stefan Zweig, who had introduced them, that "it would be very interesting to explore analytically the growth of a picture like this." [www.tate.org.uk/art/artworks/dali-metamorphosis-of-narcissus-t02343/text-summary].

A more extensive examination of the interaction of mythology with modern art can be found here: Loreti, Silvia, *Modern Narcissus: the lingering reflections of myth in modern art*. Papers of Surrealism, 9. pp. 1-29. ISSN 1750-1954 (2011).

In the field of literature, much notice has been taken of Stendhal's (Marie-Henri Beyle) novel *The Red and The Black* (1830) in particular because of his acute analysis of his characters' psychology, a quality that has caused him to be considered the creator of the psychological novel. In the book, Mathilde de la Mole, the bored daughter of a marquis, is in emotional conflict between her romantic attraction to Julien Sorel, a social and political *naïf*, for his appealing personal and intellectual qualities, and her distaste at the prospect of a sexual liaison with a lower-class man. Twice, she seduces and then rejects him. He is in despair, filled with self-doubt and happy only with having won her over her other more socially desirable companions.

Mathilde has been seen as a classic narcissist who looks at herself only and sees the protagonist and potential lover Julien "as the hero of her dreams and not yourself as you really are." A modern reader might well conclude from Stendhal's description of the tangled, exploitative, and self-serving personal relationships of his characters in the milieu of early 19th-century French society that it was difficult for sincerity of affection to gain foothold, that many could feel that they were projected constructions of other persons and "not seen as who they really were."

Herman Melville alludes to the myth of Narcissus in *Moby Dick*, in which Ishmael explains the myth as "the key to it all," referring to the theme of discovering the essence of Truth through experience of the physical world.

In the realm of poetry, there has been enduring resonance with the antique version of the Narcissus myth. Chaucer and Shakespeare both read and made use of Ovid and borrowed from his themes, the former in the tale of *Pyramus and Thisbe* and the latter in his first long play, *Titus Andronicus*.

The 17th century saw an important upswing in interest in classical mythology, partly through the availability of the work of Ovid in new translations. John Milton, the great English poet of the period, makes the Ovidian story of Narcissus an important element in his epic work *Paradise Lost* (1667).

In a more nearly contemporary vein, Rainer Maria Rilke (1875-1926), thought by some to be the most significant poet of mystical transformation, of spiritual search, of the twentieth century, created a small gem in his poem "Narcissus":

> Encircled by her arms as by a shell,
> she hears her being murmur,
> while forever he endures
> the outrage of his too pure
> image...
>
> Wistfully following their example,
> nature re-enters herself;
> contemplating its own sap, the flower
> becomes too soft, and the boulder hardens...
>
> It's the return of all desire that enters
> toward all life embracing itself from afar...
> Where does it fall? Under the dwindling
> Surface, does it hope to renew a centre?

Seamus Heaney (1939-2013) reflects in "Personal Helicon" on a childhood interest in wells and pools ("As a child, they could not keep me from wells") and ends with the mature poet's persistent search for a reflective surface ("Now, to pry into roots, to finger slime, To stare, big-eyed Narcissus, into some spring, Is beneath all adult dignity. I rhyme to see myself, to set the darkness echoing.")

The acclaimed English poet Ted Hughes created in 1997 a highly praised translation of 24 tales from Ovid's *Metamorphoses*. Some of these, including the Narcissus myth, were later reshaped in versified dramatic form and presented in a world premiere in 1999. Hughes wrote, in a commentary on these adaptations: "*Different aspects of [Ovid's] poem continued to fascinate Western culture, saturating literature and art. And by now, many of the stories seem inseparable from our unconscious imaginative life . . . The act of metamorphosis, which at some point touches each of the tales, operates as the symbolic guarantee that the passion has become mythic, has achieved the unendurable intensity that lifts the whole episode onto the supernatural or divine plane.*" [*Ted Hughes's Tales from Ovid*, adapted by Tim Supple and Simon Reade, Faber & Faber, London, 1997]

In the area of musical composition, the American choral composer Morten Lauridsen created a very popular short work titled "Dirait-on" (". . . So they say" [listen on YouTube]). The second stanza of the work, though addressed to a Rose, clearly invokes the Narcissus story (*It is your own center that you caress, Your own reflection gives you light, and in this way, you show us how Narcissus is redeemed.*). Among "pop" artists, a variety of bands, including Genesis, Tool, The Like and Threshhold have made allusion to the Narcissus theme.

The profound allusions in Western culture to the Narcissus myth across a wide spectrum of artistic creativity, including creative work in the so-called "popular" realm, make it clear that this theme of human endeavor for being, for relationship with self and others, for experience of transformation, runs through history like an eternally resonant, archetypal motif. We cannot escape the tragic aspects of living in a field of splitness and the phenomenal opposites like multiple Narcissi trying to find, and inhabit, our true identity.

What is the fate of the archetypal experience of identity formation in an age like ours when technical aspects of our civilization create a rapidly shifting ground for psychic development, for, in the words of Bishop Irenaeus of Lyon in the first century, *"becoming that which we already are"*? Dealing in understanding, compassion and empathy with the devastation of narcissistic wounding has not been a defining achievement of Western culture. What are the accommodations that we must make as well as those we mustn't make in order to flourish in the Digital Age, when the Internet spins around us its web of escalating connectedness and interactivity? Good? Not good? Both? These kinds of questions we take up in the next Section.

Narcissus on Line: Personal Spirit in the Age of Radical Connectivity

On or about December 1910, human character changed...
The change was not sudden and definite ... but a change
there was.

~ Virginia Woolf, *Mr. Bennett and*
Mrs Brown (Essay, 1923)

Virginia Woolf's serious joke that "on or about December
1910, human character changed" was a hundred years
premature. Human character changed on or about
December 2010, when everyone it seemed, started
carrying a smartphone.

~ Edward Mendelson, *In the Depths of the Digital Age,*
(Essay, 2016, New York Review of Books, 23 June 2016)

Ms. Woolf's "serious joke" and Mr. Mendelson's riposte seem to reflect the historical perception of acute observers that every so often, the time that we call our own has, in fact, suddenly gone, as in a whirlwind. We are left to contemplate a profoundly changed scene when new ontological and epistemological flags fly over the landscape—it is not as it once was.

It was the great Spanish liberal philosopher and essayist Jose Ortega y Gasset (1883-1955) who spoke directly and with wisdom about these matters when he said, for example, *"I am I and my circumstances"* ("*Yo soy yo y mi circunstancia.*"). "The World" and its "circumstances" continually approach and recede, and we remain as a kind of evidence of its passage. Heraclitus of Ionia already knew this in the sixth and fifth centuries BCE) in declaring *"panta rhei"* ("everything flows").

There can hardly be a doubt that with the sudden, even explosive, digitalization of the world and the virtually universal connectivity of the Internet, we have been thrust into a new age that asks, and gives, a new standpoint and unlimited new possibility for modes of human relationship. A great gift, to be sure—but what does it take away and what hides in its Shadow? Has human character changed, again? And how may the new world interact with the nature, dynamics, and persistence of the phenomena of narcissistic character disorders and the acquisition of personal identity? It will take decades to find good, albeit provisional, answers to these questions. In the meantime, we can reflect on the nature of connection and reflection in a time when an individual can speak with, and share perceptions and values, in principle, with every person on the planet.

Since the revolutionizing events of the Enlightenment of the 17th and 18th centuries in the West, the material elements of a culture have been in rapid flux. The creative potential of individuals and the collectives they form have been prodigious in transforming Western and planetary life with material novelty, with new wealth, power, almost every kind of increase in ease of life. In this barrage of new things, it has been rare that there has been a general awareness of the reality of the Shadow or many questions asked about the dark aspects of so much brilliant transformation of life for the better. We can, and must, ask such questions about any new technology, sparing none, if we are not to be engulfed by what we do not know and thus are unprepared to question. As the stream of new human beings pours into the world in a swelling tide, does the Digital Age offer the prospect that these humans will find more and more, increasingly effective ways of finding the mirrors that body/psyche requires for healthy and stable development of personality? If yes, we can celebrate; if not, it is time to review the process of ego development in self-formation.

The archetypal image of the reflecting surface, the Mirror, is central in mythopoeic representations of the process of self-formation, the acquisition of a relatively steady and durable version of Ortega's "I." The human embodiment of "mirror" quality is shown vividly in an iconic photo in Schwart-Salant's "Narcissism and Character Transformation" (1982, p. 47). I have shown this image for near 30 years to virtually every person who has sat in my consulting room. I regard it as an imagistic course of study in the care of the Soul. It has been relevant, even a compulsion of mine, since the majority of analysands I have seen impress me with evidence of their narcissistic wounding.

The image is of a "mothering person" (her identity is not disclosed) who holds an infant of only a few months of age, its left hand enveloping her right thumb, her left hand supporting its body, while her smiling face, slightly elevated and rich with welcome and admiration, is gazing directly into its eyes. The infant is rapt, and "wrapped-in-Mother," in joy and the radiant bliss of recognition and affirmation of its being, or so it seems to this observer.

When I ask the viewer, "What is she seeing? And, what is it seeing?" only a few will say, "she sees the child, and it sees *itself*." The text on this page remarks: "*Unless this mirroring takes place, a child will not readily have the inner ground for development. All change will be fraught with anxiety and fear, and its sense of identity will be chronically diffuse.*" Is the ubiquitous practice of making a "selfie" (it has even created a small subtechnology of rods and extensions to maintain control while holding the camera at arm's length) an unconscious effort to summon the reflecting "face" to bear witness to our lives and beauty? Will that work, and will it portend an Age of Increase of healthy, intact psyches? We do not know at this moment.

In almost any public place that I now frequent, I see clumps of people, a family at dinner, students sitting on grass park lawns, patrons of a cinema sitting and waiting for the film, all hunched forward so as to make a chiropractor weep, the magic screen cupped in both hands, and thumbs either poised over the reflecting "mirror" or rapidly tapping out a response. In groups where one might expect the surrounding beings to offer satisfying mirroring in conversation, mutual acknowledgement and affirmation, exchange of loving attention, it is the machine that comforts, acknowledges the holder, and comforts anxieties that the world imposes. No one looks up to see the faces; and yes, the "selfies" abound.

What do these scenes portend? Is this some ominous sketch of a future when "identity" pours in *via* digital magic while human connection languishes? Has a collective fear been ignited that unless there is a constant renewal of contact with "another," one will not be seen and simply fade into abstraction, like Echo and Narcissus, with no flower left behind to mark us? On the contrary, there is a prospect that extension of one's personality further into the world can generate a healthy sense of self, a more effective use of talents, a deeper and more balanced ego consciousness.

Perhaps we are witnessing merely the early days of a technological romance that will flame out, and a "real-time" equilibrium of human attention and interaction will be restored. What is certain is that careful thought at every level and through every form of inquiry in the culture must happen. There is evidence this discrimination of Light and Shadow is already underway.

In an online monograph, the authors Janna Anderson and Lee Rainie (find at: www.pewinternet.org/2014/03/11/digital-life-in-2025/) report conclusions of some 2,500 experts and technology builders and list 15 *Theses About the Digital Future*. Eight of these are described as "hopeful," six as "concerned," and one as "neutral." The reader is referred to the paper for a full listing. Only one of each is given here, with my comments in brackets.

> » **Hopeful**—The spread of the Internet will enhance global connectivity that fosters more planetary relationships and less ignorance
>
> *[How will this benefit those with narcissistic disorders already well-developed? Could it repair damaged self-images?]*
>
> » **Negative**—People will continue, sometimes grudgingly, to make trade-offs favoring convenience and perceived immediate gains over privacy; and privacy will be something only the upscale will enjoy.
>
> *[This already seems to be happening in its early stages.]*
>
> » **Neutral**—Foresight and accurate predictions can make a difference; "The best way to predict the future is to invent it."
>
> *[Invention of a future that we want implies a socially conscious and psychologically astute insight that we do not have now.]*

It is exciting to be in this current historical epoch when the arc of technical and social change is rising steeply, even as it may outpace the increase of our collective consciousness. Even while we celebrate human genius and accomplishment, I feel drawn again to another kind of genius, that I find "spread upon the world—although men cannot see it"—manifest in the poetry of Rainer Maria Rilke.

He wrote about Love in a letter to a young poet who had written a love poem, and his words remain powerful and penetrating more than 100 years later as he imagines a new kind of love in the world:

> "And this more human love (that will fulfill itself, infinitely considerate and gentle, and kind and clear in binding and releasing) will resemble that which we are preparing with struggle and toil, the love that consists in this, that two solitudes protect and border and salute each other." ["Letters to a Young Poet" (1934), No. 7 (1904)] This is the mirroring Love that sees us as we are with empathy and compassion and lets us see and own ourselves in its light. It is something that neither Echo and Narcissus nor their psychic heirs of our own time, could achieve.

Alden Josey, PhD, had a successful career of 27 years as a research chemist and manager that included publication of 23 technical papers and seven patents. Following his retirement, he completed training at the C.G. Jung Institute for Analytical Psychology in Zürich and has lectured widely in this country and abroad on various topics. He is a Member Emeritus of the Philadelphia Association of Jungian Analysts where he served as past President, Director of Training, and Director of Admissions.

Narcissism in Our Collective Home, Our American Culture

BY NANCY SWIFT FURLOTTI, PhD

Introduction

Our early relationships are fundamental to the development of our personalities. They determine whether or not we feel secure and resilient, able to embody the compassion and empathy that leads to sustaining and healthy relationships with others. These primary relationships have a huge impact on how we affect others, how we live our lives, and the footprint we leave on this planet. The narcissistic wound, on the other hand, impedes one's ability to maintain and value healthy relationships with others. Narcissism creates a large group of people who are its victims, suffering in silence and frequently voiceless. They are affected again on a cultural level when the narcissists find their way into positions of power in companies and politics. Here, the rules change for all of us to reflect their need for power and to be seen and appreciated to support their sense of grandiosity. Money is power. The narcissist, who lacks a basic internal sense of security, seeks power through materialism to fill the hole within his psyche. Unfortunately, it is only a temporary fix that leaves the narcissist compulsively seeking attention from others, which is afforded by money, power, materialism, sex, food, drugs, etc. Not only do individuals in relationships with narcissists suffer profoundly from their amorality, but the cultural values of institutions run by narcissists do, too.

We have witnessed a slow degradation of moral values in our country that favors money over people. Companies are beholden to the stockholders and no longer accountable to the community nor concerned for what is right for humanity. An example is pharmaceutical companies that have shifted from a long-standing focus on helping people with their products, to maximizing profits. This shift is consistent with narcissistic behavior. We are seeing the result of this phenomenon play out in the 2016 political race. This shift in values is at the core of why many find themselves dissatisfied with the state of our country. Many complain that their voices are not heard by politicians, their concerns about equitable pay and decent jobs, their families' health and well-being are ignored while the economy and political agendas move along in the directions supported by the interests of big business. Business interests are more important than people.

Power, advantage, and wealth supersede relationship. A powerful example of this is the drinking water crisis in Flint, Michigan, where saving money became more important than the health of the community. People are emerging from their complacency and beginning to voice their concerns with increasingly louder objections.

How Does Individual Narcissism Affect the Collective?

Relationships carry the potential to offer us tender support and security or to hurt us with the rage of uncontrollable affects. Many of us live with these early wounds that are then passed onto to our children, our loved ones, and our friends. The feelings of fear, sadness, insecurity, and inadequacy become intolerable to bear for both the narcissist and his victim. Instead, these affects are deposited into the unconscious pool, called the shadow, of both the individual and the larger collective of our country. Individual patterns become cultural patterns. This shadow contains all that is rejected, abandoned, pushed away in us. As it falls into the collective shadow, it contains everything that is the antithesis of how we consciously think of ourselves as Americans living in the land of opportunity. Consistent with the prevailing American myth, we describe ourselves as strong, independent survivors who work hard, are creative, and are able to better our lives with each generation. The shadow, on the other hand then, represents all that is weak, a failure, lazy, unimaginative, and spiraling down into helplessness and neediness. What is also there is rage at perceived inequity and envy for what one does not have, yet sees in the other. People and groups who are different become easy targets as an outlet for this rage.

We discard all our insecurities together into this collective pool and then try to ignore it. As the economic situation becomes more difficult, the shadow grows, and it simmers dangerously beneath the surface until the pressure gets too great and it blows out in destructive ways such as overt racism, sexism, riots, shootings, wars, corruption, manipulation, and fraud. Over time, it becomes like a volcano that, when punctured, releases an explosion of affect. Every one of us gets charred by the heat and is then forced to pay attention to what we have collectively created. We can decide to allow the raw instincts of anger and envy to take over, much like in the narcissistic individual, or we can find our way to begin dialogue with others, to reach out for relationships to find ways to address problems and imagine solutions.

As in a narcissistic relationship when the victim has been silenced for years, it is easier to unleash one's rage than confront the powerful and demeaning "other" directly. This is true for us politically, as well. So many voices in our country have been silenced and ignored for a very long time. People are angry and want to be seen and heard. They want to be a significant and vital part of the workings of our country, not left behind, ignored, and disdained. But, unfortunately, that is precisely how the narcissistic complex works both for the individual and the collective in our own country. Understanding what it looks like in the individual helps us to see the same pattern on a larger scale.

Narcissism is a fusing of the ego, i.e. one's sense of identity, with the positive side of the greater Self, which represents the wholeness of the unconscious, its animating life force. The negative side of the greater Self, containing destructive and negative forces, remains in the shadow, unseen and unconscious. We know that what remains unconscious is expressed in uncontrollable and unpredictable ways against others and against the ego. The wounded and debilitated ego cannot grant conscious awareness to the dominance of the Self. As C.G. Jung said, "The experience of the Self is always a defeat for the ego" (Jung, 1976, p. 546/ CW vol. 14 par. 778). Without connection to the unconscious and the wholeness represented by the Self, everything becomes black or white, much like the saying, "You are either with me or against me." There is no in-between. Empathy and compassion are emotions that reside in that in-between space, and here they are not available. Things, including people, are just concrete objects to be used. While the narcissist remains identified or fused with the positive side of the Self, all this power is co-opted by him. The dark side is pushed away. Any chance for spirituality becomes repulsive and terrifying because it means allowing the separate, omnipotent Self into one's life. Stepping into relationship with the Self creates an "I thou" relationship, which means giving over control to something more powerful, and that is exactly what the narcissist cannot allow to happen. Without this "I thou" or ego-self relationship, there is a loss of access to the life-giving symbols of the unconscious that allow us to reanimate and recreate our world. We see these symbols in our dreams, for example, and they animate our living myths, the stories that give our lives meaning. We change and become more conscious through the movement of these symbols in our inner world. Without them, we stagnate and ossify.

The weak, insecure ego is always at great risk of being overwhelmed by the destructive forces of the unconscious. Instead, these forces are frequently discharged outward onto other people, groups, or objects. The narcissists' persona helps keep these forces in check to a small extent while in public, but the anger, envy, the need for control, and the grandiose/exhibitionism that satisfies the ego's thirst for bolstering itself up by tearing others down is ever-present. The shadow of wild, uncontrollable emotions from the negative side of the Self cannot remain beneath the insufficient mask of any persona for very long.

Narcissists describe themselves as smarter, more successful, more charismatic, more everything than everyone else. No one can tell them what to do, and they don't ask for advice because they rely only on themselves. They may seem as if they change or become more humble, but they don't. They know their perceived humility is a temporary game to arrive at some benefit for them. This game is played by the narcissist's persona, which is like an ever-changing chameleon, like Woody Allen's portrayal of the lead character in his movie "Zelig," who intuitively knows exactly how to elicit the response he wants and takes on the power of those around him. Narcissists are snake oil salesmen, full of charisma and charm. One easily falls for the shiny glitter that sparkles all around them as they perform their magic, making one think their charm will rub off. But just as quickly as this false hero/savior appears, he will disappear and leave a dark, smelly mess in his wake as he shifts from Dr. Jekyll to Mr. Hyde. Narcissists are not differentiated individuals but instead are driven by the "narcissistic complex" that reflects the archetypal pattern underlying the pathology. They exhibit predictable behavior typical of the complex.

Recognizing that individual pathologies are microcosms of the larger collective allows us to begin to understand why our culture functions as it does. Our country can be likened to a family with many diverse members and viewpoints, while other countries, like other families, have different cultures, different religions, different ideals and dreams. When we as individuals haven't come to terms with our own inner diversity, being able to accept the whole of who we are, and when we have not developed the inner strength and flexibility to accept the "other," we can be sure our country hasn't either. We see the effects of narcissism on the nuclear family. The effects are the same in the larger culture.

It is also interesting that the number of people on the autistic scale is increasing exponentially. The reasons why may be quite tragic—it might be toxins in our environment. The key feature in this disorder is self-focus and lack of interest in relationship. This and narcissism seem like two sides of a coin, both dysfunctional in different ways but both with relationship problems. The person on the autistic scale will not be interested in mirroring the narcissist, though. There is always a counteraction to every action, and this may reflect one way the opposites are playing out psychologically in the collective.

Our Collective Shadow Is Leaking out of its Vessel

What is our cultural shadow? We can surmise what it is from the positive side of our American myth. We think of ourselves as hardworking, creative, fiercely independent, and self-sufficient. If we work hard enough, we can improve our lives. The flip side would represent the shadow, which is a fear of being inferior, weak, and powerless. It is this side that is negatively expressed in racism, sexism, violence, and envy toward the other as individuals, as groups or foreign countries. It is generally held in check by ethical and moral codes of behavior, but as the social fabric continues to weaken, more hostility erupts into our so-called civilized world.

There was a long period of time when most of us were contained by religious beliefs in seemingly safe, cohesive communities of like-minded people. The dogma and the group's underlying myths contained symbols that were potent, giving our lives greater meaning. We believed in a spiritual process, a right way of being and living. Morality and ethics played an important role in our code of behavior as we lived in close relationship to others. We depended upon and cared about each other.

What seems to be universally true, seen from history and the workings of the psyche, is that nothing remains static for long—continuous change is the norm. The symbols that hold our belief systems together lose their potency, leaving us with a lack of meaning. We have no choice but to wait until new living symbols emerge from the psyche and offer us meaning and purpose. Religions change over time, some become mythologies as they lose their potency, their gods relegated to the underworld. As strongly as fundamentalists of all religions try to hold the cracking vessels of their beliefs and communities together during periods of cultural change, they ultimately find it increasingly difficult. Jung spoke about the approach of this inevitable event in our time as being part of the cosmic psychological shift from the age of Pisces to the age of Aquarius. Astrologically, it will take many years to complete this transition. Evidently, there is a large shift at the end of each astrological age, before the next age settles in. This was true for the shift from Ares to Pisces, for example, where the god of war ruled and colored the world for about 2,000 years with his wide brush of influence. The ruling astrological sign determines the character of the age. During our shift, we are no longer acting as the "metaphorical" fish swimming in water, quite unconscious of the medium in which we swim, but instead we are called upon to become the individual vessels that now contain the water of the unconscious. During the earlier Piscean age, we were psychologically held in the containers of religious organizations as our living myth. In Aquarius we are on our own, acting as our own containers, holding ourselves without the help of religious communities and their dogmas. We are much more on our own.

This shift is reflected in the world today as people feel isolated and alone, finding others on social media sites instead of in community activities, texting instead of talking, spending an inordinate amount of time on their devices rather than in active relationship with others. Our world is becoming more shallow and horizontal as we distract our introversion and introspection with internet-related activities. We are moving into that narrow band of existence inhabited by the narcissist. The chaos that the religious communities held in check is now smoldering just beneath us, and we don't dare dip down into it, unless we have jumped right in by joining a radical group that thrives on the power of chaos and destruction.

Religions serve an important function to help contain and keep the dark forces of chaos at bay. This is done in many ways, not the least of which is to project all the evil, demonic impulses onto a devil or Satan figure. Heaven and hell are seen as two distinct locations, one containing the light while the other contains the dark. Upper-world and under-world represent the same concepts. Whatever names are given to these realms, they are containers for humans to hold the wild, titanic and demonic forces of the unconscious, keeping them safely away from affecting or taking control of us. Without these collective containers, we more easily become the victims of the collective shadow.

As the system of religious belief that was put in place thousands of years ago by the rich and intuitive imagination of the human psyche continues to break, we as individuals find ourselves less and less contained by anything. We have moved into a postmodern world where anything goes. There are no boundaries. We see what happens to a baby with no containment: It quickly decompensates and experiences trauma. We are in a tough situation because we don't yet know how to contain the many instinctual, chaotic forces within ourselves, to make that transition to being our own "water-carrier." Instead, out of fear we harken back to olden times, when America was Great, when whites ruled the world, when there was security in hard work and jobs, when our natural resources were plentiful and available for our every whim, in other words, when our God ruled the world and some of us participated in his grace.

How Does Technology Contribute to Our Collective Plight?

Wars have spawned the development of technology that civilian populations have taken advantage of with enthusiasm and a view toward the future. I am reminded of the hopeful push in the 1950s to modernize the home with electric appliances and all sorts of new devises that promised to make life easier and free up time for other activities. Telephones, televisions, a car in every garage, the promise of everyone being able to own a home and children being better off than their parents. The prevailing American myth was one of upward mobility and optimism for all. That myth has pushed us on and upward to greater and greater technological developments where we now find ourselves slaves to the constant demand for updates on all our devices, a movement from obsolescence to new technology that runs at a pace never before seen. In the process, many jobs have disappeared that don't support this "new economy." People have been left behind with no way to catch up. A huge disparity has been created in our country not unlike the period of the great industrialists, nicknamed the Robber Barons, of the late 19th century. "Robber Baron was a term applied to a businessman who engaged in unethical and monopolistic practices, wielded widespread political influence, and amassed enormous wealth" (history1800s.about.com, 6/12/16).

As technology continues to progress, benefiting certain classes of people more than others, the disparity will grow even wider. Anger and envy will be unstoppable, along with the fear of what is on the horizon in the form of our changing and degraded environment, wars, migrations, and newer technology that will continue to take over for humans. Before long, humans will not be able to keep up with the independent, self-creating robots and bioengineered organisms that are the spawn of the shadow side of our defunct cultural myth. We are becoming its prisoners. This realization lingers in the shadow and causes tremendous anxiety and uncertainty in all areas of our culture. Rightly so, as there seems to be a widening gap between what we are capable of creating with technology, specifically powerful weapons to kill, and our moral and social evolution as individuals and as a culture to understand the implications of these developments (Thomas Friedman, New York Times, Op-ed, 6-15-16).

The rules have changed. The economy seems to be carrying the lightning rod for anger right now. Certain jobs are gone forever, there is no longer the same stability or certainty of the past 100 years, and people are rightly insecure. The level of economic and political frustration at a system that seems to have shifted to benefit the elite at the expense of everyone else is very high, resulting in an upsurge of anger against this status quo. Charles Homans wrote an interesting article called 'The End of the American Dream." He says:

> The aspirational idea of the middle class spoke to the notion that even if Americans were in various stages of prosperity, they were all understood to be heading in the same general direction. But what happens when that's no longer true? On one end of the "middle class" spectrum is a dream inexorably receding from view; on the other is a pair of socioeconomic blinders obscuring the harsher economic realities of those further down the scale. "The upper middle class are surprised by the rise of Trump," Reeves told me. "The actual middle class are surprised we're surprised. (New York Times Magazine, May 1, 2016)

Without our sustaining cultural myth, we are faced with the question, "Which God now rules our world?" Whatever God that is seems to now show a very dark side, full of destruction, racism, terrorism, and hate. Indeed, it seems the dark side of God has been released and roams freely. Psychologically, this is the dark side of the Self, the collective shadow. People are scared, and rightly so. As Jung said in his interview with Dr. Richard Evans in 1957: "The world hangs by a thin thread, and that is the psyche of man. Suppose certain fellows in Moscow lose their nerve or their common sense for a bit, then the whole world is in fire and flames... We are the great danger. The psyche is the great danger" (Jung, C. G. *Jung Speaking*, 1977, p. 303). Using the dangers of the Cold War as an example, Jung points out how, in our ignorance of the destructive forces in the unconscious, we are capable of destroying human life. It is up to us to direct our future consciously or to defer to the dark passions that have been let loose out of the collective unconscious. The only solution we have is greater consciousness, seeking to recover our inner sense of morality and come together as a community to look after each other in mutual relationships. The projection of our own fears and inferiorities onto others, the near other and the distant other—in other words, our neighbors or the strangers from across the seas—must stop. It feels good to get rid of one's own hated parts, but in so doing we are left split from the potential for real relationship and become as dangerous as the narcissist.

One wants to say, "I had nothing to do with the changing values; it was the bankers, the politicians, the hedge fund managers, or CEOs." But the truth is that each and every one of us has to take a bit of responsibility for this happening to our culture. We are all intrinsic and important to the functioning of our country, whether we feel so or not. Inviting the devil into our home in the form of a narcissist to ostensibly lead us back to when America was "great" is not the answer. Pushed by the collective shadow and motivated by self-serving grandiosity, that would only lead to destruction, a disassembling of all that is established and currently contains us. Until we carefully create a new container to hold our new myth, we need to proceed with caution through the transition. We saw what happened in our Civil War, in World War I, World War II, and the Vietnam War, to name a few. Yet, we easily forget. It is dangerous to forget the shadow that resides right below the surface, ready to twist life into a different and unhealthy form.

The Narcissist in Our Collective Home

Narcissists live close to this shadow, in mortal fear of it destroying them. They are clever at dispensing it to others and pointing it out to us, saying everything we don't dare say out of our own fears and insecurities. Most people keep these accusatory thoughts to themselves, their fears, hatred toward change and differences. It can be a relief for those who harbor accusatory anger, though, when someone else disparages the "other," e.g., Mexicans, Muslims, environmentalists, hedge fund managers, bankers. In the past, the targets have been blacks, Asians, Poles, Irish, Italians. Jews are always at the top of the racist's list. It seems new groups of immigrants arriving on our shores have to pass through this initiation of hatred and humiliation until they assimilate. I am reminded of the many Polish jokes that were familiar in my youth. Unfortunately, some of these groups never get removed from the category of "other." During President Obama's two terms, the reality of racism in this country has been ever-present.

Groups of like-minded people find each other, and collectively their voices get louder and carry further. Individuals lose their own voice and instead chant the group mantra. Mass mentality results in everyone falling to the lowest common denominator. In groups we do what we would never do on our own. Examples of this are the increasing brutality of Hitler's and Mussolini's fascist parties. Outbreaks of violence have not been uncommon at political rallies during this election cycle, encouraged by the narcissistic rage present in the politicians.

We are taken by surprise by the narcissist because he is so good at changing colors according to the situation to maximize mirroring and support for his grandiose self. He easily manipulates and uses the unsuspecting other, not as a person but as an object, used then discarded. This happens before we even realize it, and then the narcissist has morphed again. We are left wondering what just happened, what was real, what was the truth. Everything he says is a manipulation of his audience. He will change his opinions but not necessarily to something better. We, the general public, are left wondering what is honest and what is fantasy. The narcissist moves between the two realms of reality and subjective fantasy with ease. Usually, however, the rest of us make an effort to remain in reality where facts are testable. It is as if we are living in one dimension while the narcissist lives in two and moves between them with ease, leaving us on the sidelines bewildered by what just happened. Mostly, we dismiss the craziness of it and fall back into our belief that the world is rational and consistent. The subjective fantasy world is so far outside any remnant of a myth we thought we lived by that it is hard to accept the reality of the experience.

Jung faced this same phenomenon before World War II, and we know what happened then. Years later, he wrote about Hitler in a paper titled *After the Catastrophe* (Jung, 1970, Vol. 10). He says:

> Clearly these misgivings came much too late; but even so, it is just conceivable that Hitler himself may have had good intentions at first, and only succumbed to the use of the wrong means, or the misuse of his means, in the course of his development... But I should like to emphasize above all that it is part and parcel of the pathological liar's make-up to be plausible. Therefore it is no easy matter, even for experienced people, to form an opinion, particularly, while the plan is still apparently in the idealistic stage. It is then quite impossible to foresee how things are likely to develop and Mr. Chamberlain's "give-it-a-chance" attitude seems to be the only policy. (p. 206, par. 421)

We know, psychologically, destruction can lead to re-creation, but unfortunately without any consciousness, it rarely achieves that goal. One gets lost in the destruction without any possibility for transformation, as was the case in World War II. The National Socialist Party had a complete ego-identification with the dark shadow side of the greater Self, and only destruction followed, millions died. Hitler, an insignificant narcissistic psychopathic man, found himself capable of tapping into the dark, destructive forces of anger and envy present in the collective unconscious of Germany at the time and set fate on a very bleak path. When there is no compassion or empathy, it is easy to kill or harm people because they become "objects." That door is being knocked on again. We see this rage acted out by individual mass murders in our country. They are wounded and dangerously brutal men who act on the inner urgings of their demons against individuals and our society. The result is tragic.

The narcissist candidate is popular because he unleashes the unspeakable, which touches on the collective shadow of our country right now, what people feel but have not dared to verbalize. Morris Dees of the Southern Poverty Law Center, who has spent his life fighting racism and bigotry, describes with shock what he sees in politics right now:

> It is hard to believe that, in 2016, a candidate for president has to be asked whether he disavows the endorsement of a former Klansman. It's even harder to believe that the candidate demurred. Donald Trump finally did, half-heartedly, disavow David Duke, but he has not denounced the racism and violence that has erupted at his campaign rallies where numerous protesters have been punched, kicked, and shoved by his supporters...but the violence is not the only problem. It's also troubling that candidates are naming far-right extremists as campaign advisors—people with long records of hate and bigotry. (Spring 2016 Newsletter)

There are 892 active hate groups in the U.S. right now, and they are being activated by the demagoguery. The political and cultural issues that we are dealing with now are not about the individual, but, as Paul Krugman aptly points out, they are horizontal inequalities affecting racially and culturally defined groups. He is pointing to the collective shadow issues of our country.

The world has changed, and many are rightly unhappy about it, feeling unheard and left behind. They relate to the man who speaks their mind, who has tapped into their collective grief and rage. We see the reality of this collective shadow leak out in police shootings, mass violence of all kinds, hate groups, and racism, while blame for this changing world is projected outward onto the typical shadow targets of narcissists, the many faces of the "other." He has found a voice to support his power aspirations and uses it well. He welcomes the demons to sit beside him, seductively and powerfully, drawing others in, as well. There is great power in destruction. Even the children of our country are affected by the demagoguery of such a politician. It is estimated by the Southern Poverty Law Center that when "We surveyed more than 2,000 teachers across America, they reported a sharp increase in the bullying, harassment, and intimidation of students whose races, religions, or nationalities have been the verbal targets of candidates" (Morris Dees, Letter to Friends of the Center, 6-6,2016). It is very sad to see our children hurt by this lack of containment and maturity. Children don't understand why someone would hate them without even meeting them. This is truth from the mouths of innocents.

The cry across our land from all across the political spectrum is the need for change. Our country is becoming further and further split, but splits don't last long before the two sides swing back and crash into each other. We are seeing this begin to happen. We need to find that middle ground between the opposites. This would include literally strengthening the middle class, which has acted as the buffer between the two opposing sides of society and held the system together like glue. Psychologically, when there is no middle, you end up with neuroses and unhealthy and dangerous acting-out behavior either from the left or from the right. The best way to move in a constructive direction is simple but, unfortunately, immensely difficult. It boils down to honest communication about not only the light and good, but most especially the shadow, containing the dark and destructive impulses that are intrinsic to being human. If we can accept this, there is a chance—if not, then we are in for a long and wild ride.

Conclusion

It seems we humans have more weaknesses than we like to acknowledge. We have not been responsible stewards of our world and could easily destroy it and ourselves with our self-serving, short-sighted, emotionally driven choices. We forget or ignore what a gift this world and life is for us. For reasons we cannot yet fully explain, we are a unique species capable of consciousness and hope. But in the end it seems it could be our unconsciousness, our animal instincts, that prevail.

It is ironic that the group of candidates in this election cycle, some of whom have exhibited outrageous narcissistic tendencies, are the very ones who have brought forth the shadow that needs to be explored and talked about. One in particular has unleashed the voices of the narcissistically wounded people of our too narcissistically focused society. Perhaps it is a coincidence that the candidates tapped into the shadow of the disenfranchised or maybe it is a good example of how complexes and opposites attract for the purpose of further development. The risk, though, is that we don't shake free but get locked into our collective narcissistic family and don't find a way to stand up for ourselves, or to find a way to transform the system and its values, and ourselves along with it. If the narcissist pathology prevails and becomes too powerful, which would be a sign that our culture has not learned from the insidious effects of narcissism in the home, we are heading toward troubled times.

Nancy Swift Furlotti, PhD, is a Jungian Analyst, co-chair of the C.G. Jung Professorial Endowment in Analytical Psychology, UCLA, and board member at Pacifica Graduate Institute. She is a past president of the Los Angeles Jung Institute, and past co-president of the Philemon Foundation. Her longstanding interests include Mesoamerican mythology, the nature of evil, dreams, and the environment. She has written numerous articles, and co-edited *The Dream and its Amplification* with Erel Shalit. Through her publishing imprint, Recollections, she brings into print works by first generation Jungians, such as Erich Neumann.

The Demonic and Narcissistic Power of the Media in Shakespeare's *Macbeth*

BY SUSAN ROWLAND, PhD

> I have heard
> That guilty creatures sitting at a play
> Have, by the very cunning of the scene,
> Been struck so to the soul that presently
> They have proclaimed their malefactions.
>
> Hamlet in *Hamlet*. P. 308

Not Narcissistic Enough?

Writing in June 2016, the Republican primaries and Shakespeare's play *Macbeth* share the spectacle of a radical disruption to conventions of political legitimacy. Moreover, although the primaries are without the murders, witchcraft and criminal behavior, and with major differences of culture and era, both theatrical events share an instability in the discourse of narcissism. In this paper, I want to explore how this equivocal portrayal of narcissistic personalities amounts to a productive *magic*, mesmerizing the political and psychological landscapes of both early 16th-century England and 21st-century America.

Narcissism is unstable here because the drama of the Donald Trump nomination and the character of Macbeth's tragic and tenuous grasp of the monarchy both rely on the protagonists inhabiting, and yet failing to be entirely and wholly possessed by, Freud's secondary narcissism, the problematic failure to accept the separation between self and objects (Samuels, Shorter and Plaut, 1997). Persons possessed by such secondary narcissism typically demand excessive admiration from others, self-aggrandize to the point of deception and assert their own innate superiority without requiring external evidence for it. Narcissists are unhealthily fixated on their own power and fame; they exploit others without remorse to gain their own success and are consumed with envy of other people. Convinced that such envy characterizes attitudes to themselves, narcissits are prone to outbursts of rage when they do not instantly get what they want.

Whereas Freud theorized that primary narcissism was a wholly plausible stage in infantile development prior to the capacity to relate to others, secondary narcissism is a pathological "stuckness" in fantasies that ought to have been reframed if the Oedipus complex had been negotiated successfully.

> The point is that his omnipotence and grandiosity are a distorted version of the selfhood he might have attained in relation to his parents, but did not. Ibid. p. 98

By recognizing the father's presence and potential to separate mother and baby, the infant of either sex must relinquish fantasies of omnipotence that his or her unbounded union with the mother has previously fostered. Following the path of Oedipus, as Freud considered proper for the male child, means that desire for the mother's exclusive love has to be renounced under threat of castration. The tiny boy therefore represses incestuous desires to form the ego/unconscious structure and is compensated by assuming the social and phallic power of the father. That Oedipus' father is a king and not just any man is not considered by Freud, just as he has far greater difficulty in positing an Oedipal route for the small girl.

Arguably, C.G. Jung's far greater sense of the cultural factors in psycho-social development may offer a way of looking at the issue of relating to a paternal icon of extreme power. Although narcissism as a pathological disorder is little considered in his *Collected Works*, its key indication of being erotically obsessed by a mirror image is significantly reworked. Twice in CW12, *Psychology and Alchemy*, gazing rapt at a mirror image is regarded as a potentially productive part of individuation. This process for Jung signifies the gradual accessing of a greater psychological coherence by means of learning how to unite and separate from the unconscious (p. 114-5, p. 116).

The problem for Jung with looking into a mirror is overreliance upon what the glass signifies to the person, "his" superior intellect. Much more preferable is a more mysterious type of reflection, the mandala circular image as a mirror of wisdom (CW13, p. 22). Here, the mirror does not reflect the outer being of the person, either in the Freudian erotic obsession or the Jungian risky reliance upon rationality or persona (the public presentation of being). Rather, the mirror indicates the deeper ordering principles of the self, icon of wholeness and majesty that cannot be swallowed by the ego in omnipotent fantasy.

So where does this leave the current Republican nominee for United States president and Shakespeare's Macbeth, who, I suggest, share a break in the assumption of narcissism that has a magical effect on their audiences? Donald Trump's success in primary elections is predicated upon his playing the role of political outsider, one who is not narcissistic enough to assume presidential trapping in conventional language. He is rather narcissistic enough to nakedly reach after power *without* recourse to the traditional antecedents.

Narcissism surely *also* inheres in his claim to the presidential throne without the usual political qualifications. These are accompanied by assertions of superior intelligence and business acumen. At a rally in Waterbury, CT, on April 23, 2016, he said, "I'm like a really smart person." While it is useless to speculate on what a political candidate 'really' believes, Trump is nevertheless playing the role of genius who is fit for office because he is not "fitted" to the office, not one of the elite insiders.

Macbeth's tragedy is different but similarly structured on his own perception of being unfit, illegitimate. Successful in obtaining the throne of Scotland by murdering the true king and exiling his sons, Macbeth is carrying out an archaic myth unacceptable to his present-day society. The myth is of a potent young man killing an aging king and taking his place as lover of a queen signifying the sacred fertility of the earth. Such an underlying structure is visible in several of Shakespeare's tragedies, including *Hamlet* and *King Lear*.

These plays are tragedies because ritual murder is no longer permissible within the consciousness of the times and its Christianized culture. Macbeth is haunted by his illegitimacy in the actual figure of his friend Banquo, for whom a royal descent is prophesied. Childless Macbeth has been goaded into his great crime by a feminine part of himself left over from his earliest bond with his mother. Such a fragment of his being now is constellated in his relationship to his wife, Lady Macbeth. In fact, Macbeth's psychic dysfunction is imaged in Lady Macbeth (and himself) as having no living child. Her "infertility" is his land without fertility—a wasteland. Let us take a closer look at this protagonist's narcissistic maneuvers.

Macbeth's Primary and Secondary Narcissism

I want to consider the witches in *Macbeth* as having a magical effect similar to the media in the modern presidential race. This comparison is not a precise equation, since these witches are secret, witnessed in the drama only by Macbeth and briefly by Banquo, whereas the modern media are public and ubiquitous. They are a feminine unconscious to the political order of reality in the play inhabited by kings, thanes and two very different wives. Rather, it is in the magical effect of the witches on this character, and possibly the play's audiences then and now, that parallels can be drawn with contemporary events.

In fact, the witches form a supernatural arena of psychic transformation for Macbeth. They are his dynamic and dramatic psychic mirror, and as Jung indicates, it is his too great reliance upon them as mirror that is his downfall.

Witches:	Fair is foul, and foul is fair:
	Hover through the fog and filthy air.
	Macbeth, Act 1, sc.1 l. 11-12.
Macbeth:	So foul and fair a day I have not seen.
	Act 1, sc.3 l. 38.

Macbeth's very first line echoes the concluding chant of the witches in the very first scene. He is already their creature, although only the audience can sense it in the auditory repetition. Moreover, as well as undoing moral and aesthetic categories, "fair is foul...," the witches suggest that they can defy the very bounds of gravity as they "hover" in atmospheric dirt. Here indeed is a pre-Oedipal state of fusion that is *confusion*. The witches proclaim the *powers of horror* that give the title to Julia Kristeva's book on the pre-Oedipal as the realm of the abject as the not-yet subject (Kristeva 1982). Without clean and proper boundaries, being is a world of terrifying invasion of monsters and evil. No territory is protected, no body is safely a *body* with psychic integrity.

In his opening words, Macbeth reveals his pre-Oedipal predilections in straying into the wilderness of mirroring the abjecting witches. When they hail him successively as Thane of Glamis, Cawdor and King, they conjure him into a world in which time and agency are similarly detached from social and physical realities. Macbeth knows he is already Thane of Glamis. He does not know that he has been given the traitor's title of Thane of Cawdor. To be king would be to go outside social and moral rules because he would have to kill the incumbent and push away that man's natural bodily successors.

Such a move would transfer the primary narcissism (constellated by the witches taking him back to pre-Oedipal lack of subjecthood) to a secondary narcissism in which he cannot separate himself from the object of desire—being king. Symptomatically, after committing the murder, primary narcissism overtakes him again. He loses a sense of his own body as whole and bounded.

Macbeth:	What hands are here? Ha! They pluck out mine eyes.
	Will all great Neptune's ocean wash this blood
	Clean from my hand? No, this my hand will rather
	The multitudinous seas incarnadine,
	Making the green one red. Act 2, sc. 2, l. 58-62

Hands wanting to destroy eyes show a horrifying sense of bodily disintegration. Bloody hands that can dye whole seas indicate the psyche trapped in a world without end, without limits to his crime. Transfixed by pre-Oedipal enchantment in the witches reincarnating his primary narcissism, Macbeth has struck down his king, his father figure who was the obstacle to his deepest and forbidden desires. Such a perversion of the Oedipal situation propels him into a secondary narcissism in which his crime traps him in an endless mirroring of his murder.

The psychic dysfunction is even more marked in his premurder exchanges with his wife. She overtly rejects any primal bond of love that could provide an-other to his Oedipal fantasies.

Lady Macbeth: When you durst do it, then you were a man...
                   Does unmake you. I have given suck and know
                   How tender 'tis to love the babe that milks me:
                   I would while it was smiling in my face,
                   Have pluck'd my nipple from his boneless gums,
                   And dash'd the brains out, had I so sworn
                   As you have done to this. Act 1, sc.7, l. 49, 54-8.

Such graphic destruction of maternal love effectively cuts away the "normal" Oedipal path by which fear of castration by the actual father is succeeded by the boy Macbeth eventually becoming a father. It is later made explicit in the play that the Macbeths have no children, giving Lady Macbeth's terrible lines the visceral context of babies that have died, typical for the period. In these lines we sense a rejection of a potential mirroring of love. Macbeth cannot see himself being mothered safely and lovingly in the person of a baby son.

Imaging his own mother, Lady Macbeth fuses all possible Eros, or in Jung's terms, feeling and connection into Thanatos, the sacred drive to death. All her relational energy is predicated on Macbeth removing the father-king as obstacle to *her* desires that cannot be separated from his desire, which has to be repressed if he is see himself as separate from the kingship. Lady Macbeth unrepresses his Oedipal drive by choosing iden-tification with it instead of mother love that feeds the baby. She pushes him into the mirror of secondary narcissism in portraying the alternative as the feminine that annihilates the defenseless child. She channels a pre-Oe-dipal mother that he can never appease nor escape once he has submitted to her desire as his desire and killed the king-father.

Unsurprisingly, murderer Macbeth is haunted by children. Since the witches proclaimed his sometime companion Banquo as the father of future kings, he has his friend murdered with the command to execute the child also. Banquo's son escapes, as do King Duncan's progeny but not so fortu-nate is the family of defector, Macduff. The only other woman in the play only appears as a loving mother. We see her affectionately playing with her children until the entire family is murdered by Macbeth's henchmen. It is time for Macbeth to visit the witches again. They show him a mirror.

Secondary Narcissism and Relying Too Much Upon the Mirror

Trapped in his secondary narcissism, Macbeth cannot stop killing because he cannot see himself as a legitimate ruler. He keeps murdering to repeat the primal crime that got him the throne, but none will give him that separation from the object, kingship, that would stabilize his identity. Rather he is trapped in the mirror of murdering to achieve his desires, and each murder takes him further from his lost desire, to take his father-king's place, to be king like Duncan —respected, loved and a father. So Macbeth returns to the scene of his primary narcissism, the abject feminine of the witches. His visit awakens narcissistic possibilities in the play's audience.

> Macbeth: I conjure you by that which you profess...
> though the treasure
> Of nature's germens tumble all together,
> Even till destruction sicken, answer me
> To what I ask you. Act 4, sc. 1 l. 50, 58-61.

Assuming the position of the witches as the chaos energy of the planet ("I conjure you..."), Macbeth proceed by envisioning terrifying destruction in which fertility itself, "nature's germens," is distorted beyond repair. Such is the psychological position of a fertility rite, in the archaic myth, or an Oedipal process, literalized in secondary narcissism.

The witches enable Macbeth and the audience to receive three supernatural messengers, an armed head, a bloody child, and a crowned child carrying a tree. The messages are successively a warning about Macduff, that none of woman born can kill Macbeth, and that he will not be defeated until Birnam Wood comes to Dunisnane, his fortress. Macbeth, now a creature of the abjecting world without inner sight or in-sight, interprets all three messages disastrously. The armed head is right that Macduff is a particular danger because he is Macbeth's future killer. Macbeth sees the fragment of a warrior and thinks he can kill part of his being, his family. Instead of incapacitating Macduff, the atrocity actually spurs him on.

Thinking that no person of woman born means no human being is a similar mistake, for the bloody child suggests the power of the infantile psyche in the narcissistic mirror that Macbeth is trapped in. In a fight to the death, Macduff will tell his opponent that he is that man of no woman born because he was from his mother's body "untimely ripp'd" (Act 5, sc.8, l. 16). The crowned child carrying a tree branch is another false mirror in Macbeth's secondary narcissism. Macbeth interprets Birnum Wood coming to his castle Dunsinane as a mere statement of impossibility. Now nothing can detach him from his throne; he is fused with it as object.

More pertinent would be to see the bloody child and the crowned child as emblems of his own catastrophic failure to negotiate his Oedipal desires for kingship. The bloody child recalls Macbeth's own first appearance in the play, covered with the blood of a traitor. At the end of the play, he will be that traitor and appear finally as the first vision, a decapitated armed head. In between he metaphorically, then intentionally, and at last actually kills children. He accepts his wife's horrible narcissistic identification with his desire in her statement about being willing to murder their child. Once Oedipal killer of Duncan, Macbeth intends to kill Banquo's son, the play's icon of fertility and generation. With the slaughter of Macduff's family, the tyrant's journey to literalism and narcissistic identification with the act of murder in an Oedipal mirror is complete.

Each time Macbeth commissions murder, he is killing part of himself because he fatally embodied his desire to be father-king instead of being able to repress it and take the place of child-who-will-be-father in a familial overcoming of primary narcissism. Rather, murder continues his libido stuck in secondary narcissism where he is the bloody child and needs to kill the bloody child. He is also, of course, the crowned child, the child who killed his father and became king. However, in holding a tree and speaking of Birnum Wood moving, this third vision cements Macbeth's secondary narcissism by imagining what kingship itself might mean, if Macbeth could be the king that he can never be; that is fertile, as in the archaic myth part of the renewing fertility of the land. And Macbeth cannot be that king because he killed a father rather than becoming one.

It is this crowned child with branch who makes absolutely explicit that it is loving, loyal Banquo who is king-lover of the land as goddess.

A show of eight kings, the last with a glass in his hand;
Banquo following.

Macbeth: Thou art too like the spirit of Banquo: down! ...
             What! Will the line stretch out to th'crack of doom?
             Another yet? – A seventh? – I'll see no more –
             And yet the eight appears, who bears a glass,
             Which shows me many more: and some I see,
             That two-fold balls and treble scepters carry.

             Act 4, sc.1, l 112, 117-21.

When Birnum Wood *does* come to Dunsinane (as the soldiers are commanded to carry a tree branch in order to conceal numbers), and the wood appears to march, the land itself appears to regenerate by rising up against Macbeth. The crowned child with a tree that Macbeth thinks speaks of the impossible, a moving wood, shows merely what is impossible *for him*. He commands a show of kings who will be descended from Banquo as father whose family relation did not fall in to fatal secondary narcissism.

Additionally, these phantom kings make explicit something about *Macbeth*, the play as well as Macbeth, the man. What if the intimate Oedipal and archaic nature of this drama tempted *the audience* into a secondary narcissism? Extraordinarily, such a dangerously tragic psychological trap is written into this very dramatic script.

Kings, Politicians and their Narcissistic Audiences

"Glass" in Shakespearean English means a mirror. The eight Banquo descended kings hold a mirror out to the audience and invite them to see themselves in what Macbeth next howls, a line of kings with the balls and scepters of the throne of England. The explanation for such a reference is made even more magically potent when we consider this interaction in a Jungian context, as we will see. In a straightforward sense, these lines confirm that this play, first performed around 1604, was conceived for the new monarch, James I, who was legendarily a descendent of Banquo. As a complement to the new king-father, who fortunately was already a father, the mirror held out to the audience invites the king himself to see his own legitimacy confirmed upon the stage.

And yet this is a crucial violation of the stage as boundary between realities in a play full of the violation of sacred, nature, political and familial boundaries. The mirror invites new king James to a secondary narcissism of seeing stage phantoms as performing his own political claims to his very new role. After all, James became king of England as well as native Scotland by *familial* ties, as the most intimately living relation of dead Queen Elizabeth. That these familial ties are bloody is shown by the fact that James inherited the English throne via his mother, who plotted to kill her cousin Elizabeth and was in turn executed.

And what does James I see? He is now invited to identify through an actual and literal mirror with a play in which a good king is murdered and a bad king is overthrown by force—and, a play claiming, enacting, prophetic powers. C. G. Jung suggested that a visionary work of art, one vibrating to the music of archetypal themes not fully present to the artist, would be to the collective society like a dream to the individual (CW15, para. 161, p. 104). It could show where she/he or society, was going. So where is England of 1604 going?

In 1605, James I and his parliament suffered the Gunpowder Plot, a failed bomb plot against the government leading to brutal executions. Less than 20 years later, an army did march against a king they called tyrannical, James' son, Charles I. After a trial, the defeated king was beheaded, suffering the same fate as semifictional Macbeth. His son, Charles II, achieved the throne with the consent of the forces who defeated his father and wisely chose to forgo revenge against all but the signatories to his father's death warrant. Some of these found refuge in the American colonies, whose leaders refused to hand them over in an early act of defiance to the English crown. Otherwise unlike Macbeth, Charles II, a notorious womanizer, had no legitimate children. His brother, James II, and his son, Charles, were not able to hold onto power.

Charles I was not inevitably doomed to the fate of Duncan and Macbeth of violent death. Rather, he summoned his own downfall by foolishly refusing to recognize any legitimate political power but his own. He famously believed in the divine provenance of kings, which gave him a narcissistic identification with the role. He could not separate himself from the mirror that was kingship. Here, a dream commented upon by C. G. Jung seems illuminating.

Dream

> The dreamer, a doctor, a pilot, and the unknown woman are travelling by airplane. A croquet ball suddenly smashes the mirror, an indispensable instrument of navigation, and the airplane crashes to the ground. Here again there is the same doubt: to whom does the unknown woman belong? (italics in original, CW12, para. 147, p. 113)

Significantly the theme of flight heralds disaster just as the witches' *hovering* proves unfortunate for Macbeth. Jung comments pertinently on the fate of the mirror.

> The "mirror" as an "indispensable instrument of navigation" doubtless refers to the intellect, which is able to think and is constantly persuading us to identify ourselves with its insights ("reflections")... The term "instrument of navigation is an apt expression for this, since it is indeed man's indispensable guide on pathless seas. But when the ground slips from under his feet and he begins to speculate in the void, seduced by the soaring flights of intuition, the situation becomes dangerous. (Jung, CW12, para. 149. Pp. 114-5).

For Jung's dreamer, the croquet ball smashes the mirror, so preventing the danger of seduction by ungrounded intuition, whereas Macbeth's perilous mirroring is not so interrupted. He is seduced by the witches as an ungrounded feminine intuition. As in Jung's reading of the dream, the witches mirroring persuades Macbeth to identify himself with the visions they bestow. Having failed to negotiate Oedipal distance from his desires, he is unable to conceive that these visions or intuitions do not serve his fantasy identification with the crown.

Similarly, had a croquet ball interrupted the fateful mirroring of the play's procession of fertile and just kings in the implied royal audience—who are James I and his family—perhaps they too would have been more aware that their people's *reflections and insights* were not wholly favorable. How far does the play *Macbeth* anticipate the narcissistic downfall of the Stuart dynasty? Jung would have said that literature is a form for archetypal evolution within a culture in supplying what is absent from conventional social mores.

> Therein lies the social significance of art: it is constantly at work educating the spirit of the age, conjuring up the forms in which the age is most lacking. (Jung, CW 15, para. 130, p. 82)

Art conjures. It is capable of witchcraft on a collective social level as well as its effect on the audience and artists. But who is the unknown woman, Jung asks of his dream above? What both the dreamer and Macbeth lack is grounding. Macbeth for sure has missed his chance to be grounded through his relation to his wife and the potential mother of his children. The visions of bloody and crowned children mock his ungrounded and infertile narcissistic kingship.

For Jung the unknown woman will prove to be that necessary feminine psychic relation, the *anima*. For Macbeth, the ground he cannot connect to, cannot love, is the land itself. In his narcissistic tyranny, he has made a wasteland of Scotland. Far from incarnating the lover of the goddess in taking the place of an aging King, he has rather been the destroyer of the earth as sacred feminine. His slaughter of the Macduff family is only the most graphic metonym of his desecration of the Earth-Goddess through his catastrophic secondary narcissism.

So in what sense are Macbeth's fateful witches, the demonic mirror, comparable to the modern media. Crucially, *Macbeth*, the play, is not so much *about* magic as an enactment of it. The witches chant spells; that is all they do. In that sense, they are dramatists, not supernatural beings. Their spells liberate the potential for secondary narcissism in Macbeth. Once trapped in their ungrounded narcissistic mirroring, he himself does the rest.

Moreover, arguably the play is a rite rather than a dramatic entertainment. If it really does conjure up the forms that are lacking in the age, does it promote the likelihood of James I and his son, Charles I, being unable to dis-identify with the divinely appointed king? Or does conjuring up the forms reduce the likelihood? I am suggesting that the play is magic because it demonstrates and promotes narcissistic temptations. In this sense, it anticipates the distorting and productive mirror of the modern media.

While ostensibly claiming to inform and communicate, no one could assume the modern media to be a neutral or transparent medium. With its internet-enhanced range from the latest social media to venerable news-papers, the media reflect back powerful figures in ways that permit or even seduce (them and us) into narcissistic (mis)identification. Media energies are multiple, unpredictable, capable of being manipulated but not wholly controlled. Such a perspective suggests that the media are a form of the psyche itself, or, in the language of this old Shakespearean world, *magical*. Ultimately, what might matter in elections to the populace is which candidates can love and make fertile the ground we stand on.

Susan Rowland, PhD, is the Chair of Engaged Humanities & the Creative Life at Pacifica Graduate Institute, has degrees from the Universities of Oxford, London and Newcastle, UK, and was the first chair of the International Association of Jungian Studies (IAJS). She is author of many studies of Jung, literary theory and gender including *C.G. Jung and Literary Theory* (1999), *Jung: A Feminist Revision* (2002), *Jung as a Writer* (2005) and also edited *Psyche and the Arts* (2008). Another recent book is *C.G. Jung and the Humanities* (2010), showing how Jung's work is a response to the creative, psychological, spiritual, philosophical and ecological crises of our age. In 2012, Her book, *The Ecocritical Psyche: Literature, Complexity Evolution and Jung* was published by Routledge, showing how the Jungian symbol is a portal to nature. Additional works include *C.G. Jung and Literary Theory; Jung: A Feminist Revision; Jung as a Writer; Psyche and the Arts* (editor); *From Agatha Christie to Ruth Rendel; C.G. Jung in the Humanities; The Ecocritical Psyche.*

References

Jung, C. G. (1944) *Psychology and Alchemy, The Collected Works of C. G. Jung, volume 12,* Trans. R. F. C. Hull, edited by Sir Herbert Read, Michael Fordham, Gerhard Adler, William McGuire, Princeton: Princeton University Press.

Jung, C. G. (1966) *The Spirit in man, Art and Literature, The Collected Works of C. G. Jung, volume 15,* Trans. R. F. C. Hull, edited by Sir Herbert Read, Michael Fordham, Gerhard Adler, William McGuire, Princeton: Princeton University Press.

Kristeva, J. (1982) Powers *of Horror: An Essay on Abjection.* Trans. Leon S. Roudiez. New York: Columbia University Press.

Samuels, A. (1985) *Jung and the Post-Jungians,* London: Routledge & Kegan Paul.

Samuels, A., B. Shorter and F. Plaut (eds) (1986) *A Critical Dictionary of Jungian Analysis,* London and New York: Routledge.

Shakespeare, W. (1998/2011) *Hamlet, The Arden Shakespeare Complete Works*, revised edition, eds. Richard Proudfoot, Ann Thompson, and David Scott Kastan, London: Methuen Drama, pp. 291-334.

------------------ (1998/2011) *Macbeth, The Arden Shakespeare Complete Words*, revised edition, eds. Richard Proudfoot, Ann Thompson, and David Scott Kastan, London: Methuen Drama, pp. 773-800.

"The Opposite of Loneliness is not Togetherness; It is Intimacy"

from *The Bridge Across Forever* by Richard Bach

BY LAURENCE DE ROSEN, PhD

Introduction

In order to fully embrace narcissism, I decided to come back to the Latin text, written by Ovid around 1 B.C.E. In other words, like Narcissus, I decided to go to the source: the source of the story, the source of many translations, the source of the narrative. Two scholars who specialize in ancient Greek and Latin helped me: Together we, slowly, translated, verse after verse, the part of the book III of the Metamorphosis focused on Narcissus (from verse 407 to verse 510). Why slowly? Because it is a difficult study and translation. To study this poem and to translate it requires looking at the text in great detail, the reflection of the words, the tenses and modes of the verbs and the grammatical structures. For the reader, each thought and feeling give rise to deep waters. Ovid uses specific words, often mistranslated when translators wanted to give some aesthetic to the writing or for other reasons. Ovid plays also with the tenses of the verbs and their modes to indicate subtleties that are important to completely understand the story.

As typical in ancient drama, Ovid uses the voice of the chorus in his narrative (to express the collective unconscious) and gives to Narcissus the voice of the main protagonist (to express the personal and individual unconscious).

To come back to the original text allows us to be observers of the interactions between them. This is extremely important because to write about narcissism is to take the risk of being caught in Narcissus' eyes and his reflected image, to be inflated, grandiose and disconnected. Indeed, Ovid writes not what he sees, but what Narcissus sees and feels. The other risk is the opposite: to be stuck with an intellectual, unemotional, and brilliant narrative. Writing about this myth leads to a third risk: to be caught in the muddy waters where all clarity is lost and the text disappears.

I gazed at the text for hours and hours, as Narcissus did at the pool, to let the words and the way they were used and choreographed by Ovid mirror within me. It took time for the waters to clear and for the text to take shape like a dream to be translated and interpreted with the main motifs (Cf Y. Kaufmann, *The Way of the Image: The Orientational Approach to the Psyche*).

The setting of the dream is a paradise—virgin place—and the protagonist, Narcissus. Then we read the culmination of the drama, with the turning point of the story. Finally, comes the *lysis* of the story with the result produced by the dream/story work.

I. The Paradise

1)The motif of the source

Verse 407 starts with *fons erat illimis....*, i.e. "the fountain was clear." Ovid uses a very precise word, which is fountain/source. It has often been mistranslated as "a pool, a pond." In fact, the pool, the pond, lies at the bottom of the fountain. The origin of the word "fountain" is a place where baptism took place with, therefore, a religious dimension. The fountain symbolizes a return to the source, to the origin, a place of death and birth. It grounds the story.

It is useful to remember that Narcissus' father, Cephisos, was the god of the river. He was associated with the shrine of Apollo at Delphi. The river Kephisos was also said to run near Eleusis, place of the Mysteries, place of transformation. The water of a river flows, whereas a pond is still water. Obviously, the psychic attitude is not the same in each of the two cases.

In the alchemical treatise of the *Rosarium Philosophorum* (16th century), cornerstone of the depth psychology studied by Jung, the first image of the alchemical process of transformation is precisely a fountain. Jung saw in alchemy a projection of the psychic process at stake in a process of individuation. In both cases, for Ovid and for the alchemists, the bottom of a fountain/source is seen as a sacred space, a symbolic womb. There a gestation could take place leading to a possible transformation. Ovid uses the Latin word *illimis*, for the water of the fountain, from "limus," meaning "mud." *Illimis* means "not muddy," therefore clear. It is this clearness, this limpidity that allows Narcissus to see himself, more exactly to mirror himself.

2) The motif of Virginity

The story of Narcissus starts in a paradise as a virgin place. A virgin place is an idyllic and archetypal place symbolizing the Mother world, the *Mater Natura*: "There was a clear pool with silvery bright water, to which no shepherds ever came, or she-goats feeding on the mountain side, or any cattle; whose smooth surface neither bird nor beast nor falling bough ever ruffled." (Verses 407-410) The killing of any wild animal is a transgression against the mother world. Ovid insists on making this point: Nothing was touched, things were pure. By doing so, Ovid represents the psychic structures where the protagonist of the dream is in the archetypal realm. In this world, there is no place for the personal. According to Jung, "In actual psychic experience, the mother corresponds to the collective unconscious and the son, here Narcissus, to consciousness which fancies itself free but must ever succumb to the power of sleep and deadening unconscious." (Jung 1952, vol V, par 393)

A virgin forest is a forest where no human being ever came, which is precisely what Ovid wrote. Virginity implies the concept of purity. And what lies under such a concept is the most fundamental taboo: the incest. The word "incest" means "impure." The incest taboo gives rise to the situation of virginity.

Because of Ovid's insistence on that motif of virginity, there is a sense of urgency, that one can feel through the lines, to leave that realm where there is no place for the personal. Narcissus has to lose or/and is going to lose his virginity. As a matter of fact, at the beginning of the tale, Liriope, Narcissus' mother, asks the blind seer, Tiresias, whether her son would live to reach a well-ripened age, and the seer replies: "if he never knows himself." To know oneself means to grow, to separate from the Mother world, so to lose one's virginity. Narcissus needs to separate the subject from the object, to leave the confusion.

3) The motif of onesess/sameness

Narcissus lives in a oneness, with no relationship with his surroundings. He is alone. Narcissus is one not whole. For Narcissus, the Other doesn't exist: "Many youths and many maidens sought his love; but in that slender form was pride so cold that no youth, no maiden touched his heart." (verse 353-354(1)) In fact, there is no other character in the myth which emphasizes the sense of loneliness. We also know from the beginning of the story that "Narcissus had mocked her (Echo), thus had he mocked other nymphs of the waves or mountains; thus had he mocked the companies of men." (Verses 402-403) To know oneself supposes relationships to oneself; that is precisely the issue in this myth. Narcissus is not differentiated from any otherness. The topic in the myth is not about the sameness but about the otherness. Fordham speaks of "deintegration," that is the process that unblocks the ego/self-fusion and then allows the One to become multiplicity.

What is clever in the way Ovid writes the story is that he describes what Narcissus sees in the water, meaning we see what he sees. In verse 420(1))," *Prone on the ground, he gazes at his eyes...*" In other words, the reader sees only what Narcissus looks at, meaning the reflected image/ shadow: "That which you behold is but the shadow of a reflected image." (verse 416(1)) The Latin text differentiates between Narcissus and his view rather than identifying Narcissus and his view. This illustrates, I believe, a common place where analysts (and others in common life) find themselves as they work with narcissistic features. There is a touching moment where Narcissus tries to raise himself a little, as if to separate from himself to get a better view, but he fails. (Verse 440) There is in the text a rise of anxiety when Narcissus speaks to himself with the second person of the singular: "O fondly foolish boy, why vainly seek to clasp a fleeting image? What you seek is nowhere; but turn yourself away. ... That which you behold is but the shadow of a reflected form and has no substance of its own." (Verses 432-436, (1)) The way Ovid uses the different personal pronouns helps to situate where Narcissus is psychologically.

Narcissus needs to separate the subject from the object, to leave the confusion, to be able to relate. Narcissus, following Ovid, tries to get through his bubble, to separate from his archetypal container and to break down his loneliness. "Identity doesn't make consciousness possible; it is only separation, detachment and agonizing confrontation through opposition that produce consciousness and insight." (C.G. Jung and Kerényi, Essay on a Science of Mythology) The word "separate" comes from a Latin word, *pario*, which means to give birth.

4) The motif of fixedness

At the beginning of the story Ovid describes a picture. Everything is still, like a postcard, not like a movie. Ovid stops our gaze at the description of the first scene, which is like a painting. Everything is so still that it becomes fixed, almost petrified. In fact, reading directly in Latin has one holding one's breath. There is a crescendo with this experience of stillness pushed to its extreme. Narcissus is first "smitten" (verse 415), then in verse 417, (1), he "is speechless" and he "wonders," he "hangs motionless with the same expression" (verse 418, (1)), and finally,"he is carved like a statue" (verse 418, (1)).

After such a succession of verbs comes a succession of nouns, where Ovid zooms in on Narcissus' body and face, from verse 420 to verse 425. Here Narcissus is described in the same way one would describe a statue. So when Narcissus looks at his image, we know in the Latin text that as a statue he cannot move or be moved. This reminds me the movie *The Blood of The Poet*, from Cocteau, where an artist sketches a face and is startled when its mouth starts moving. He rubs out the mouth only to discover that it has transferred to the palm of his hand. The artist places the mouth over the mouth of a female statue and the statue speaks to the artist, cajoling him to pass through a mirror.

In verses 420 through 425, there is a great amount of details but no interaction, no movement. There is no motion because there is no emotion. These words share the same etymology: from the Latin word *movere* meaning to move. When there is no movement there is ultimately death. Narcissus doesn't move and is not moved. He is going to die. What is lacking is fluidity, motion, life. We can see the psychic energy, the libido is stuck

This scene reminds me of patients who keep speaking, providing many details and thus compensating and hiding the overwhelming emotion that they are not able to be articulate. At the same time, the archetypal energy is too powerful to allow Narcissus to relate at the personal level. "While he seeks to slake his thirst, another thirst springs up." (Verse 415, (1)) The emotion is stuck behind the words and cannot go through. I remember how satisfied I was as a trainee to have long dreams from patients with many details to explore. I realized later on that I was caught in a kind of grandiose exploration where the intellect was the main force. It was not all bad, but truly I missed the flow, I missed the emotion.

This scene of no (e)motion illustrates the scene of trauma. In Greek, trauma means "wound." In Ovid's text, Narcissus briefly lets his defenses down when he becomes aware that he is looking at the image of himself. Indeed, he realizes for a quick moment that "Oh I am he," (verse 463, (1)) "Tis I in you" (verse 463, (2)). His world is shattered: "... his tears disturbed the water and ripples on the surface, troubled now, made dim his mirrored form." (Verses 475-476, (2)). This is what happens when emotions overwhelm and bring confusion and trouble, sometimes even chaos. But soon Narcissus comes back to his previous position and status illustrated by clear and transparent water. "As soon he sees this, when the water has become clear again." (Verse 486, (1))

II. Paradise Lost

1) The motif of deception

Deception is an ever-recurrent theme in the story until verse 463, where Narcissus understands that "he is he." From this moment onward, Ovid gives many names to describe deception: lies, mistake, simulacra, error, and deception. In addition, a trickster energy is activated, and Narcissus is surprised at first. He wonders at himself until the pool becomes elusive (verse 427); "the same delusion mocks and allures his eyes ... why vainly seek to clasp a fleeting image?" (Verse 432, (1)); "he gazes on that false image" (verse 439, (1)); "I see and what charms me I cannot find, so serious is the lover's delusion" (verse 447, (1)); and finally "Why, O peerless youth, do you elude me?" (Verse 454, (1)) Progressively, the deception becomes a lie in Narcissus' eyes. Ovid is explicit at that point, writing that Narcissus doesn't know what he sees.

Ovid uses three different words for "eyes" to insist on their role. (Verse 420) The first meaning is the organ, the second is the light coming from the eyes, and the third is the eyes as stars. I remind the reader that what we see about Narcissus in the story comes from and through Narcissus' eyes. That is the genius of Ovid. And I had to say that I had to read and reread and reread again to be able to come out from within Narcissus' eyes, like anyone has to do in the presence of narcissistic people. The main reason comes from the fact that Narcissus is caught in his own reflected image/shadow: "Narcissus loves an unsubstantial hope and thinks that substance which is only shadow." (Verse 417) Ovid often uses the passive mode of the verbs to illustrate Narcissus' passive position during most of the story; he is devoured, he is consumed, he is burnt, and he perishes by his own eyes.

2) The suffering of Narcissus

From the very beginning of the story, the reader apprehends the surge of a suffering: "While he seeks to slake his thirst, another thirst springs up." (Verse 415, (1)) The suffering of Narcissus comes first from the experience of the "mistake." In fact, Narcissus doesn't really know that he suffers. The "mis-take" implies a shadow piece within the take. Nevertheless, at that point, Narcissus is trying to find the nature of the error and blames the outside.

It is only when he finds and recognizes his image as separate from his shadow/the reflected image that he starts to suffer. Or at least to have an idea of what suffering is. It goes against his willingness and defenses. Narcissus "becomes the victim of a decision made over his head or in defiance of his heart." (Jung, CW, Vol 14, par 778) When Narcissus recognizes himself (verse 463, (1)), the Latin text says "I felt it," implying that Narcissus has an intuition of a possible relationship with himself but he doesn't say "I know."

Narcissus can no longer endure the suffering brought on by looking at himself (verse 487). Ovid uses two different verbs to express the nature of the suffering. Indeed, in Latin, there are two words to say "to beat." One is *percusare*, which means a concrete beating of the body. The other is *planxare*, which means to beat oneself as a sign of grief and mourning. In most translations, it is this second sense that is referred to. That is wrong. Ovid does describe the naiad-sisters beating their breasts out of grief and mourning. But he describes Narcissus differently, still caught in his defenses.

Narcissus is going to die. Ovid uses a specific verb *"liquitur,"* which means "to liquefy." The word is used in a passive mode. This word is close to what analysis calls a symbolic melting. The etymology of analysis is first made of "ana," meaning a motion from the bottom to the top, also a motion going back and forth. "Lysis" comes from a Latin verb meaning "to dissolve." Narcissus is going to dissolve. Is not water the source of life? Dear reader, remember that one of the names of Dionysus, is Lysios, from lysis.

3) The motif of desire and love

The word "desire" is very present in the story (verses 415,425,426, 450, (1)), and most of the time it is connected with the motif of fire. The etymology of the word "desire" is "stops seeing, to notice an absence." Stop seeing is not very far from being blind. And that is the irony of this story with its sources being found in the motif of the eyes, the seeing, the regard, the mirror. Recall that the myth is introduced by the blind seer, Tiresias, who also introduced the Oedipus myth. The idea is to close the eyes to improve one's sight. As long as one is caught by desire, one cannot close one's eyes. This is what happens to Narcissus: His desire enflames him and makes looking an obsession. Narcissus suffers deeply from his desire.

He doesn't love (nor does he hate) himself for the simple reason that he doesn't know that the reflected image is his Self until he realizes he is he. But even then he backs off. Until then, Ovid does not use an active form of verb with Narcissus as the subject. Ovid uses the passive form with the love of the nymphs who love Narcissus. (Verse 457, (1)) The closest Ovid comes to the experience of love by Narcissus is by using the "We," approaching the differentiation of Narcissus from his image. Even after Narcissus understands that his reflected image is part of himself (verse 463), Narcissus doesn't say that he loves. It is the passive form of the verb to love that is used: "I burn with love of my own self, I suffer (by) the flames." (Verse 465, (1))

It is only in verse 477 that Narcissus is the subject who loves. It is a crucial point that is rarely well-translated. For instance, the main common translation (like the Loeb Classic Library) is "stay here, and desert not him who loves thee, cruel one!" The Latin text shows explicitly that it is not about "him" but about "I" ("me" in Latin"). It is the "I" who loves, and because it is the only place in the story where Narcissus, the subject, loves, it is worth noticing. It is also worth noticing that the construction of that sentence puts "crudelis" ("cruel" in Latin) between the subject "I" and the verb "love," to show that real love will make him suffer.

III. The Underworld

1) The motif of the body

The myth of Narcissus starts with a question about a body and ends with a question about a body. Echo is a nymph who loves Narcissus and tells him so with her own voice. In fact, she can only repeat the words she heard in concluding phrases of a speech. At the beginning of the story Echo has a body: "... up to this time Echo had a body" (verse 359,(1)) but then she loses it: "She becomes gaunt and wrinkled and all moisture fades from her body into the air. Only her voice and her bones remain: then, only her voice." (Verses 397-399, (1)) The understanding of Narcissus's myth cannot be completed without Echo; it would be colluding with Narcissus to let her aside. Echo represents the other side of the narcissistic coin.

Narcissus starts the story with a body largely described by Ovid: "Here the youth, worn by the chase and the heat, lies down ..." and "prone on the ground he gazes" (verses 412-413), "he plucks away his tunic at its upper fold and beats his bare breast with pallid hands." (Verse 481) This description is completed by Narcissus himself, through his own eyes. Ovid's insistence on the object of a body seems to compensate for the lack of Narcissus' relationship to his body.

This focus onto the body is reminiscent of Michelangelo's painting in the Sistine Chapel at the Vatican, *The Last Judgment*. It is a description of the Second Coming of Christ and the final and eternal judgment by God of all humanity. In the painting, the souls of humans rise and descend to their fates. The original subject of the mural was the resurrection. Michelangelo shows figures equalized in their nudity, stripped bare of rank. What Michelangelo celebrates in his painting is the transfiguration of the body. Those created a scandal at that time, and the Pope considered destroying the painting. Indeed, Michelangelo's conception of the body was not accepted and not in accord with the vision of the Catholic Church at that time. The Pope eventually changed his mind and asked Michelangelo to "dress" the bodies a little bit. And for many years, several Popes continued to ask—and get—more clothes.

I have to emphasize the repetitive confusion about the word "body" in different translations, which is often mixed up with the form, with the shadow, with the reflected image. The Latin text helps to differentiate between them. But what is tricky is that along the story, it is easy to be caught in Narcissus' eyes and see only what he sees because, like Narcissus, we can be "smitten by the sight of the beautiful form he sees. He loves an unsubstantial hope and thinks that substance which is only shadow." (Verses 416-417, (1)) For instance, the Latin word "forma" is not a body. Its first meaning is "a mold." In other words, a forma doesn't have a body, it contains the body. It has the silhouette, the appearance of a body but no substance of the body, no physical body. In the ancient culture (cf. Aeneid and Odysseus), the form refers to the underworld where the dead are in search of a body. The soul/form then was not seen as amorphous: There were the images of the departed but not corpselike images. They had nothing of the living corpus.

The descent into the body is of crucial importance for self-awareness. Trans-formation(in Latin), like meta-morphosis (in Greek), signifies a passage from one form to another. It doesn't mean any crescendo in the quality or nature of the new form. Sometimes, I believe, there is, in the psychoanalytical world, a mystification of the word transformation implying a change for the best (cf. J.W. Goethe, "The Metamorphosis of Plants"). In the *Metamorphoses*, Ovid sets a place for transformation but doesn't speak about the end result of it.

2) The motif of intimacy

What is striking at the end of the poem is that Ovid writes very clearly "Narcissus' body was nowhere to be found," (verse 509, (1)) "Where he (Narcissus) had been, alas he was not there." (verse 509, (2)) There is no body. In my experience, staying with this loss is more difficult than jumping directly to what has been found instead, a flower named narcissus. It seems to me that the empty chair, with no body in it, haunts the practice of psycho-analysis. It is possible for psychoanalysis to become disembodied.

Up to the point when Narcissus becomes aware of his body, he is caught in it. After his realization, Narcissus is split from his body because of the suffering induced by living in a body: "Oh, that I might be parted from my own body! and strange prayer for a lover, I would that what I love were absent from me" (Verses 467-469) Against his will, Narcissus takes us down to the underworld: "And even when he had been received into the infernal abodes, he kept on gazing on his image in the Stygian pool." (Verses 503-504) As Jung put it: "The experience of the self is always a defeat of the ego." (Jung, CW vol 14, par 778)

Narcissus doesn't have a relationship with his body: he doesn't relate to his body. When it hurts too much, as in the case of trauma, there is disso-ciation. Trauma in Greek means "wound." For Narcissus to discover himself is to open a wound. Ovid writes that Narcissus cannot bear the suffering of seeing himself anymore. (Verse 488) The lack of relationship with his body and therefore with himself is indeed a very painful experience. On this theme, Kerenyi refers to the mother-daughter relationships and writes: "Mother divided from daughter is a symbol of something unspeakably painful that is hidden in the Demeter-aspect of the world." (Kerényi, 1978)

Narcissus cannot dive into his inner landscape no matter how hard he tries: "How often did he plunge his arms into the water seeking to clasp the neck he sees there, but didn't clasp himself in them." (verse 428, (1)) For Narcissus there is no IN, there is even a terror of going IN. Narcissus cannot get close to intimacy: "I would that what I love were absent from me." (Verse 469) The etymology of the word "intimacy" comes from the superlative of the preposition "in," meaning very much inside. A second meaning derives from the first one; intimacy in Latin also means the center of the earth, in a sense of the underworld, also called by the ancient the Infernal (cf Dante).

The loss of sight gives Tiresias the power to see inside and into the future; paradoxically, Narcissus cannot see with his open eyes. He would need to close his eyes to see but *"... he ever loves to gaze on his reflection in the Stygian wave."* (Verse 505, (2))

In place of Narcissus' body, a flower is found, a narcissus. The Greek word for narcissus (narkissos) comes from the Greek word "narke," numbness, drowsiness. The Greek and Roman cultures made the flower of narcissus a flower of death. The flower was the entry into the infernal world in the chthonian cult of Demeter at Eleusis. The hymn of Demeter attributes a decisive role to the flower of narcissus in the abduction of Persephone. In fact, in picking up a narcissus, Persephone was drowned to the infernal world. The flower of narcissus tells us where Narcissus is going into the darkness of the underworld, also place of the mysteries where transformation could take place. The flower of narcissus and the word of intimacy come together to lead the reader to the center of the earth, into the underworld, namely the world of the unconscious.

IV. Conclusion

The lysis, which is the solution, of the story indicates the place where Narcissus has or is to go: into the underworld. Narcissus starts his journey alone in a paradise. He ends it in the Infernal realm of the underworld. His journey symbolizes a descent in general and a specific descent into this body, which is estranged to him. In *The Divine Comedy*, Dante's journey makes the reverse trajectory; it starts in the *Inferno* and ends in the *Paradisio*. For Dante, the journey of the soul toward God from the Inferno describes the recognition and rejection of sin.

In the myth of Narcissus, Tiresias keeps his consciousness in the underworld. It is in the darkness, place of the mystery, which I first mistakenly wrote « "misery," that transformation is going to take place and that Narcissus is going to experience a possible rebirth. It is in the realm of Dionysius, who was said to have his grave under Apollo's temple at Delphi.

As Erich Neumann beautifully put it: "It is not under the burning rays of the sun but in the cool reflected light of the moon, when darkness of unconsciousness is at the full, that the creative process fulfills itself; the night, not the day, is the time of procreation. It wants darkness and quietness, secrecy, muteness and hiddenness." (Spring 1954).

Are the *Metamorphoses* of Ovid about impossible and failed transformation, or about a potential transformation? It seems that to equalize transformations to a "better something/someone" would be to accommodate modern psychology to ancient mythology. Modern psychology would then be caught in its own narcissistic wounds and narcissistic fantasies of transformation, as well as fear of a failure to transform. Modern psychology needs to honor and to bear patiently (from "pathos" in Greek, meaning to suffer) the mystery of transformation.

Ovid, as a poet, intuitively traces the place of transformation. As in psychoanalysis, when one enters analysis, one never knows if transformation will occur or not. Narcissus opens the gate to the mystery: "The Greek word for mystery has the meaning of the Latin 'initia,' that means 'beginning, the entry,' and the word 'initiate' means in Greek 'to close' and is used for eyes and mouth alike. The initiate remained passive, but the closing of the eyes and the entry into darkness is something active." (Kérenyi, "Essay on a Science of Mythology") Togetherness is not the opposite of loneliness: paradoxically only intimacy can help create relatedness.

Laurence de Rosen, PhD, is an alumna of the Ecole des Psychologues Praticiens, at the Catholic Institute of Paris (1979). She worked with Dr. M. Seligman and Dr. A. Beck at the University of Pennsylvania (1995-1998). She is a graduate of the C.G. Jung Institute (1996-2005), New York, and a licensed and certified Jungian analyst. She worked in both the clinical context and in private practice in France (1979-1993) and in the US, where she taught, published, and was the recipient of the Gravida Award in 2011. Having returned to France, Laurence studied wood sculpture for three years under the supervision of master woodworker Pierre Leron-Lesur at la Maison de l'Amandier in St Rémy de Provence. Today, Laurence lives and practices her therapy and sculpture in Paris.

References

J.W.Goethe, 1790, *The Metamorphis of Plants*, British Journal of Botany, 1863

Jung, C.G, --1956 *Symbols of Transformation*, Collected Work, vol 5.

Princeton, N.J.:Princeton University Press 1978.

-- 1955. Mysterium Coniunctionis,Collected Work, vol, 14.

Princeton N.J.:Princeton Universtiy Press, 1963.

Kerenyi, K. 1978, *Essays on a Science of Mythology*, Princeton University Press,

Kaufmann, Y.2004, *The Way of the Image, The Orientanional Approach to the Psyche*, published by the Assisi Foundation.

(1) *Ovid Metamorphosis*, translated by F.J.Miller, Revised by G.P.Goold, Loeb Classical Library.

(2) *Ovid's Metamorphoses*, translated by B. More, Marshall Jones Company.

America in the Grip of Alpha Narcissism
The Predator Within and Amongst Each and All of Us

BY JACQUELINE WEST, PhD

Preamble

Having been invited to write this paper as an expression of my personal thoughts, I prepared it as if I was engaged in a collegial conversation rather than as a formal seminar or polished journal article with appropriate references. I hope that it stimulates conversation and that the ideas I discuss are understood as exploratory, and nourishing "food for psyche".

Introduction

In February 2016, the weekend before I was to give a talk on the American psyche, I took a break from my writing to watch the Super Bowl halftime show. There it was: the American story, in so many of its psycho-political dimensions. I was particularly amazed by the show-stopping performance by Beyoncé and her chorus.

This cadre of forceful black women, in a powerhouse proclamation of self-assertion, sexuality, and celebration, was a force to contend with. Beyoncé's performance stirred up endless media debates. Beyond the level of gossip about her personal life, both heated reactions and thoughtful reflections about the substantial issues in our country were ignited and discussed.

A few days later, I showed a video version of this performance at the end of my lecture in order to launch our discussion time. It did indeed heat up our reflections, handing us images of racism, grit, wit, talent and power—along with an unquestionable dose of narcissism. In the talk, I had suggested that there are gifts of narcissism that arrive when narcissism is not employed in the service of defensive dynamics. It seemed to me that we could see an intriguing mixture of both defensive and creative narcissism in this performance. Giving close consideration to these dynamics took our discussion into deep and creative waters individually and politically.

Whether or not you actually saw Beyoncé's performance, I hope you can sense the force of it and can let this enliven your engagement as I turn toward reflections about the various forms of narcissism at play in the American psyche.

Psycho-Political Reflections about America:

The psycho-political issues raised by Beyoncé's performance addressed one essential slice of the problems that are at a near boiling point in the U.S. America, as a nation, and as an international citizen, is in a startling state. Within the nation, the unease, unrest, and disturbances are palpable, while the pervasive violence is relentless. It is a time of chaos, of volcanic polarities, of increasingly exposed racism, along with surprising reorganization. Meanwhile, the world we are undeniably a part of is in an uproar: Plagued by eruption and strain, dismemberment and fragmentation, and a startling emergence of mongrel forms of warfare, it is being asked to redefine itself, geographically and politically. Some of us think this may be ruinous; others think it may be creative, perhaps creative through its destructiveness. Others simply tremble with terror. As a nation, facing a world full of what we have been known to label as "evil," we are being asked, in one way or another, to do something, to make a difference.

It seems imperative to emphasize what we can and must do and that we devote time to reflect on the nature of our individual and national psychodynamics. Through most of the 20th century, psychological reflections concentrated upon the dynamics of individuals. But gradually, a noticeable shift toward interactive dynamics emerged. Increasingly, attention was extended into various perspectives about the relationships between people, as well as between groups of people. The dynamics within a group as well as between groups began to come into progressively clearer focus. These developments widened and deepened as psychoanalytic theories were woven into these studies. This relatively new tradition provides the context for my explorations in this paper. My focus here is on the United States of America, on its psyche as seen through its narcissistic character structures and the impact of its structures on its interactions with the other countries on this planet. Yes, the U.S., like every other nation, has a personality. It is an organ within the psyche of our world, to some degree a conscious organ, emerging from the presence of each and every American. This nation requires, and deserves, our attentive and caring reflections, our heartfelt engagements, and our active participation.

The process of applying psychological language to a nation is controversial not only on grounds of its questionable reliability but also its vulnerability to political misuse. Nevertheless, given that an informed perspective may enhance our capacity to forge responsible choices about both our national and international behaviors, it seems that active, well-considered explorations about our psychodynamics are well worth these possible shortcomings.

Informally, America has been referred to often as narcissistic. This off-hand reference was effectively grounded and scholastically substantiated by the quite popular book by Christopher Lasch *The Culture of Narcissism*, published in 1979. But in the ensuing decades, the word "narcissism" has continued to be loosely flung around, typically as a pejorative slur, in our everyday talk and in our public discourse and debate about America and certain individuals. Used repetitively in our newspapers, TV shows, novels, etc., the word itself has become overused, overloaded, distorted, and misunderstood.

What are we to make of a word when it is used to describe blatantly different dynamics. For instance, at one moment, we may hear "narcissism" used judgmentally in reference to the escapism of the boy down the street who won't grow up. In another moment, it may appear in an exasperated description of the entitlement, along with the hidden and crippling alcoholism, of the extraordinarily beloved principal of the local school. And just minutes later, it may be inserted as a definitive conclusion about the remarkably intense, apparently ruthless but simultaneously compelling rants of a popular politician. Yes, each is caught in a disturbed and disturbing pattern that involves the classical narcissistic dynamics of exhibitionism, grandiosity, and omnipotence. But their differences are unmistakable. When these differences are blatantly ignored and the word is reduced to name-calling, its underlying accumulated archetypal and clinical wisdom is effectively erased. Furthermore, it blocks our ability to develop a sophisticated differentiation of different forms of narcissism.

The Three Faces of Narcissism:

Some years ago, a colleague of mine, Nancy Dougherty, and I undertook an extensive project to understand the puzzling fact that while the meaning of the word "narcissism" remains remarkably mercurial despite its frequent and wide use. The inconsistencies that riddle clinical discussions about narcissism became much clearer to us once we realized that different forms of narcissism were related to three archetypally informed patterns of relating to others. Throughout this chapter, I'll be discussing the role of narcissism in our lives through the lens of these three patterns. In order to launch into these reflections, I'll present a very short description of the work that is presented in far more detail in the book that we co-authored, *The Matrix and Meaning of Character: An Archetypal and Developmental Approach.*

We began our work with a clear intention to interweave the depth and richness of archetypal explorations with robust clinical reflections well-informed with diagnostic knowledge. Focusing on the archetypal themes that appeared in the various stories and the patterns of a variety of diagnostic categories, we realized that three discrete wellsprings of archetypal energy underlie our character structures. Under the inevitable stress of entering and developing a human life, some of us, inspired by archetypal *mentation*, tend *to withdraw from* interactions. Others of us, informed by archetypal *affect*, tend *to seek* relationships with whatever and whoever is available. And yet others, informed by archetypal *action*, tend *to meet the world antagonistically*. One can frequently sense these different adaptations to others in the movements of a newborn as she adjusts to her mother's body during their first contact hours, days, weeks—and on into life.

We also recognized that stories and classic diagnostic profiles that shared similar images easily fell into three phases of pre-Oedipal development. During the earliest phase, *The Primal Phase*, roughly from birth to 18 months, the infant is occupied with separation. Sorting out her infant body from her mother's, her nascent consciousness from the archetypal realms, her hunger from her satisfaction, her power to affect the world from her powerlessness, happiness from sadness, she grapples with separations—and with the relationships between separated parts. From that time onward until roughly 3 years old, the child, primarily through her interactions with the mother, is exploring and managing what can be seen developmentally as narcissistic dynamics. Discovering the dimensions of her individual presence, in *The Narcissistic Phase*, she establishes her selfhood in the world. From 3 years to roughly 4.5 years, in *The Pre-Oedipal Phase*, the child's psychic attention revolves around the various dynamics that further support the strengthening of a conscious perspective grounded in a more well-defined sense of self. These developments ultimately enable her to extend her primary relationship with the mother, turning toward embracing the father and, subsequently, the larger world.

As we progressively integrated numerous archetypal and developmental images, stories, and profiles, it gradually became clear that the coincidence of a developmental age with an archetypally rooted pattern of relationship informs a distinct character structure. What emerges from these coincidences is a *Matrix* of nine archetypally informed diagnostic personality patterns. When we study the *Matrix*, we can clearly observe how diagnostic categories that we generally think of as discrete and disparate can be seen as dynamically interrelated.

We can also see how and why narcissism has three quite different faces. We had originally imagined that a single narcissistic profile would be rooted in a particular archetypal wellspring, given that this was becoming the case for the other diagnostic profiles. But surprisingly, after reviewing our material innumerable times, what we consistently found was that narcissistic profiles find expression in all three of the relational patterns. Thus, empirically, we concluded that there are three narcissistic character structures: the Counter-dependent Narcissist (withdrawing), the Dependent Narcissist (seeking), and the Alpha Narcissist (antagonistic).

For instance, let's return to the personality sketches presented above. When we consider the narcissistic escapism of "the boy down the street who won't grow up," we can sense that a pattern of defensive *withdrawal* is coincident with a considerable amount of difficulty handling how to integrate desires to be seen, understood, appreciated, and adored, as well as how to choreograph an effective sense of "I" as one who can assert himself in the world. Archetypally, we recognize, for example, Peter Pan, inspired by adventures into an imaginary magical faraway place called Never Neverland. Likewise, we can see that "the exaggerated entitlement, along with the hidden and crippling alcoholism of the extraordinarily beloved principal of the local school" portrays a narcissistic pattern of defensive *seeking* that is coincident with a desperate, insatiable desire to be loved and engaged in order to experience that her assertion in the world, as full of feeling as it is, is valued. Here, we recognize, for example, Don Juan, aflame with seductive charisma, heading for the ashes. And in the intense, self-righteous stridency of a political, or corporate, or institutional ideologue, we feel the impact of a pattern of defensive *antagonism* that fuels a determined and driven need to "remain on top," to win and dominate at all costs in order to avoid any sense of failure, defeat, or vulnerability that hints that her narcissistically claimed privilege and security in this world are not guaranteed. Here, we recognize any number of envious stepmothers, vampiric characters, the well-veiled psychopath or, perhaps, a malicious trickster.

The Ascendency of Alpha Narcissism in America

The three faces of narcissism are seldom differentiated in clinical discussion and in public discourse and political debates. This not only leaves us faced with recurrent riddles, but it also robs us of more creative and generative insights that could serve us well regarding both our individual and national realities. Focusing on the differentiations of narcissism, we find ourselves in a position to free ourselves from the confusion created when they remain undefined. This enables us to turn toward the task mentioned above, the task of attending to the psyche of the United States of America.

If we step back, take a breath, and view the nation diagnostically, it is difficult not to see that Alpha dynamics have been our predominant form of narcissism. The archetypal wellspring of raw action that lies in the roots of Alpha dynamics has fueled the U.S. since its birth. These dynamics served both the adventurous settlers and the subsequent inhabitants of these lands both creatively and destructively. Historically, they supplied the forceful energy required to explore and develop, to establish new communities in the face of innumerable, raw hardships. Plenty of robust power, a daring stride, and the courage to undertake demanding explorations, as gifts of Alpha dynamics, have clearly served us well. However, these dynamics have also inspired the settlers to ruthlessly take over these lands from their current Native American inhabitants—at the cost of so many deaths that this process is now quite openly seen as genocide. This raw archetypal energy also fueled a merciless industry of slavery that established a racist rift in the fabric of our nation that we are still struggling to repair. In the midst of all this, our western "heroes" slaughtered—truly slaughtered—innumerable herds of buffalo that roamed the prairies. To this day, these undeniably destructive early expressions of Alpha dynamics lie deep within American Narcissism, driving us widely and wildly into ruthless domination over and over.

Currently, this ruthless determination to dominate appears pervasive. There is a well-acknowledged and unprecedented gap between the "haves and have-nots" in terms of money, power, and the ability to obtain justice. Also, it is generally acknowledged that in our public interactions, within government and economics and on the street, there is a significant increase in vituperative language, startling aggression, simmering violence, and astonishing inequalities. In addition, we remain consistently intent upon waging numerous international wars that were persuasively presented initially as a determination to rid the world of "evil" and bring democracy to all. Just a few years ago, the fear and despair generated by the boldness of these dynamics were expressed in numerous images of the apocalypse appearing in the news, films, Internet conversations, etc. And now our wars continue at an alarming rate, even though they are minimally recast as efforts to support the fights for freedom abroad. These aims are expressed with intrepid gallantry accompanied by indisputable assertions that we have the strongest military in the world; we are, in all accounts, No. 1, without question. Sensing the expanding inflation and self-righteousness at the core of each of these national behaviors, many people recently have expressed fears that we are becoming an authoritarian, if not a fascist, state. Fears of global disorder have "come home" and now include a deep dread that we might well lose our essential democratic values and be faced with totalitarian control. Forecasts of doom aside, it does seem apparent that Alpha dynamics not only fuel our country, but that *they have us in their grip*.

Earlier in this paper, I suggested that America is in the grip of Alpha Narcissism. At that point, I referred to our many forms of destructive dominance, ruthlessness, aggressive entitlement, and impenetrable superiority, along with a tolerance of, if not outright approval of, blatant economic inequalities. We are in the grip of these dynamics to the extent that alpha dynamics steer our behavior—and it does appear that they play an astonishingly large role. This is particularly evident in the fact that alpha dynamics infuse the nation's management of its resources, most centrally its wealth. It becomes progressively clearer the drive to win serves and preserves the elite and devalues, in effect dismisses, all others. Overtly and covertly, huge amounts of America's national wealth, both economic and environmental, are in the hands of people for whom amassing more wealth with minimal regulation is a thrill, a challenge, and another star on their shield. Insatiable greed partners with the drive to win, each and every time. Alpha dynamics also hold a tight grip on our various forms of national security. Perhaps more than anywhere else, when we perceive that our international security is in any way questioned, not only a deter-mination to protect, but a fierce determination to dominate quickly reigns supreme. Within our boundaries, we see a penchant for punitive action applied to the disadvantaged, to someone whose vulnerability calls out the predator. Any number of other examples demonstrate that in America vulnerability, in any form, is soundly denied or devalued; it is consistently defended against.

A Clinical Vignette:
An Analytic Profile of Alpha Narcissism

In order to explore in more depth what these observations suggest about America, it will serve us well to delve further into the analytic dimensions of Alpha Narcissism. The following brief clinical vignette offers a glimpse into these dynamics on a scale that will help clarify America's national structures. Therefore, while our attention at this point will be focused explicitly on a single individual, through this experience I am implicitly setting up a vocabulary that may enhance our explorations as we return to our concerns about America. (This vignette is a composite of a number of clinical interactions. It presents experiences and insights that have arisen in my work with a variety of clients, and it does not present a profile that fits any particular individual.)

I once worked with a woman, I'll call her V, who was a veteran Alpha. She had torn through her life recklessly but with such great talent, charisma, and cunning that neither she nor others could identify why the fabric of her life, her profession, and the full spectrum of her relationships, including husband and kids as well as a large network of friends, were all on the verge of being torn into shreds. People around her, including her husband and kids, occasionally joked about being afraid of her but clearly they were deeply attached to her. Mostly, everyone remained silent and obedient; just as she ordered, they stayed in her life. Amid her roaring successes, she was occasionally told that she was astonishingly harsh, sharp, or insensitive, but she dismissed these remarks as envy of her strength and/or simply as proof that the person who said this was an oversensitive wimp. She came to see me when she began to have repetitive fantasies and impulses to physi-cally tear her daughter apart. V had always experienced her daughter, who was nick-named "doll," as a paragon of a well-behaved little star who won applause wherever she went. Now a midadolescent girl, she was beginning to talk back, argue, resist, and rebel. Over the years, V had had plenty of images of viciously attacking many different people whom she thought had stood in her way, often through language that cut like a knife, frequently accompanied by brutal physical assaults. She had never flinched at these thoughts; in fact, she recognized that she generally experienced them as somehow satisfying. She didn't mention concerns about her daughter's apparent distress, nor was there any indication that she herself felt guilty about her violent images of attacking her daughter. Her concerns were focused on her sense that the images had "stealthily" started to disturb her; she felt increasingly annoyed by them and wanted me to help her "exorcize" them.

Our work proceeded very slowly, since V deftly diverted moments that might question her authority or approach her vulnerabilities. Nevertheless, she did commit to and stay engaged in the process for a very long time, long enough for us to noticeably reduce the grip of the structures that had bound her for so long. In the midst of our work, V and I unearthed the memories and images that I'll briefly describe below. These do not reflect the essential nature of the relationship between us that allowed her to form these narratives, but they do offer us, in the context of this paper, an outline of the dynamics involved in the development of Alpha Narcissism.

While V's childhood was materially quite lavish, it was emotionally unusually harsh. Her rocket-wealthy father received constant praise and prestige, while the shady schemes that created his wealth were bragged about at home but were never exposed publicly. His swaggering was mated to a wife whose cunning, sly, self-promotions and showy success exceeded his, both at home and publicly. They were a classic powerhouse couple whose single child, V, was virtually neglected as an infant and as a youngster was constantly criticized and summarily dismissed except when she performed brilliantly.

Given this paucity of positive attention, love, and empathic mirroring, V took her first steps into the world with a fragile sense of self, with minimal attachment to others, and with virtually no sense of belonging. These interpersonal challenges were co-existent with the reality that archetypal action was at the root of her antagonistic pattern of interpersonal relatedness. I mentioned above that one of three archetypal wellsprings underlying character structures is archetypal action. These wellsprings are a never fully identifiable force appearing in human reality; being archetypal, they are in and of themselves neither creative nor destructive, good nor evil, adaptive nor defensive. V's "fate" was that she was psychically rooted in archetypal action.

Jung and many post-Jungians frequently remind us that entering the human world involves inherent separation, personally from our mother's body, archetypally from a unified state. Intra-psychically the birth and progressive development of consciousness naturally creates a psychic dissociation, a presence of differentiated elements within our psychic reality. The emergent reality of consciousness as *other than* unconsciousness and the relationship between the two become the intra-psychic art of personal development. This entails a continuous dialogue, a consistent dance between what has become separated. While this exchange between severed opposites is often understood as a process of withstanding the tension between the opposites, it also can be seen as a process that allows the psyche to accept both and accept whatever this may lead to.

During each phase of development, at best, the child learns to meet the challenges of that period with creative and flexible adaptation rather than constricting and rigid defenses. Adaptation allows for a continuous deepening of the relationship between consciousness and unconsciousness, as well as between the myriad possible expressions of archetypal realities. However, V's fragile sense of self seriously limited her capacity to access the sort of creative dialogue mentioned above or meet challenges adaptively. While her parents' narcissistic cruelty was not physically enacted, it was violent, abusive, emotionally traumatic, and soul-slaying for V. Terrifyingly alone, in the face of the overwhelming force of the unconscious, she experienced it as destructive and she defensively focused on its dark side. Sacrificing her connection to the creative sides of archetypal action, she tragically crippled her relationship with the depths of her being and consequently left her consciousness defensively rigidified. When her compromised consciousness was then roughly buffeted by the overwhelming power of her archetypal wellspring, she became all the more threatened and defensive.

When consciousness meets archetypal reality, it brings with it an experience and perception of opposites *within* the archetype as well as between consciousness and archetypal reality. Accordingly, as V faced into the destructive side of archetypal aggression, she was challenged to mediate archetypal forces of both sadistic aggression *and* masochistic victimization, predatory dominance *and* inescapable submission. V's minimal capacity to hold these archetypal opposites in dialogic tension left her psyche in the position, unconsciously, of "choosing" one or the other. By splitting the opposites, her psyche could then rid itself of the incompatible other by projecting it into the world. The predatory pole of archetypal action offered V the option of antagonistic aggression, in effect the option of identifying with the archetypal and personal aggressors, or perpetrators, who had robbed her of a well-rounded and trustworthy sense of self and others. Protected by this identification, she could establish herself as impenetrable, invulnerable, and entitled to win, hands down. Meanwhile, the victim, the looser, the wimp, as manifestations of the dissociated and rejected pole of archetypal action, were exiled into the shadow and projected onto others. These intra-psychic maneuvers enabled V to defend herself interpersonally as well since they supported her sense of herself as the victor, not the victim, and thus as invulnerable. This enabled her to protect herself at least somewhat from the unusual and deeply wounding cruelties of her parents.

Splitting and projection, employed in order to handle the stress inherent in separations, are the defining defenses of the primal phase of development. As inhabited by splitting and protected by projection as V's psyche was, she apparently managed to develop a sufficient amount of consciousness that her identification with the predator did not drive her into acting out her aggression. This may be, in part, because in these early months of her life, her most basic physical needs were met and she was not bodily abused. The cruelty entered psychically and deeply impacted her interpersonally as well as intra-psychically but apparently did not result in archetypal aggression forming an uncompromising grip upon her life. If she had not been able to at least minimally contain her raw and violent aggression during this primal phase, she probably would have developed a psychopathic character structure, driven to wound or kill off the other, literally or psychologically. She may also have become bedeviled with paranoid fantasies about being under constant attack by inner or outer sources. However, armed with an identification with the aggressor and successfully hiding her vulnerability from herself as well as from others, V managed the early dynamics of the Primal phase without apparent disorder.

But as V entered the narcissistic phase of development, armed and split as she was, she carried quite a handicap as the natural narcissistic dynamics of grandiosity, exhibitionism, and omnipotence began to come into play. When these dynamics are well met, both intra-psychically and interpersonally, they can initiate and nourish the development of self-esteem, the establishment of personal values, and the capacity for empathic relatedness. Unfortunately, V's interpersonal world was strongly colored by her parents' cunning domination, criticality, and now punitive neglect, all of which were intensified in reaction to V's increasingly demanding behaviors. Meanwhile, intra-psychically, her already defensive and inflexible consciousness was not well-equipped to participate in a dialogic process with these expansive forces. Quite the contrary, her identification with the aggressor took over and claimed them for her further defensive use.

Not mediated by a give-and-take with consciousness, narcissistic dynamics tend to inflate the ego, which is generally imaged as the structural center or seat of consciousness. Inflated with grandiosity and omnipotence, the ego becomes the authorized center of the psyche, stridently independent from the unconscious. This uncompromising opposition between consciousness and unconsciousness renders a person inordinately self-absorbed "master of the universe." Tragically, it also renders her relatively unable to enter and maintain authentic personal relationships. At odds with the *other*, both internally and externally, she lives a life of alienation.

This indeed became V's reality. Given that her natural surge of narcissistic grandiosity, exhibitionism, and omnipotence was generally in the hands of her defensive identification with antagonistic aggression, as a toddler she charged headlong, with fierce determination, into claiming her space. Throughout her "terrible 2s" she was indeed terrible. She began to test her parents, claim her own power, and establish herself as a princess, if not the queen. Driven by her very young but very powerful drive to dominate, she went all out every chance she had. No question, she was quite a handful. And, no question, her parents responded in kind. They quite ruthlessly and consistently won each battle, and V eventually retreated into a sturdy standoff. As she backed into further entrenchment in her identification with the perpetrator, she hardened her heart and vowed to never, ever truly submit to anyone, anytime. She never asked for help, never cried a tear, and never really relaxed. This sealed the grip that Alpha Narcissism had upon her psyche, and she set off into a lifetime unconsciously driven by a determination to rule. She polished her aggression, perfected her aim, and never lost the opportunity to impress, win over, and ever so subtly skewer anyone and everyone in her path. The tenaciously unconscious drive to dominate left her virtually no capacity to own her aggression and therefore to assume responsibility for it.

Three Faces of Narcissism and Their Shadows at Play

Earlier in this chapter, I suggested that America is in the grip of Alpha Narcissism and I pointed out that this is apparent in our destructive dominance, ruthlessness, aggressive entitlement, and impenetrable superiority. I noted that as we explored the personal dynamics of V's life, we would be detailing a perspective that might enhance our capacity to make sense of these observations. Recognizing that the same patterns of behavior that appear in V's profile also appear in our collective behaviors, it is possible to extrapolate that the dynamics in her profile are simultaneously descriptive of and informative about our collective reality. We can now see how our national behaviors are scripted by Alpha defenses. We can also surmise more confidently that vulnerability, the unacceptable possibility of being prey, lies in the Alpha shadow of our country.

While it is informative to see that America is in the grip of Alpha Narcissism, the story about our collective psyche doesn't stop there. Additional perspectives emerge when we reconsider the Matrix of character structures that I described earlier. The Matrix clarifies how much of our individual lives are choreographed by the particular character structure that is one's fundamental ground. It is this basic notion that supports our "diagnosing" our nation, as a collective entity, in terms of one particular structure, which I have been suggesting is Alpha Narcissism. Furthermore, this central character structure can be seen as dynamically interrelated to the other structures. Thus, the dynamics inherent to the other structures will also play a part in our national character. In effect, subgroups within our national psyche, both individual people and multitudes of subcollectivities composed of groups of people, contribute to the dynamics of the whole. Although currently our collective attention is seriously caught in an Alpha web, it is essential to also identify the ever-present roles of Counterdependent Narcissistic and Dependent Narcissistic dynamics in terms of how their interrelatedness with Alpha dynamics impact us nationally.

As Americans, here we are, more at odds with each other than ever, to put it quite mildly. The interrelatedness of the various character structures stimulates us to inquire, particularly, about the lines of shadow play between the three forms of narcissism. What about the shadow-ridden sides of Counterdependent Narcissistic and Dependent Narcissistic character structures? How are these shadows dynamically interrelated to the Alpha Narcissistic structures?

In general, each character structure tends to project its shadow onto those structures that are rooted in the *other* archetypal wellsprings of psyche. I noted above that what lies in the Alpha shadow of America and is insistently projected onto others is vulnerability, the unacceptable possibility of being prey. Individually, when we project our shadows onto someone else, we naturally see them as fitting our perceptions. Given that an Alpha Narcissist is attempting to get rid of his vulnerability, he will look for another whom he sees as vulnerable. He will dismiss and diminish the other so as to guarantee that he remains free of this disowned part of himself. For example, he will diminish a Counterdependent Narcissist for hollow, impotent intellectualisms and he will diminish a Dependent Narcissist for his soppy emotions that waste time and energy in the illusory field of love. With each of these maneuvers, he feels relieved to be free of vulnerability and is thrilled to be more and more triumphant—as a predator. Meanwhile Counterdependent Narcissists, bathed in the wellspring of mentation, sense that raw action is so utterly other that they disidentify with it altogether, committing it to their shadow that finds an "easy hook" in a nearby Alpha. And Dependent Narcissists, inflamed by archetypal affect, do the same.

All this rejected and projected archetypal, raw action is easily seized and put to predatory use by both Alpha individuals as well as by the collective psyche of our nation. This is one of the trickiest dynamics at work today in the United States. Bottom line, those of us who disidentify with aggression of any sort and then proceed to project it onto Alpha individuals, as well as onto Alpha-spirited collective movements, are in effect handing over our share of this wellspring of energy to Alpha Narcissists. This amounts, in essence, to a collusion with Alpha values.

An essential difficulty arises in our collective psyche when all this happens. The Counterdependent and Dependent individuals and their collective projects evict not only the creative power within themselves that is naturally generated by this wellspring of raw action, but they also throw away, through projections, their own destructive power, their own inner predator. Once we have thrown out part of ourselves, we're not only psychically much poorer, we have lost the possibility, and the responsibility, to maintain a relationship with these disowned parts and thus contribute to their integration. I noted above in reflections about V that her split-off drive to dominate left her virtually no capacity to truly own her aggression and therefore to assume responsibility for it. In each case, whether through disidentification from raw action altogether or from identification with the split-off predator, the key individuals involved as well as our national psyche collectively are ill-equipped to enter into a creative dialogue that might release them from such rigid oppositions.

It seems apparent that in order to deal with the current predomi-nance of unbridled Alpha dynamics in the United States, each and every one of us must be challenged to assume responsibility for and to address the individual integration of his or her split and dissociated inner selves. Naturally, this would entail not only our developing the capacity to recog-nize whom we choose to have carry our projections and why, but it also entails our endeavoring to withdraw our own projections. Inherent in this process would be the development of the capacity to perceive the other internally and externally. Redressing the grip held by Alpha dynamics is naturally going to have to start with those of us who are minimized by these dynamics since at this point the Alpha herself is consistently satisfied by her triumphs. The potentially effective challenge then becomes for the Coun-terdependent or Dependent Narcissist to boldly renew her relationship to archetypal action, to insistently withdraw her projection of raw action, to own it herself, and thus to effectively empower herself. This would render her unavailable to receive the projections from the Alpha, who would then have to wrestle with her own vulnerability. These observations take us back to my opening appreciation of Beyoncé's performance. From a histor-ical and personal place of having been "assigned" a one-down position, she fiercely claimed her strength and value. In a prize-winning challenge to predation embodied in both racism and misogamy, she empowered herself and her "chorus."

In our current political chaos, steadily studying the tricky dynamics of the predator at work in our world may prove to be invaluable. Each step along the way may well prompt further, deeper explorations: for example, deliberations about the nature of responsibility, considerations about conscience, questions about the conscious use of violence, ponderings about what it takes to discern/to smell a predator, and what it takes to further the development of empathy, generosity, and caring.

Truly understanding the potential power accessible to us through such psychological work is a first, and perhaps essential, step in loosening the grip of Alpha dynamics. Asserting our knowledge about individual and collective transformation through the development of integration and balance within psyche would be, in itself, a form of creative aggression, one we can offer with conscience. It may well be one of the most effective and responsible steps we can take.

Jacqueline J. West, PhD, is a Jungian Analyst practicing in Santa Fe, New Mexico. She is a member and Training Analyst in the New Mexico Society of Jungian Analysts as well as in the Inter-Regional Society of Jungian Analysts. She has served as both President and Training Director of the New Mexico Society and also as President of the Council of North American Societies of Jungian Analysts (CNASJA). She is co-author, along with Jungian Analyst Nancy Dougherty, of *The Matrix and Meaning of Character: An Archetypal and Developmental Perspective - Searching for the Wellsprings of Spirit.* She lectures widely on the dynamics of archetypally informed character structures and their interplay with art and politics.

Section 5
Closing Thoughts

"Come, There is Much That We Can Yet Do!"

BY ROBERT MOORE, PhD

(Excerpts reprinted from *Facing the Dragon: Confronting Personal and Spiritual Grandiosity* by Moore, with permission of Chiron Publication LLC 1996, Asheville, NC)

On Sept. 11, an ancient scourge of the human species came out of hiding once again. The power of radical evil broke through our denial just as it did on Dec. 7, 1941.

What does this new escalation in violence and terror mean for us and for a prognosis of the human future? The increasing anxiety and chaos of our time have been fed by an arrogant and malignant secularist narcissism and nihilism that increasingly fosters arrogant fundamentalisms in response. At this time in history, it is imperative that we realize that both kinds of arrogance are being fueled by compulsive intrusions of archetypal energy tantamount to possession states.

J. R. R. Tolkien's *The Lord of the Rings* portrays a world in which a seductive and demonic lust for power over others grows in strength until it threatens to overwhelm the entire world. This fantasy masterpiece reflects an accurate intuition that such a process is active not in Middle Earth but on Planet Earth.

Working as both a Jungian psychoanalyst and spiritual theologian, my recent research has focused on the powerful, grandiose "god-energies" that burn fiercely in the heart of every human being. When we face these energies consciously in faith and with authentic respect, they reflect in us the numinous, creative, and transformative power of the divine presence. But when the human ego engages in a pretentious "unknowing" of the reality and significance of this presence, the result is existential idolatry and malignant narcissism.

Existential denial of the divine presence creates a demonic alchemy that hijacks the sacred energies of the soul and twists them into destructive powers of hideous strength, powers of aggressive nonbeing that reveal themselves as addiction, racism, sexism, homophobia, all forms of political oppression, ritual violence and war, and the ecological destruction of our planet. These same grandiose energies fuel both corporate greed and religious fundamentalism.

Carl Jung was the first modern psychological researcher to see clearly the great dragon of grandiose energies lurking within us, never sleeping but waiting for the light of our awareness to grow dim before striking at the heart of humanity and civilization. Traditional mythologies often used the mythic image of the dragon to indicate an intuition of these great and dangerous forces that lurk within the human soul and turn satanic when left unconscious or treated with disrespect. Jung called us to face the reality of these great energies and take moral and spiritual responsibility for their conscious and creative incarnation in psyche and history. In his *Answer to Job*, he accurately assessed our current situation in the following terms:

> Everything now depends on man: immense power of destruction is given into his hand, and the question is whether he can resist the will to use it, and can temper his will with the spirit of love and wisdom. He will hardly be capable of doing so on his own unaided resources. He needs the help of an "advocate" in heaven . . . . The only thing that really matters now is whether man can climb up to a higher moral level, to a higher plane of consciousness, in order to be equal to the superhuman powers which the fallen angels have played into his hands. (quoted in Stein 1995, p. 168)

Never before has Jung's psychology and prophetic vision been so timely or so urgently needed as now.

We must all be vigilant to the insidious—usually unconscious— temptation to open the door to these forces within ourselves and act them out in a demonic way. These psychic invasions and archetypal colonizations often coerce us into terrible acts of hate, violence, and inhumanity. We have seen what individuals possessed by these grandiose archetypal forces are capable of.

Is there any antidote to this powerful lust for the "ring of power"? I agree with Carl Jung and Paul Tillich that the antidote is present, effective, and far more powerful than the toxins that afflict us. Where is this antidote? It lies in increasing the light of our spiritual and psychological awareness and respectful acceptance of the dragon within and the implications of its presence.

Facing the Dragon shows how pathological narcissism results from archetypal energies that are not contained and channeled through resources such as spiritual disciplines, ritual practice, utilization of the mythic imagination, and Jungian analysis. In the larger social sense, unconscious and uncontrolled grandiosity all too often leads well-intentioned groups into a malignant, pathological tribalism that wreaks havoc on their neighbors and threatens the rest of the world.

The issues addressed here have significant implications for the future of human civilization on Planet Earth and must be faced by all of us. Not just religious leaders and psychotherapists but people from all areas and walks of life should look within themselves for evidence of these recurring phenomena and set themselves upon a path of increasing awareness. The problem, in other words, is not only "out there" but also always "in here" as well.

We are now beginning to understand that contemporary culture has this one little fly in the ointment: the epidemic of unregulated human grandiosity. Every concerned person needs to stop and think about this question. Why might grandiosity become a growing problem in modern, secular culture? What is there about secular-oriented culture that might cause an increase in problems of psychological grandiosity? Not theological problems. Forget theology for a moment. This is just a question about the psychology of narcissism. We can bracket theological issues here and talk about psychodynamics.

Very simply, "grandiosity" means you have larger fantasies and wishes for yourself than your real life experience can support, so they either make you *manic*, running around trying to keep up with their demands, or they make you *depressed because* your desires are so high and unachievable that it soon seems useless to try to do anything at all.

Periodically, in families, communities, and in larger groups, the pressure of grandiose energies builds to intolerable levels, and people turn to desperate, unconscious pseudoritualizations expressed in ritual violence that includes warfare and the quest for the human sacrifice of those weak enough to serve as scapegoats. Violent catharsis may lower the pressure for a while, but soon the dragon, cloaked in the darkness of unconsciousness, returns to feed its terrible insatiable appetite. We must face the dragon consciously with our new psychoanalytic knowledge. This presents a huge and decisive challenge for our species. Meeting it successfully can bring us to a new phase of human evolution, but ignoring it means we would rather continue arranging unconsciously for our own last rites.

Psychodynamically speaking, an ideology becomes the carrier for your archetypal Self. The ideology serves as a psychological prosthesis for the individual while the grandiosity continues having a toxic effect at the cultural and societal level.

That is what happens in malignant human tribalism. You can view human religious tribalism or ethnicity in these terms. When your ethnic or racial or religious group becomes numinous for you as an individual, the group will carry the numinosity of your archetypal Self. That will protect your ego from the grandiosity, but it will not protect other people or the world from it.

Remember, there is no such thing as a person who has completely trans-formed his or her own narcissism. There are only people who acknowledge the existence of their grandiose energies and try to learn how to relate to them consciously and regulate and optimize their contacts with them intelligently.

We don't want to eliminate archetypal energies, but neither do we want them to destroy us. We want and need these energies to fuel and enrich life. That is the true meaning of human spirituality on the psychological level, to facilitate productive and creative contact with these sacred energies. That is why Jungians are uniquely able to diagnose grandiosity and the threat of pathological narcissism as spiritual problems that no one in the modern secular world can avoid having to deal with.

Jung's studies of alchemy led him to believe that the archetypal Self was imaged in what he called the *coniunctio*, the *mysterium coniunctionis*, the sacred marriage, the marriage of *rex* and *regina*, the king and the queen. Two good places to start are Jean Shinoda Bolen's books, *Goddesses in Everywoman* (1984) and *Gods in Everyman* (1989).

The main problem with a narcissistic personality disorder, technically speaking in terms of the syndrome, is sensitivity to criticism. If you are a narcissist and people criticize you, you may experience great anxiety and fragmentation. When they are not criticizing you, and especially if they are constantly mirroring you, you may feel pretty calm with little fragmentation anxiety. You do not have to vibrate a lot as long as people are mirroring you, but people dominated by the king-queen configuration are usually very sensitive to criticism. Your anxiety level will stay fairly low only as long as you can arrange for everyone to adore you, because that serves as a camouflage and no one can detect how easily you become anxious and subject to fits of rage.

That is why so many of these narcissists rise to positions of leadership. They get a lot of adulation, and as long as they get uncritical adulation, they can look very calm and self-assured. They are calm because they are getting adored, but when criticism comes, their world begins to disintegrate. When the truth comes out, then everything begins to fragment.

Grandiosity experienced unconsciously forms a "Lucifer complex" that becomes incarnate in our homes and communities as well as in world affairs. We become the actual enemies of cosmos, or creative ordering. I recently saw a sign that said, "Your hate becomes you." We need to deal with that. We must wake up and withdraw these things. Without awakening, we will never become more truly human and humane in our dealings with each other, other species, or the environment. Unresolved, these grandiose claims always lead to havoc. We never quite get around to the actual slaying, except maybe in "Jack and the Beanstalk," but you intuit the need to "slay" your same-sex giant or dragon, because it represents this grandiose presence within. The great dragon cannot be killed. No matter how old you are, *you are not an adult until you have slain that unconscious identification with the grandiose presence within.*

Unconscious gods have no limits in their fantasies. This is the satanic manifestation of the God image. The satanic impulse always has no limits. It is the mark of a Lucifer complex when you have no limits on your behavior or your claims. That is widespread, not just in men, but particularly in men. The boy kings, however, or the boy warriors, will use the enormous AK-47 firepower they have and turn it against their own community and against civilization.

Without authentic and grounded relationships, you can easily get a little bit crazy, because you have no one to challenge your inflation. Human relationships in and of themselves are obviously not enough, however, because most people in relationships still have enormous struggles with their grandiosity. You need to form a conscious internal connection with what the Jungians call the archetypal Self as a center beyond the ego. This helps the ego begin to get down off its throne.

To understand the dynamics of human evil, whether in the personality or the human community, you must look at the underlying dynamics of pathological narcissism. Narcissistic pathology is more like sin, a condition common to all. If we didn't have the Soviet Union, Reagan's "Evil Empire," it would be harder for Americans to deal with their own personal grandiosity. We wouldn't have such a demonic enemy to be superior to. If they (Russia, China, or an Enemy of America) stopped being difficult, we couldn't project the evil shadow upon them quite so easily, and that would force us to start dealing with our own emotional problems and shadows. America would face a psychological crisis. That is how it works. When someone refuses to carry your projections, it creates a psychological crisis for you. Your displacement mechanisms no longer help you regulate your own grandiosity, so your ego must look for another way to avoid the truth.

World leaders need to learn about these archetypal pressures toward either transforming or destroying our global grandiosity epidemic. In my view, we must either have a new spiritual revolution that *consciously* confronts global human grandiosity, or we will soon engage in a literal but *unconscious* sacrificial ritual that seeks to cure this human cancer by self-destruction. In other words, if humanity will not consciously face its problem of grandiosity and spiritual narcissism, then the unconscious alternative will try to cure the malignancy by nuclear cauterization. We must either face the global initiatory task consciously or be doomed to act it out unconsciously.

Unconscious grandiosity is the main engine of racism, classism, sexism, malignant nationalism, and terrorism. When dragon energies are present unconsciously, we have little concern for even the most blatant inequities. Injustice is not high on our list of concerns. We look for ways to stay in denial, to rationalize our acceptance of poverty, disease, political oppression, and environmental despoliation. Our "let them eat cake" attitude ignores the degradation and despair in refugee camps all over the world. We have no time to cooperate with compassionate action on behalf of people who cannot help themselves.

We declare our lack of interest in nation-building among the abandoned, dispossessed, the "wretched of the earth." In deference to so-called national security, we engage in the grandiose fantasy that we can live safely inside our gated communities while children elsewhere die of starvation and treatable diseases in the laps of their emaciated mothers. Thus the grandiose attitudes and behaviors of rich and powerful nations help create a fertile soil for extremism in the poor and weak ones.

Possessed individuals hijack the symbols of their tradition to rationalize and channel the emerging compulsive necrophilic and nihilistic energy and behavior, so they can be demonically creative without becoming personally chaotic, planning and executing acts of mass murder, so to speak, with a clear conscience.

Why shouldn't you be so creative? Like Faust, you can channel the hideous strength of satanic energies into the purity of your hatred. This is how Hider's elite SS corps, Hirohito's samurai, and bin Laden's Al-Qaeda all became so terrifyingly effective in their missions of hate and destruction.

This excerpt from *Facing the Dragon* is published posthumously. Robert L. Moore (August 13, 1942 - June 18, 2016).

Robert L. Moore, PhD, was an internationally recognized psychotherapist and consultant in private practice in Chicago. He served as Distinguished Service Professor of Psychology, Psychoanalysis and Spirituality at the Graduate Center of the Chicago Theological Seminary, and served as a Training Analyst at the C.G. Jung Institute of Chicago. He is Co-founder of the Chicago Center for Integrative Psychotherapy.

Do Not Lose Heart, We Were Made for These Times

BY CLARISSA PINKOLA ESTÉS, PhD

Mis estimados queridos, My Esteemed Ones:

Do not lose heart. We were made for these times.

I have heard from so many recently who are deeply and properly bewildered. They are concerned about the state of affairs in our world right now. It is true, one has to have strong cojones and ovarios to withstand much of what passes for *good* in our culture today. Abject disregard of what the soul finds most precious and irreplaceable and the corruption of principled ideals have become, in some large societal arenas, "the new normal," the grotesquerie of the weak.

It is hard to say which one of the current egregious matters has rocked people's worlds and beliefs more. Ours is a time of almost daily jaw-dropping astonishment and often righteous rage over the latest degradations of what matters most to civilized, visionary people.

...You are right in your assessments. The lustre and hubris some have aspired to while endorsing acts so heinous against children, elders, everyday people, the poor, the unguarded, the helpless, is breathtaking.

Yet ... I urge you, ask you, gentle you, to please not spend your spirit dry by bewailing these difficult times. Especially do not lose hope. Most particularly because, the fact is—we were made for these times.

Yes. For years, we have been learning, practicing, been in training for and just waiting to meet on this exact plain of engagement. I cannot tell you often enough that we are definitely the leaders we have been waiting for, and that we have been raised, since childhood, for this time precisely.

...I grew up on the Great Lakes and recognize a seaworthy vessel when I see one. Regarding awakened souls, there have never been more able crafts in the waters than there are right now across the world. And they are fully provisioned and able to signal one another as never before in the history of humankind.

I would like to take your hands for a moment and assure you that you are built well for these times. Despite your stints of doubt, your frustrations in arighting all that needs change right now, or even feeling you have lost the map entirely, you are not without resource, you are not alone.

Look out over the prow; there are millions of boats of righteous souls on the waters with you. In your deepest bones, you have always known this is so.

Even though your veneers may shiver from every wave in this stormy roil, I assure you that the long timbers composing your prow and rudder come from a forest greater. That long-grained lumber is known to withstand storms, to hold together, to hold its own, and to advance, regardless.

... We have been in training for a dark time such as this, since the day we assented to come to Earth. For many decades, worldwide, souls just like us have been felled and left for dead in so many ways over and over—brought down by naiveté, by lack of love, by suddenly realizing one deadly thing or another, by not realizing something else soon enough, by being ambushed and assaulted by various cultural and personal shocks in the extreme.

We all have a heritage and history of being gutted, and yet remember this especially ... we have also, of necessity, perfected the knack of resurrection.

Over and over again we have been the living proof that that which has been exiled, lost, or foundered—can be restored to life again. This is as true and sturdy a prognosis for the destroyed worlds around us as it was for our own once mortally wounded selves.

...Though we are not invulnerable, our risibility supports us to laugh in the face of cynics who say "fat chance," and "management before mercy," and other evidences of complete absence of soul sense. This, and our having been 'to Hell and back' on at least one momentous occasion, makes us seasoned vessels for certain. Even if you do not feel that you are, you are.

Even if your puny little ego wants to contest the enormity of your soul, the smaller self can never for long subordinate the larger Self. In matters of death and rebirth, you have surpassed the benchmarks many times. Believe the evidence of any one of your past testings and trials. Here it is: Are you still standing? The answer is, Yes! (And no adverbs like "barely" are allowed here). If you are still standing, ragged flags or no, you are able. Thus, you have passed the bar. And even raised it. You are seaworthy.

...In any dark time, there is a tendency to veer toward fainting over how much is wrong or unmended in the world. Do not focus on that. Do not make yourself ill with overwhelm. There is a tendency too to fall into being weakened by perseverating on what is outside your reach, by what cannot yet be. Do not focus there. That is spending the wind without raising the sails.

We are needed, that is all we can know. And though we meet resistance, we more so will meet great souls who will hail us, love us and guide us, and we will know them when they appear. Didn't you say you were a believer? Didn't you say you pledged to listen to a voice greater? Didn't you ask for grace? Don't you remember that to be in grace means to submit to the Voice greater? You have all the resource you need to ride any wave, to surface from any trough.

...In the language of aviators and sailors, ours is to sail forward now, all balls out. Understand the paradox: If you study the physics of a waterspout, you will see that the outer vortex whirls far more rapidly than the inner one. To calm the storm means to quiet the outer layer, to cause it, by whatever countervailing means, to swirl much less, to more evenly match the velocity of the inner, far less volatile core—till whatever has been lifted into such a vicious funnel falls back to Earth, lays down, is peaceable again.

One of the most important steps you can take to help calm the storm is to not allow yourself to be taken in a flurry of overwrought emotion or despair—thereby accidentally contributing to the swale and the swirl. Ours is not the task of fixing the entire world all at once, but of stretching out to mend the part of the world that is within our reach.

Any small, calm thing that one soul can do to help another soul, to assist some portion of this poor suffering world, will help immensely.

It is not given to us to know which acts or by whom, will cause the critical mass to tip toward an enduring good. What is needed for dramatic change is an accumulation of acts—adding, adding to, adding more, continuing. We know that it does not take "everyone on Earth" to bring justice and peace, but only a small, determined group who will not give up during the first, second, or hundredth gale.

...One of the most calming and powerful actions you can do to intervene in a stormy world is to stand up and show your soul. Soul on deck shines like gold in dark times.

The light of the soul throws sparks, can send up flares, builds signal fires ... causes proper matters to catch fire. To display the lantern of soul in shadowy times like these—to be fierce and to show mercy toward others, both—are acts of immense bravery and greatest necessity. Struggling souls catch light from other souls who are fully lit and willing to show it. If you would help to calm the tumult, this is one of the strongest things you can do.

...There will always be times in the midst of "success right around the corner, but as yet still unseen" when you feel discouraged. I too have felt despair many times in my life, but I do not keep a chair for it; I will not entertain it. It is not allowed to eat from my plate.

The reason is this: In my uttermost bones I know something, as do you. It is that there can be no despair when you remember why you came to Earth, who you serve, and who sent you here. The good words we say and the good deeds we do are not ours: They are the words and deeds of the One who brought us here.

In that spirit, I hope you will write this on your wall: When a great ship is in harbor and moored, it is safe, there can be no doubt. But ... that is not what great ships are built for.

...This comes with much love and prayer that you remember who you came from, and why you came to this beautiful, needful Earth.

Clarissa Pinkola Estés, PhD, a Mestiza Latina, a long time activist in her seventies now, continues to testify before federal and state legislatures for social justice causes of disenfranchised persons. She is a poet, an author whose books are published in 35 languages, and a post trauma recovery specialist, serving 9-11 survivor families; and students, teachers and community after the Columbine High School massacre. She is a senior diplomate Jungian psychoanalyst in practice for forty-seven years, the former Chair of the Colorado State Grievance Board, and is the first recipient of the Joseph Campbell "Keeper of the Lore" award.

Coda

The original title is *Letter To A Young Activist During Troubled Times* with the subtitle, *Do Not Lose Heart, We were Made for These Times.*

Copyright

CPSIA information can be obtained at www.ICGtesting.com
Printed in the USA
LVOW11s1800040916

503171LV00004B/381/P

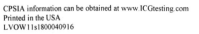